Portraits *from* Memory

Praise for *Portraits from Memory*

'Testimony to her long engagement with the best of modern Hindi literature, *Portraits from Memory* brings together Ruth Vanita's translation of two timeless gems—Mahadevi Varma's *Ateet ke Chalchitra* (1941) and *Smriti ki Rekhayen* (1943)—that have lost none of their lustre over the last eighty years and more. It opens with an introductory essay about Mahadevi's life and work that, besides being comprehensive, is refreshingly free of the kind of anachronistic ideological presuppositions that often mark critical assessments of masterpieces from earlier times. The importance of Mahadevi Varma, the iconic forerunner of modern-day feminists, can never be overemphasized.'

—GEETANJALI SHREE

'Oral histories, the nuanced view, the startling philosophy, and the music of Mahadevi Varma's prose—its assonance and alliteration—informed by experience and analysis, are skilfully brought to life in Ruth Vanita's layered new translation of the iconic Hindi text.'

—SARA RAI

Portraits *from* Memory

MAHADEVI VARMA

translated from the Hindi by

Ruth Vanita

HARPERPERENNIAL
An Imprint of HarperCollins *Publishers*

First published in India by Harper Perennial 2025
An imprint of HarperCollins *Publishers*
HarperCollins *Publishers* India, Cyber City,
Building 10-A, Gurugram, Haryana – 122002, India
www.harpercollins.co.in

2 4 6 8 10 9 7 5 3 1

P-ISBN: 978-93-6989-090-3
E-ISBN: 978-93-6989-300-3

Typeset in 11.5/15.2 Adobe Caslon Pro
by HarperCollins *Publishers* India Pvt. Ltd

Printed and bound at
Thomson Press (India) Ltd

FSC www.fsc.org MIX Paper | Supporting responsible forestry FSC® C010615

This book is produced from independently certified FSC® paper
to ensure responsible forest management.

HarperCollins Publishers, Macken House, 39/40 Mayor Street Upper, Dublin 1,
D01 C9W8, Ireland

MAHADEVI'S HANDWRITTEN DEDICATION

whose tears have cleansed my path
whose scattered stories have linked life's events for me
whose affection has been beautiful, simplicity auspicious, and humanity true
who are unaware of their kindness to me and of my gratitude to them,
to those ever-radiant sources of my cloudy moving pictures

—Mahadevi

TRANSLATOR'S DEDICATION

This translation is dedicated to the memory of my aunt, Evelyn Sarah Desai (1933–2001), who completed her MA in medieval history at Allahabad University, and was therefore in Prayag at the same time as Mahadevi Varma. The only member of her generation in my family who knew both Hindi and Urdu, she wrote me a birthday card in Urdu after I learnt the *Nastaliq* script.

—Ruth Vanita

Contents

Lines of Memory (*Smriti ki Rekhayen*), 1943

Translator's Introduction

Like most Indian schoolchildren, I first read Mahadevi Varma's poetry and prose in Hindi class in middle school. While the poetry did not remain with me, her prose sketch 'Gheesa' was unforgettable. Even today, I find her prose more compelling than her poetry. I engaged deeply with her work when I translated 'Lacchma' in 1984 in *Manushi*, the women's magazine that I co-founded and volunteered on as co-editor for thirteen years. This was the first-ever English translation of 'Lacchma'.

Even among the many remarkable women and men of her time, including her unconventional fellow-poets who belonged to the *chhayavad* group, Mahadevi's life stands out as extraordinary.[1] In her book, *Mera Parivar*, which is about her animal companions

1 I refer to her throughout by her wonderful name Mahadevi (Great Goddess) rather than as Varma, a common surname among the many Kayastha Hindi writers of the twentieth century. *Chhayavad* was the name given by literary critics to a type of mystical but modern Hindi poetry that dominated the mid-1910s to early 1940s. The word *chhaya* or shadow derives from Hindu philosophy, wherein the universe is viewed as an ever-changing projection of an immutable reality. The four great Chhayavad poets are Suryakant Tripathi 'Nirala', Jaishankar Prasad, Mahadevi Varma, and Sumitranandan Pant. Their poetry deals with social and political issues but in the light of love, the natural world, and eternal things. It engages with Vedic and Upanishadic thought.

(I translated it in 2021 as *My Family*), she recounts how all her prose writings arose from an experience she had as a student of Class Five in a boarding school. Homesick and distressed by the school's rules, she found a refuge in the orchard, where she would sit and read on the branches of a tree, surrounded by flowers, birds, and animals. Here, she befriended a hen and her five chickens. One day, a chicken disappeared and she found out that it had been taken away to be cooked for a teacher. Mahadevi wept so much for the chicken, whom she called her child and had named Munga [Coral], that the cook returned him to his mother. Mahadevi writes that she then listed in her notebook the distinguishing features of each chicken, and 'all my memoirs sprouted, budded, and bloomed from this childhood prose expression of mine'.

Mahadevi was a child prodigy and became known as a poet while she was an undergraduate. Most biographers claim that she was born in 1907 but some say the correct date is 1902. Either way, her genius is evident in the fact that she wrote her first sketch of a human, entitled 'Rama', in 1930 when she was quite young. As soon as she completed her MA in Sanskrit, she was appointed principal of the women's school (and later college) Prayag Mahila Vidyalaya, in the city then called Allahabad but which she almost always refers to by its ancient and continuing name Prayag, as was customary among most Hindi writers.

Her father had got her married as a child and she was supposed to go to her husband's home after completing the BA. But although she had met her husband and was kind to him, she absolutely refused to live with him. She also refused her father's offer to convert the whole family in order to get her divorced and remarried.

Unlike her friend and fellow-poet Subhadra Kumari Chauhan, Mahadevi had no husband or children and therefore was free to shape her life as she wished. She lived in the principal's house adjoining the girls' college, and there developed a household of staff, workers, and many rescued animals, from peacocks to deer and cows, and a wide-ranging network of friends as well as students and ex-students. She travelled widely, often following pilgrimage routes, and had a home in the Himalayas where she retreated to write in the summer vacations.

Among her friends were writers such as Suryakant Tripathi 'Nirala' and Sumitranandan Pant, whom she considered her brothers. She created portraits of these fellow writers in her book, *Path ke Saathi* (Companions on the Path), 1946. But also among her friends and companions were the people, mostly illiterate or semi-literate, whom she sketched in her first collection, *Ateet ke Chalchitra* (Moving Pictures of the Past), 1941, and then in *Smriti ki Rekhayen* (Lines of Memory), 1943. The present collection includes all the sketches from these two books. The only English translation of *Smriti ki Rekhayen* was published in 1976 and the only one of *Ateet ke Chalchitra* in 1994.[2] I glanced at these two translations after I had completed mine but did not read them through.

Both these earlier translations have trouble with the many Upanishadic words which Mahadevi employs throughout her writings, both in their original meanings and in creative ways. For example, *samskara* is not merely 'upbringing' as the 1976 translator of *Smriti ki Rekhayen* renders it. It refers to deeply engrained patterns of thinking, feeling, and behaving, which one inherits both from one's family and from one's former lives. Similarly, translating *kalpavas* as 'observe anchorage' is very odd. Kalpavas

2 Radhika Prasad Srivastava and Lillian Srivastava, *A Pilgrimage to the Himalayas and Other Silhouettes from Memory* (Delhi: Clarion Books, 1976). Neera Sohoni, *Sketches from My Past: Encounters with India's Oppressed* (Boston: Northeastern University Press, 1994).

is the practice of spending a month bathing, praying, singing on the banks of Ganga at Prayag. Likewise, when Mahadevi, dedicating *Ateet ke Chalchitra* to her subjects, calls them *satya, shiva, sundar*, translating these words as 'pure,' 'eternal', and 'genuine' (as the 1994 translator does) loses the force of applying Shiva's epithets to these common people. This 1994 translation omits almost all Mahadevi's literary allusions, thus missing the layered nature of her writing.

The 1994 translation of *Ateet ke Chalchitra* throughout translates forms of address like *Maalik* [used for an employer] and even *Mata* [mother, used for an older woman in 'Sabiya'] as 'Ma'am' even though Mahadevi discusses at some length (in 'The Chinese Vendor') why she intensely disliked the foreign word Mem [the Hindi form of Ma'am] and preferred kinship terms. These kinship terms give both translators trouble. The 1976 translation of *Smriti ki Rekhayen* calls Thakuri Baba 'Grandpa Thakuri' but 'Baba' in India is as often used for a father as for a grandfather.

Indian kinship terms are indeed hard to translate but they are at the core of Mahadevi's world-view. In 'Bibiya' she explains that in her parents' villages, everyone, regardless of community or status, was called by a kinship term. This practice continues in Indian villages, and it is only recently that the English-educated in the cities have begun to mock the Indian-English way of addressing all and sundry as 'Aunty' and 'Uncle'.

In her preface, Mahadevi acknowledges that her own life also appears in these pen-portraits of other people. We learn many things about her—her writing habits, the rituals she observed, her diet, her travels, and above all, her emotions. But all her prose portraits are centred on other people or animals. This is a particularly Indian way of thinking about oneself. One is not so much a supposedly unique individual but is defined by the constellations in which one is embedded. In the 1990s, when asked to write essays on 'Myself', my students in India almost always began with information about their parents and siblings, while my students in the US often began with their individual predilections. Even Mahadevi's contemporary, Pande Bechan Sharma 'Ugra', in his *Apni Khabar* (1960), considered the first autobiography in modern Hindi (I translated it as *About Me* in 2007), names eight out of his fourteen chapters after other people.

Both Mahadevi and Ugra focus not on their biological families but on wider networks. Employing kinship terms, Mahadevi constructs an expansive network, including both people from many backgrounds and animals, as her family. These people and animals also have kinship relations with one another. The girl students and the workers come to the kitchen for snacks and tea; the animals play with and nurture each other.

This environment is created in part by Mahadevi's temperament, in part by the nationalist climate in which she flowered, and in part arises from the traditional Indian ethos in which people take seriously the kinship relations that they establish. The washerwoman tells Mahadevi that she wears her clothes when she takes them to wash and Bhaktin just laughs when Mahadevi tries to dismiss her from employment. Mahadevi points out that for this reason, Bhaktin cannot be called an employee, and to call her a servant would be like calling the darkness and light that come and go in the house one's servants. Mahadevi feels compelled to buy items she does not want from the Chinese vendor because she calls him brother.

Although Mahadevi is forthright in denouncing systemic social oppression, she does not make the mistake of blaming all suffering on society or on any particular group, such as Brahmins or men. This is because she is in touch with reality, not driven by ideology. She perceives the suffering of near-destitute Brahmins like Munnu, the child of a poor Brahmin reciter. Munnu works as an agricultural labourer as well as a construction labourer, and her family is no better off than that of Sabiya, the sweeper-woman.

The 1994 translation of *Ateet ke Chalchitra* tacks on a subtitle that Mahadevi did not write, 'Encounters with India's Oppressed'. But the suffering depicted in these sketches is not peculiar to India. Wife-beating and rape are universal, and the treatment of vulnerable women, such as unwed mothers, women discarded by their husbands, first wives supplanted by second wives, and even widows, is found in many parts of the world, such as the Middle East and Africa. The woman who sells her little stepdaughter into sex work is not Indian but Chinese-Burmese.

The translator also terms Mahadevi a 'feminist' and an 'activist', which are terms she did not use for herself. Mahadevi is not a typical feminist. She does express disgust and anger at the behaviour of men who spend their wives' earnings on gambling, drink, and other women, or gang up with other men to drive women to death. In her book, *Shrinkhla ki Kariyan* (1942), she analyses injustice to women and discrimination against them. But she also depicts women mistreating not only other women but even men and boys, a reality that feminists rarely discuss.

Fear of strengthening a stereotype does not deter Mahadevi from telling the stories of stepmothers who overwork, neglect, and torture their stepdaughters ('Binda', 'The Chinese Vendor'), and drive their stepsons away through ill-treatment ('Rama'), or sisters-in-law who gang up on their husbands' sister ('Bitto'). If an adopted son abandons his doting, disabled mother ('Gungiya') and numerous husbands mistreat their wives, a wife, too, robs and abandons her disabled husband ('Alopi') and, most tellingly, an apparently submissive, veiled wife bullies her husband and probably drives him to death ('Rama'). The cheerful, childlike Rama's woman employer first forces him into marriage with a view to doing him good and then forces him to return to his unpleasant wife in order to be fair to the wife.

Nor is Mahadevi a typical 'activist'. She helps out when she can but she does not wish to overthrow the existing order nor does she try to change the lives of all those she encounters. Her typical response is to become a client for workers in the trade they pursue, for example, she buys vegetables from Alopi, cloth from the Chinese vendor, and employs Bhaktin even though she hates her cooking. Only on rare occasions does she go out of her way to find work for someone, as in the case of Gheesa's mother and the nameless unwed mother. The sex-worker's daughter realizes that the work Mahadevi gives her is in the nature of charity so she quits.

Mahadevi's language is far from what would be considered politically correct today. She states that she cannot see much variety in the faces of Chinese people, and unabashedly describes various people as dark or ugly, and the faces and homes of the poor as dirty. First, it is important to stress that we cannot and should not import twenty-first century criteria of political correctness or present-day ways of writing into earlier times. To do so would require censoring or rewriting or banning numerous major writers in every known language.

Second, some of these descriptions are the outcome of realism. For instance, the children of the poor whom she teaches in 'Gheesa' are described as skeletal and wearing dirty rags as clothing. This is clearly intended not to condemn the children but to condemn the terrible conditions in which they and their parents live, wherein they do not have enough to eat and cannot afford a second set of clothes or even soap to wash themselves and their clothing. Mahadevi condemns herself for having preached her ideas of cleanliness to the children: 'I cannot forget the day when, without providing clothes for them, I foolishly exhausted those poor children with my exhortations regarding the importance of cleanliness.' Any sensible reader can see throughout this justly famous essay and other essays where she describes such poverty-stricken children and adults, for example, 'Badlu' and 'Munnu', that her whole soul revolts against the suffering and deprivation she sees. She is also critical of and sarcastic about the callousness of the rich, for example (in 'Munnu'), the wealthy Thakur Gopalsharan Singh, who refuses permission to use his unused and broken-down house as a schoolroom for village children.

Fortunately, the nature of poverty has changed in India. Most working people and artisans, such as potters and vendors, no longer live in the abysmal conditions that Mahadevi describes with precision. Many construction labourers and agricultural workers are still badly housed and clothed, but even they have more than just one set of ragged garments. Even when I was a child in the 1960s, most domestic workers in Delhi were barefoot and covered in dust, much as Mahadevi describes them. Today, almost all are neatly dressed, have footwear, and also cellphones. These sketches give us a clear picture of that not too distant past from which India is emerging.

The comments she interjects into her narratives are sometimes didactic, even judgemental, arising from social reformist ideas, but her thought process is not inhibited by her theories. Thus, she is angry that the young widow Bhabhi is forbidden to remarry but she also sees how social reformers' promotion of widow remarriage can work against women, for instance, when Bitto's brothers and their wives force her to remarry against her will because they do not want her to live in her parental home and share the property.

Similarly, she makes negative statements about Hindu rituals, but the interesting contradiction is that she observes many of these rituals. She tries to explain away this contradiction. For example, she says that she observes the annual kalpavas gathering because it gives her a chance to fulfil her curiosity about people. But, of course, there are many other ways of fulfilling this curiosity.

These sketches are framed by Mahadevi's astute analysis. For example, she suggests that Hindu pilgrimages and gatherings like kalpavas encouraged people from different parts of the country to share their cultures. Diana Eck, in her 2011 book, *India: A Sacred Geography*, shows how, over millennia, ordinary people understood the idea of India by following pilgrimage routes from Kashmir to Kerala, Dwarka to Puri.

Mahadevi's judgements are balanced by her ability to value those who are different from her. Thus, she may not share her housekeeper Bhaktin's Hindu piety and rules of purity but she does not interfere with them. She accepts and sometimes even admires others' choices that differ from her own. Thus, she herself would not put up with male misconduct. She criticized her beloved father and the husband whom she refused to live with, for hunting and eating animals. Yet she appreciates the selfless devotion of Sabiya to her abusive husband, his difficult mother, and his nasty second wife, and Munnu's mother's leaving a comfortable life in the city to return to her painful existence in the village for the sake of her selfish husband and father-in-law.

She respects these women's integrity and refusal to compromise their values even when their communities view them as eccentric. Mahadevi critiques the way men interpret the concept of a Sati, a true and pure woman, for their own advantage and to exploit women, yet she says that Sabiya is a true Sati, who lives up to her namesake, Savitri, the courageous wife from the Mahabharata who brought her husband back from death. At times, for instance, in 'Thakuri Baba', one may think that Mahadevi romanticizes rural India, but this is not true. Her love and respect for village life and community is balanced by her awareness that individual and collective cruelties are just as common there as in the city.

Mahadevi highlights her subjects' courage, strength, and resourcefulness. However destitute or helpless, they emerge not as victims or even as 'the oppressed' but as admirable and distinct individuals who are free from self-pity and envy. They are just as generous to Mahadevi as she is to them—Bhaktin offers her savings to Mahadevi, Lacchma runs through the forest to bring her fresh honey, Alopi thinks long and hard about what vegetables she would like, and, most unforgettably, the child Gheesa exchanges one of his two kurtas for a watermelon that he presents to her.

One returns to Mahadevi's sketches not just for what she says but for the marvellous way she says it. Her language draws on the deep wells of Sanskrit from which Hindi arises as well as on the many variations of modern Hindi in the heartland. She reproduces these types of Hindi when she recounts her conversations but unfortunately, their eloquent turns of phrase are lost in translation. All the different types of Hindi get flattened out in English.

I have chosen to retain the original fluid movement between past and present tenses, which is common in Hindi speech as well as writing. English writing tends to stick to one tense. Most Indian languages do not, because they more accurately mirror the flow of consciousness and the fact that we all live simultaneously in the present and the past. Recognizing this, English modernist writers like Woolf also move between tenses. Furthermore, Indian concepts of time are both linear and cyclical, thus Hindi employs the same word *kal*, for both 'yesterday' and 'tomorrow'. This is related to the concept of rebirth. What has happened is, in one sense, still happening and will happen again.

Unlike Mahadevi, most Hindi speakers today are not alive to the resonances and roots of Hindi words. Thus, under the influence of Persian and of English, the concepts of mind and heart [*dimagh* and *dil*] have come to be separated, with *man* meaning mind and *hriday* meaning heart. This works within the Cartesian world-view wherein animals cannot think but do have emotions, so emotions are inferior to thought. But in the Hindu world-view, mind and heart, thought and feeling, are inseparable. This understanding is more in tune with modern psychology—our thoughts are influenced by our feelings and our feelings by our thoughts. *Man* (Sanskrit *mana*) is the seat of both thought and feeling. It is both mind and heart. Depending on the context, I translate 'man' sometimes as 'mind' and sometimes as 'heart'.

Similarly, today, the word *mamta* is generally understood to mean parental, especially motherly, affection, as in the famous 1966 Hindi movie, *Mamta*. But this is only a derived meaning. Mamta, from the Sanskrit root *mama* [mine] means a sense of someone being one's own. There is no English equivalent for this word.

Likewise, *aanchal*, literally the free-hanging sari-end that is often used to shade one's head or a child's, to wipe things or tie things in, has a metaphorical meaning that is impossible to translate. The aanchal symbolizes protection and nurturing by a woman. It usually refers to protection of a child by a mother but can also refer to a woman nurturing her community or country. To spread one's aanchal means to beg, as when Gungiya begs the Baba to release her son; this is because beggars collect grain in the aanchal. Mahadevi extends the word to refer to a woman nurturing her husband or in-laws, or a little girl nurturing her siblings and father when her mother dies ('Badlu').

English often necessitates turning living forces, even divine ones, into objects. Thus, Prithvi and Ganga, earth and sacred river, become 'the earth' and 'the Ganga'. In Hindi, these are proper names of Goddesses (and people named after Goddesses, such as Ganga Din). I have tried to translate these, as far as possible, as proper names, without the article.

In one sense, these sketches are oral histories but when recreating dialogue from memory, Mahadevi almost certainly changes it because the original conversations were not recorded when they occurred. As she acknowledges in her preface to *Ateet ke Chalchitra*, we get not the thing itself but the thing filtered through her imagination. At times, she adds details that are not strictly factual. Thus, she suggests that she wears only white clothes because colours remind her of the pain of Bhabhi, the young widow who loved colours but was forbidden to wear them. But Mahadevi was eight years old when she knew Bhabhi, and for many years thereafter, Mahadevi was known for her fashionable clothing. It was only after she became a Gandhian that she took to white khadi.

Mahadevi was a painter as well as a writer, and in the preface, she refers to her sketches as pictures coloured by the light of memory. The sketches are also alive with the music of language. She employs alliteration, assonance, and wordplay in ways that are more commonly found in poetry than in prose. She often plays with rhyming words that have nothing in common except the rhyme, for example, in the fourth paragraph of her preface, *prateeksha* [waiting] and *pareeksha* [testing].

One of the most delightful aspects of Mahadevi's writing is her use of philosophical terms in unexpected contexts. Her usage expands the conventional understanding of these terms. Thus, she employs *sadhana* and *tapasya*, terms usually associated with ascetic practice, either to the endless struggles of the poor in the service of their families or to ordinary people's choosing dignity over comfort. When Bitto, the daughter of a prosperous family, is widowed, she wants to remain single, but her brothers force her to remarry because they do not want to share the parental home with her (even though she has a right to live there, under traditional Hindu law). Mahadevi bitterly notes that ancient stories generally show women as tempters disrupting men's ascetic practices, yet 'Men have never been able to accept that when a woman makes sadhana her nature and some particular truth her *atma* [consciousness], men are no longer important to her and do not frighten her'.

Another alluring feature of her prose is her penchant for frequently alluding to Hindi and Sanskrit literature, such as the epics, Kalidasa, and Hindi poets, especially the greatest of them, Tulsidas. These allusions are often subtle and they are the breath of her prose, since literature is the air she breathes. But if we miss the allusions, we miss her understanding of and feeling for her subjects. Thus, in 'Alopi', she humorously refers to the sensation created by the two very poor boys, the blind Alopi and his cousin Raghu, among the girl students. She quotes Tulsidas's famous line '*gira anayan nayan binu baani*' [the voice has no eyes and the eyes have no voice]. When Rama and Lakshman go walking in a garden, Tulsidas says that the beauty of these two young men is hard to describe because the voice that could describe them lacks the vision to see them and the eyes that see them have no voice to describe them.

It might seem that Mahadevi is quoting the line ironically because Alopi and Raghu, whom she has described earlier, are weak, very poor, and ill-clad. But what she actually does here is to brilliantly adapt Tulsidas's idea of the disconnect between impression, emotion, and expression. We absorb an impression through the eyes but expressing it with the tongue is difficult. Alopi and Raghu look strange and strike viewers dumb, but over time, viewers such as Mahadevi as well as her girl students perceive their beauty and find it hard to describe. This is because, unlike Rama and Lakshman's beauty, Alopi and Raghu's beauty takes time to make itself felt. Another layer of meaning emerges when we note that Raghu's name is one of Rama's names and Alopi gets his name from a Goddess.

At the same time, she perceives in the stories and songs of illiterate villagers a vast treasury drawing on the same sources as Hindi literature does. She amusingly recounts how, as a precocious child, she quoted phrases from her books to confound her younger siblings, but the unlettered Rama outdid her with his store of stories, fables, and idioms. Similarly, while she quotes Surdas, Kabir, and Tulsidas, the pilgrims in 'Thakuri Baba' sing songs about Rama, Lakshman, Bharat, and Krishna by unknown village composers.

These memoirs are illuminated by Mahadevi's love of life in all its forms. Scattered through them like gems are her descriptions of everyday occurrences like a winter sunset ('The Child-Mother'), a moonlit night, or clouds in the sky which she compares to lotuses in a river, and her detailed accounts of each feature of a person's face and clothing or of the dietary arrangements of the poor. It is fitting that the famous statement *vasudhaiva kutumbakam* is first uttered by an animal in the *Hitopadesha* or *Panchatantra*. For Mahadevi, the universe is a family, as she writes in 'Lacchma': 'I express my joy not only in art but also in the company of birds and animals, trees and plants.'

Some commentators today remark that this statement about the universe as a family is not to be taken at face value because in the *Hitopadesha*, predator animals utter it in order to entrap their prey. I disagree, because the fact that the malevolent or foolish can misuse an idea does not invalidate the idea. In *Hamlet*, it is Polonius who says, 'This above all, to thine own self be true / And it must follow, as the night the day / Thou canst not then be false to any man.' The fact that Polonius is foolish and self-serving does not invalidate his statement. Mahadevi not only stated but also lived the idea that the universe is a family, with cruel and mean people in it as there are in all families, but also with great-hearted and generous individuals of all species.

—Ruth Vanita, 2025

From Me[1]

I cannot say much about the person who inspired me to write the memoirs of those people who, at various times, have set in motion new directions and perceptions in my way of thinking. That story belongs to another era but is drenched in pathos. The mistress of a family I knew had banished an old servant for a minor offence and her arrogance prevented her from acceding to his many requests for forgiveness.

That poor old man, rich in affection, would sit on the bridge waiting for his small deities with two withered marigolds, four sugar candies melting in his warm palm, or a colourless clay toy. His eyes would be wet with tears after he had given these worthless gifts to the children who were out walking with a new servant.

In 1930, the sight of this man awakened in me the memory of my childhood and its encirclement by Rama's affection, which filled my heart with the desire to write the incomplete story of that past. Gradually, Rama's family kept growing and present-day pictures joined past pictures. I wanted the dim light of these memoirs to help me recognize those pictures of the past once more, after time had run its paintbrush over them, erasing their glow.

---

1 This is Mahadevi Varma's preface to *Ateet ke Chalchitra*.

I never thought of publishing them. Every complexity of thought or vibration of feeling does not call up for me the pleasing picture of a printer. And the persons in these memoirs are not objects for display but recipients of my unbreakable affection. It seemed better to wait rather than to right away test whether they would garner the respect of others.

My life too has entered into these portraits from memory. This was natural. We can see things that lie hidden in darkness only when we bring them into the bounds of our light, however dim or bright. Beyond those bounds, they blend into a darkness without end. People make themselves known within the bounds of life, and outside of those bounds their form changes. A storyteller brings imagined characters closer by decking them with realism; why then would I clothe the companions of my journey in imaginings that would distance them? But the details about myself that become known due to my closeness with them have no more importance than the ashes that surround the burning coals which keep the fire going. One who cannot see past this cannot reach the heart of these pictures.

There are eleven memoirs in this collection (*Ateet ke Chalchitra*). I do not want to put these wounded lives into a marketplace of toys to provide readers with cheap entertainment. This collection will be successful if anyone can find even one line of their own shadow in these half-lines and dimmed colours, otherwise I have been unjust to them by bringing them out of the safe confines of my memory.

—Mahadevi

Janmashtami, 1941, Prayag

MOVING PICTURES OF THE PAST

Ateet ke Chalchitra
(1941)

Rama[1]

Neither I nor my siblings can say when Rama came to live with us. Just as we knew Babu-ji's [father's] variegated study-table, under which our universe of toys was established in the afternoon silence and on which we slept looking like Vishnu's fish or turtle incarnations, and as we recognized Ma's Thakur-ji [Krishna] flanked by conch and bell, in the desire to swallow whose food we sat with half-closed eyes, with heron-like mental absorption, counting the bell's chimes, so also we had always known the short, black, and sturdy Rama from his long nails to his long topknot.[2]

We were well-acquainted with his palms, white as a serpent's belly, and his fingers that resembled the crooked, knotted branches of a tree, because the hostilities that prevailed between them and us from the morning hour of washing our faces up to bedtime culminated in a stable truce only at storytelling time. We knew the sound of his sturdy black feet, which, like elders of a family, were the foundation of the scattered family of fingers

1 Mahadevi writes the name as Raamaa.

2 The heron or *bagula*, who sits motionless, waiting for its prey, is a proverbial symbol of the fake worshipper who is greedy but pretends to be lost in meditation.

seeking ten directions, because however silently we ran away after doing some mischief, they reached our hiding-places as if on wings.

Childhood memories have a strange quality. When our sensibilities are serious and calm, the lines of the past effortlessly grow clearer and clearer like objects emerging from fog, but when we sit down to recall them and logically establish their utility, forgetfulness covers them up just as throwing a stone briefly disperses scum on the water that regathers itself again.

Rama's narrow forehead, thick eyebrows, and small eyes liquid with affection sometimes inscribe themselves on my memory, and, at other times, grow dim and even disappear. This is true also of his unshapely, thick nose, which was like the final mistake of a tired and irritated sculptor, his nostrils that seemed spread out by breath, his lips puffed up as if with free laughter, and his row of white teeth reminiscent of curds in a black stone cup.

Rama's hair was not allowed to grow beyond half an inch so we constantly roamed around with a pair of scissors, hoping to bestow the blessing of symmetry on his long tuft.[3] But that tuft was like the location of a cat, because its master was never asleep during our waking hours and we dared not perform this auspicious act while he was awake.[4] Today, one would have to say that Rama was ugly, but at that time it was intolerable for us to even imagine a more pleasing companion than him.

Life is the soul of beauty, but its symmetry is more often worshipped than its irregularity. As we get more and more entangled with a variety of outward forms, we forget the life in which they are rooted. Because children are not acquainted

---

3 The *shikha* or strand of hair worn by a Brahmin.

4 *Myau ka thaur*, the location of a cat, is an idiom suggestive of danger, somewhat like belling the cat.

with a variety of material things, they recognize only life. A person ignores irregular lines from which life's rays burst forth in affection and good feeling, but rejects external symmetry where life is concealed in envy and hatred.

For this reason, Rama was very dear to us. It seems that he too was unaware of his ugliness, which is why he went around in a long-sleeved jerkin and a knee-length dhoti, displaying much of his ungainly body. He did not lack the means to adorn himself because a long, lined kurta, a pre-tied turban, Bundelkhandi shoes with curled toes, and a stout, knotted *lathi* waited in his room, as if for an auspicious occasion. Inspired by their endless waiting and Rama's complete neglect, our executive committee unanimously passed a resolution to thread the lathi through the kurta as a curtain for our toys, remove the turban from its peg and honour it by making it a cradle for dolls, and make permanent arrangements for the dolls' water excursions by putting the Bundelkhandi shoes into a cistern. But Rama kept the door of his dark fortress fastened with a bolt which scolded us in creaking tones and was so high up that we could not raid the room even by standing on a *stool*.[5]

When we grew up, the story we heard about Rama's advent was as strange as he himself was. One afternoon, while Ma was putting *papad* and *badi* out to dry in the sun, a weak and famished Rama had sat down on the courtyard threshold, unmoving, his head propped up by the door.[6] Thinking he was a beggar, she went near and spoke to him, and he replied, 'O mother, this Rama is about to die of hunger,' and lay down at her feet. Ma

5 Words that are in English in the original are italicized in this translation.

6 *Papad* is a round wafer-like accompaniment to meals, which is made by rolling out circlets of lentil dough and drying them in the sun. *Badi* are sun-dried dumplings made of lentil paste.

revived him with milk and sweets but the problem grew more complicated because hunger is not an illness that can be cured with one-time treatment.

This rustic boy from Bundelkhand, fleeing his stepmother's cruelty, had begged his way to Indore, where he knew no one and had nowhere to stay. Unsurprisingly, Rama became the natural recipient of Ma's motherly love. When Babu-ji returned that evening, Rama's big shoes were at rest in one corner of the woodshed and his long lathi in another. And the somewhat bewildered Rama, with freshly washed face and hands, was being initiated into service, and trying to comprehend the meaning and limits of his duties.

Babu-ji was surprised and amused by his ugliness. Laughing, he asked, 'From which planet have you brought this being, Dharmaraj-ji?'[7] Our house was pretty much a *zoo*, thanks to Ma. When Babu-ji returned home in the evening, there would be either a lame beggar having a meal on the verandah, a Surdas with a tambourine singing a bhajan at the back door, a poor boy from the neighbourhood leaping around the yard in a new kurta, or an old Brahmin woman bundling up some uncooked grain on the threshold of the storehouse.[8]

Babu-ji never opposed any of Ma's activities but he enjoyed teasing her. He thought Rama would be a guest for a short while but Ma, unable to quickly come up with an answer, said in an agitated manner, 'I've kept him as a special servant for myself.' That the person who never rested a moment despite the presence of several servants had kept a servant just for herself was surprising

---

7 He jokingly calls his wife the God of Dharma, who is God of Justice, and is also Yama, God of Death.

8 'Surdas' is a polite way of referring to a blind man because the famous sixteenth-century poet Surdas was blind.

enough, and then he was such a strange servant! Babu-ji could not stop laughing. Still joking, he said, 'Right, a servant specially framed to frighten atheists is perfect for Dharmaraj-ji.'[9]

He did not trust Rama who hailed from some unknown clan but it was futile to argue with Ma because she measured the deserts of anyone by her own spontaneous sympathies. It was impossible for her to doubt the beauty of the simple heart she had found beneath the covering of Rama's ugliness. So Rama stayed on with us but it was hard to determine his duties. There were old servants for all tasks and Ma could not give the task of looking after her *puja*-room and kitchen to anyone. Her rules with regard to *arati*, puja, and cooking were fixed and brooked no exceptions.[10] Just as she was sure that worship was necessary for her spirit, so also she was convinced that her cooking the food herself was absolutely essential for all of our bodies.

We were all a year or two older or younger than each other, so there was not much to choose between us in the matter of developing good sense. Like demons absorbed in ruining rites and rituals, we were always hovering around, waiting to obstruct Ma's well-laid plans, so she found some relief when she gave Rama the major duty of keeping us rebels under control.

First thing in the morning, Rama cleaned the puja-room and polished its vessels with lemon, and next he woke us up. By morning, the positions and directions of our heads and limbs had achieved many revolutions in our big bed. One child's foot measured another's neck, one child's hand lay across another's body, and one child's back formed a wall to obstruct another's

---

9 Since Mahadevi's father calls his wife Dharmaraj, who is God of Death, he jokingly says that Rama, her servant, can frighten atheists because even they fear death.

10 *Arati* is a worship ritual, wherein one waves a tray with various items on it before an icon.

breath. In order to fully understand the situation, Rama's rough hand, clothed in gentleness, would roam over the quilt or sheet from one end to the other, and then he would carry off one in the chariot of his arms, another on the horse of his shoulders, a third staggering along somehow, for the ceremony of face cleansing.

Washing our hands and faces was no easy feat, for Rama had to continuously recite the mantra of 'Raja eats milk and sweets,' but none of us was willing to accept another as raja [king]. When Rama called me Raja, my little brother, opening his mouth like a bird's beak, would say, 'Lama, why do you call her Laja?' The arrogance of this small man who could not even pronounce 'r' shook me up. The fingers of one of Rama's hands would keep my head fixed in its circuit while the palm of his other hand, with its three deep lines, searched for dirt on my face like a Sudarshan Chakra.[11] To endure such hardship yet cede the right of royalty to others would be to proclaim my own insufficiency so I would use the strategies of petition, bribery, penalty, and division to compel Rama to call only me Raja.[12] Rama knew an unfailing mantra to satisfy such great warriors. He would whisper in my ear, 'You are the great Raja, not the little one,' and he probably whispered the same into the little one's ear, because my brother would happily dip his finger into the small box of tooth powder and start scrubbing his lips instead of his teeth with it. Rama had strictly forbidden us to do this, so I would look at him with scorn, as if he was a foolish soldier disobeying the general's commands.

Then we three icons were ranged in a row and Rama would sit, with small and big spoons, a cup of milk, and a tray of fruit, ready to worship strange deities, each of whom was eager to prove his

---

11 The discus of time, wielded by the Preserver God Vishnu as a weapon.

12 The four strategies, Sama, Dama, Danda, and Bheda, which Chanakya, in the *Arthashastra* (circa fourth century AD), advises a ruler to use.

or her own superiority. But he was a shrewd priest. By the power of his devotional skills, he would make the deities eager to close their eyes and receive the worship of the crows. As soon as we closed our eyes, a grape would reach the mouth of one, a biscuit the teeth of another, and a spoonful of milk the lips of a third. Of course, we only pretended not to see because with half-closed eyes we all watched the artistry of Rama's thick, black fingers. The truth was that I was afraid of the crow's hard, black, and unfamiliar beak. Had I not recognized Rama's hands and fingers in the imaginary crow's beak, I would definitely have abandoned the temptation of food and run away.

Rama's labours did not conclude with breakfast. It was Rama's duty to prevent our eyes from absorbing soapy foam and our ears from remaining dry islands while we bathed, to maintain an illogical *varna* system among the odd forms our clothes assumed as we dressed, not to allow disproportion between the quantity of food and the consumer's limits while we ate, to serve as our elephant, horse or flying vehicle when we played, and to tell us stories with many movements of his fan-like hands until he brought us to the door of the world of dreams.[13]

The excesses we heaped on Rama were as boundless as his love for us. One day, when we insisted on going to the Dashehra fair, Rama begged and pleaded with Ma until she gave him permission to take us for a little while. When he was buying toys, he put one of us on his shoulder, the other in his arms, and told me repeatedly, 'Don't let go of my finger, Raja Bhaiya.' Even as I nodded in agreement, I decided to let go of the finger and see the fair on my own. After I had wandered around and several times escaped being crushed, I began to feel hungry and naturally missed Rama.

---

13 Varna, the division of society into four categories, and by extension, any kind of categorization.

Stopping at a sweetshop, I attempted to hide my anxiety and asked, 'Have you seen Rama? He is lost.' The old sweet-seller, parental affection in his eyes, asked, 'What is your Rama like?' Pressing my lips together, I contentedly said, 'He's very nice.' Knowing the impossibility of finding Rama on the basis of this description, the old man insisted that I rest there for a while. I did not want to acknowledge defeat but my legs were tired and the platters of sweets were inviting so I sat down like an honoured guest on the sacking in a corner, accepted sweets offered by the old man, and began to tell him the story of my epic journey.

Meanwhile, dying with anxiety, Rama was scanning the fairground for me. When he reached the shop with great difficulty that evening, having made enquiries everywhere, I said, swelling with pride at my victory, 'You are so big yet you still get lost, Rama!' Tears of joy rolled down Rama's fatigued face like dewdrops. He turned me round and round to look at me from every angle, as if I might have lost a limb in the fair. When we reached home, we found out that small people's heroism is defined as an offence in big people's dictionaries, but Rama took my offence on himself and endured the reproaches and rebukes, and when he put us to sleep that night, I was the chief recipient of his affectionate patting.

One day, Rama gave us an excellent exposition on the subtle and complex differences between one's own things and another's things. Well! All of us anxiously engaged our minds with the question of what thing belonging to someone else we could obtain, in order to fill Rama's small eyes with sad dismay.

Our house adjoined the house of a Thakur Saheb in a way that made it easy to reach one roof from the other, but the path was a ridge that was a hand's breadth wide, where, if a foot slipped, one would easily measure the distance to the underworld. Having decided that the flowers in the neighbour's courtyard could be defined as things belonging to another, we set out one afternoon by that skyway to steal flowers, with the sole object of upsetting Rama. Had anyone's foot slipped, this story would have been different, but fortunately we reached the other roof safely.

We went down the stairs and on the lowest step found a bitch with her tiny puppies. As soon as we saw her, we changed our minds regarding the object to be stolen, but when we picked up a puppy, the helpless mother began to announce her rights and desires. The master of the house emerged from the sitting room, in a state of disarray, and the mistress ran out of the bedroom, awakened from her nap. Rama had not informed us what to do in such a situation, so we relied on our own wisdom and said, 'We came across the roof to steal flowers.' The master started laughing and asked, 'Why don't you take some?' We replied with even greater solemnity, 'Now we will steal a puppy.'

When we returned by the normal route, Rama had found out about our dacoity. Seeing this poisonous fruit grow on the nectareous tree of his preaching, he must have been much agitated, because he lifted the leader of the dacoits by both ears into the air and asked, 'Speak out, speak out, where did you go?' I considered it beneath my dignity to cry so, pressing my teeth into my lips, I bore this unprecedented punishment and then, with restrained anger, said to my mother, 'Rama has pulled my ears and made them crooked as well as long. Call the doctor to fix them and lock Rama in a dark room.'

She was unacquainted with our offence and Rama would not tattle on us as long as a breath remained in his body, so he had to hear a psychology-based sermon on not mistreating children. He was ashamed of his conduct, but the more he tried to make up for it, the more Raja Bhaiya remembered the pain in her ears. Nevertheless, at dusk, seeing Rama sitting outside, dejected, I proposed a truce, saying, 'Sing a song.' Rama knew only one bhajan, '*Aiso Siya Raghuvir bharoso*',[14] and the way he sang it would

14 A Bundelkhandi devotional song about how Rama and Sita protect devotees who rely on them.

have made birds, even crows, fly away from the trees above, but we were unique listeners to an unmatched singer—Rama sang only for us and we listened only for him.

My childhood was somewhat different from that of other girls of that time, which is why Rama was so important to it. At that time, families did not yearn for girls. The singers in the courtyard, the musicians at the door, and everyone in the family, from the old people to the children, waited for sons. As soon as the news was whispered that Lakshmi had arrived, sorrow spread through the house.[15] The old ladies would gesture to the silent singing women to leave and the old men would bid farewell to the quiet musicians with a wave. If the family could not bear the burden of such a guest, there were easy ways to reject and return her.[16]

Why it was so I do not know, but when no Goddess arrived in our family for a long time, anxiety grew because just as there can be no horse sacrifice without a horse, the important ritual of giving away a daughter is not possible without a girl. When I was born after much waiting, my father considered this the special kindness of Goddess Durga to our clan, and to demonstrate his respect, he forgot his knowledge of Persian and found for me an ancient name before whose magnitude no one dared to give me an ordinary pet-name.

To make me worthy of my name, everyone stuffed my head with so much knowledge from childhood onwards that my heart revolted. I doubt whether I could have become acquainted with the simplicity of life were it not for the shade of illiterate Rama's affection. The ceremony of *patti pujan* had been

---

15 A daughter, wife, or daughter-in-law is called Lakshmi, Goddess of Prosperity.

16 Alluding to female infanticide.

performed for me,[17] and I could express myself by putting my finger on the letter *Aa*, and saying *aadmi* [person], *aam* [mango], *aalmari* [cupboard], *aaj* [today], *aadi* [etcetera]. I was a virtual Shukracharya among my siblings.[18] They had to be constantly vigilant for fear of my talent for finding in books approval of or opposition to their activities. As soon as my little brother began to jump around, I would open my book and read, 'The monkey has come to dance,' and when my younger sister got annoyed, I read, 'Who can bring around an angry girl? When she needs you, she will come running.' The poor things were upset by my scriptural knowledge because they had no way to cite precedents for my actions. But the educated Shukracharya was defeated by the illiterate Rama. He had a vast treasury of stories, fables, and idioms that could not be contained in a hundred books. When my book-learning became the cause of a Mahabharata-like war, he would be the judge whose decision established accord.

Rama had no objection to my Pandit-ji, but when Maulvi Saheb, a music teacher, and a drawing master descended amidst our toys, Rama's heart was angered. Perhaps he knew that I would not be able to bear the burden of so much learning. I had begun to fear Maulvi Saheb so much that one day I hid in a big straw basket. Unfortunately, a few of the mangoes sent by Baba [grandfather] were still in the basket. Rama picked up the basket in order to take out the mangoes and put something else in; surprised by its weight, he brought it before Ma, and the problem now became too difficult for me. As he took off the lid, all I could think of

17 The ritual of initiating a child into education by worshipping Goddess Saraswati and having the child trace the first letter (Om).

18 Shukracharya was a great sage. However, there is irony to Mahadevi's choice of his name, because he became the teacher of the demons and helped them create conflict.

was to flee. Finally, Rama's and Ma's joint efforts freed me from studying Urdu.

I had no complaint against the drawing master because he did not stop me from playing. I would draw two vertical lines on every sheet of paper and a circle on top of them, thereby producing a picture of Rama. When someone else had to be drawn, I would make minor modifications to this model.

Neither Rama nor I was pleased with Narayan Maharaj. When he questioned me on the first day about learning music, I confidently declared that I learnt from Rama. He asked me to sing something, and I sang Rama's devotional song in such a strange manner that he was rendered speechless. When he did not acknowledge my servant-guru Rama as a greater and more skilled singer than himself, it was natural for me to be displeased.

We found it impossible to believe that the world's activities could continue without Rama. When Ma went to visit her mother for a fortnight, Rama had to stay behind to look after the house and Babu-ji. We absolutely refused to go with her, without Rama, so she was forced to leave us behind too.

It would be hard to find a better or more alert nurse than Rama in times of illness. When my younger brother got smallpox, Rama stayed with the rest of us on the upper floor in such a way that we did not miss our brother. It was thanks to Rama's attention that I never got smallpox.

He also saved me from another terrible illness. Indore was gripped by plague and we lived outside the city. Ma and my younger brother, who was then just a few months old, were so sick that Babu-ji had little time to look after the other three of us. At such times, Rama surrounded us with his love so completely that it was impossible to feel any lack.

One day, we were sitting on a swing that hung from a branch of a large mango tree, listening intently to one of Rama's strange stories, when I developed a mild fever and a swelling near my ear. Rama had told us a story of an old woman from whose swollen foot a heroic frog had emerged due to divine powers. I gave Rama my news, saying, 'I think the frog from the story is going to emerge from my ear.' The poor fellow was stunned. It would be hard to say how much time he spent fomenting the spot with a hot piece of brick wrapped in a wet cloth. As he did this, he kept up a muttering, in which the names of Devi, Hanuman, and Bhagvan could be heard. He did not move from my bedside for two days and two nights.

On the third day, the swelling subsided but Rama developed a high fever. He had a swelling which was incised and he was very ill, but he was content because I had been saved from illness. When he recovered sufficiently, Ma took us to see him. He was weak, but his dry lips smiled, his sunken eyes swam with joy, and a wave of energy ran though his feeble body. Ma said, 'You saved her, Rama! If we hadn't been able to save you, we would have repented it all our lives.' Rama stretched out his hand, on which the nails had grown long, to touch Ma's feet, and then wiped his tears.

When Rama recovered, Ma began to say quite often, 'Rama, you must settle down so that you can enjoy having children.' Rama would always reply, 'What are you saying? What have I to do with producing my own wretched children? May my princely children prosper—they will ferry their Rama's boat across.'[19] He made so many negative comments about his prospective children that we became well-acquainted with them and saw them as our

19 In Hinduism, this world is known as *bhava sagara*, the ocean of existence. At death, one is usually reborn. But liberation entails crossing over the ocean of existence into another realm. The metaphor for that crossing is a boat; often the divine is imaged as the ferryman. Some also believe that a child is necessary to light one's funeral pyre and start one's journey.

rivals. We were sure that had they been like us, he would not always refer to them as wretches, burnt-faces, and so on.

When Rama one day appeared in the courtyard in his pink turban and shoes, holding his lathi, we grew afraid because we had never seen him so attired. Looking suspiciously at the lathi, I asked, 'Are you going to beat those children, Rama?' Twirling the lathi, Rama answered, laughing, 'Yes, Raja Bhaiya, I will belabour those wretches.' But Rama went away and we had to think up many strategies to escape the hard hands of Kallu's mother.

After what was for us an eternity and for others a period of time, Rama appeared at the doorway in a saffron turban and pink dhoti, and began to call, 'Raja Bhaiya, Raja Bhaiya.' We ran out, tumbling over each other, but we pulled up short on the verandah. Rama was not alone. We were interested in but also suspicious of the woman who stood behind him in a red sari, bangles on her arms, anklets on her feet, and with her face veiled.

When Munni began to swing on Rama's kurta, two sharp eyes, looking through the veil that came up to the nose, silently opposed her action. When my little brother clamoured to be enthroned on Rama's shoulders, a tremor of refusal seemed to run through the covered head, and when I bent down to look at that new face, she turned around and stood with her back to me. How could we be pleased with such a guest?

As time passed, the seedlings of war took root in Rama's dark room, and the possibility of drought befalling our realm of play kept growing. Rama was both Vishwakarma, the divine artist who set up our city of toys, and the demon who destroyed it, but now he had no leisure to engage in these important duties. As soon as he came to us, that veiled figure followed him, and her silent non-cooperation suffocated not only Rama and us but even the dolls.

For this reason, our war committee was convened. The king must have an exalted place, so I sat on the table with my feet dangling in the air, the chief minister was seated on a chair, and the general on a stool. Then the king asked gravely, 'Why has Rama brought her?' The minister, solemnly shaking her head, repeated, 'Why has Rama brought her?' And the general, scowling to conceal his inability to articulate the words, said, 'Yes, why has he blought her?' Then this strange committee unanimously resolved that the being who scorned our sovereign rights must be punished in order to protect the majesty of the law. This task was allotted to the general.

When Rama's wife was cooking, my younger brother would quietly put a biscuit in her kitchen.[20] While she was bathing, he would use a stick to throw her dry sari on the ground. She received many punishments of this kind but she neither asked forgiveness nor sought a truce. She merely became firmer in her opposition and took revenge on Rama for our misdeeds. An impenetrable veil of harshness covered her dark face and the shadow of anger never left her black eyes. Rama, who was as much of an innocent as we were, was at first baffled, then upset, and finally he revolted. Perhaps he did not understand why he should lay all his time and affection at the feet of that woman or how he was to live if he did so. Then, one day, Rama's wife, enraged, went off to her parental home.

Rama seemed to have been liberated from an unpleasant bondage because he once again became the ever-cheerful creator of our unique world and forgot about his wife as if she had been a line drawn in water. But Ma could not tolerate any form of injustice. She thought it improper that Rama should throw away his wife like one of our old toys, so Rama began to receive difficult and complicated sermons about knowing one's duty.

---

20 A biscuit, being a foreign item processed in a factory, would pollute the kitchen.

This time Rama's departure seemed imbued with the pitiable helplessness of a student who, thanks to his father's affection, has to go and be beaten by a schoolmaster. And this time he was not able to return. After a long time, we found out that he was sick. Ma sent money and wrote, asking him to come, but he was meant to accompany us only thus far on life's path.

We laid our toys aside and kept gazing at the outside world with blank eyes. My brother wanted to cross the seven seas but his journey was postponed for want of a flying horse. Munni was eager to traverse the world by train but proceeding and stopping were impossible without the one who waved the green and red flags. I wanted to get my doll married but the auspicious moment kept getting delayed in the absence of an organizer and a priest.

Our youngest brother, who brought the count up to four, was now two-and-a-half years old and grew more practised every day at destroying our constructions. We would set him in the midst of our toys and take turns telling him stories about Rama, concluding with the warning that when Rama returned with his pink turban and lathi, he would prevent this mischief. But Rama did not return, not even to write the epilogue of our story.

Today, I have become so big that the insistence on being called Raja Bhaiya seems like a dream, the stories of childhood appear imagined, and the beauty of the world of toys has become an illusion, but Rama, even today, is true, beautiful and memorable.[21] Rama's vast shadow, standing in my past, keeps growing in the present—voiceless, tireless, liquescent with love.

3 July 1930

---

21 The words translated as 'true, beautiful' are '*satya, sundar*' in the original. Alluding to the phrase in the Upanishads, '*satyam shivam sundaram*', Mahadevi applies these words for ultimate reality and for Lord Shiva to the humble Rama, whose love was divine.

Bhabhi

Although so many years have gone by, my memory, in the mists fast gathering every day around the past, not only draws every line of that sad, tender face before me but also brings it alive.

The brow that looks broad in proportion to the small, round face, yet is bounded by two dry, black locks that seem to enclose childhood and maturity within them; heavy, long-lashed eyelids and moist-seeming eyes in their shadow; a straight nose that is small even for that small face; and the lips somewhat open, as if surprised by the laughter imprinted on them, can fade with the flow of time but cannot be washed away.

How can I forget those palms, tender in some places and hardened in others, wrapped in a net of grimy lines due to doing all the clean and dirty, easy and difficult household chores, those slim fingers seemingly weighed down by lustreless nails inscribed with black lines, the thin, dry but fair arms seemingly unable to bear the weight of the hands, and the two small feet, with long toes suggesting delicacy but fatigued, as it were, by the heavy encirclement of the Marwari *lehnga*! How many times, in my childhood, those hands smoothed out my tangled hair and bound it up with great tenderness. How many times those feet, forgetting their learnt gravity, ran across the courtyard to open the door for me. It is hard to say, now, how my innocent, eight-year-old intellect made her into my Bhabhi.[1] Many of my classmates had very nice sisters-in-law; perhaps, listening to their accounts, my heart, which had not known this relationship for itself or even among distant relatives, experienced a lack which that widowed Marwari daughter-in-law filled.

I remember that Mission school of my childhood, where the monotony of prayers and curriculum made me so tearful that every day, between the time I got home and the time I fell asleep, I continuously tried to think up pretexts for not going to school. In those days, the chief object of my envy was the maid's daughter, who washed dishes and cleaned the kitchen but got to stay at home. I was always in a quandary, wondering whether the harsh God, who had written constant attendance at school into my destiny, was my mother's Thakur-ji [Krishna] or the Jesus of the nuns at the Mission. My mind was always lost in deep thought about puja, arati, and prayer, because if this God was Ma's Thakur-ji, he would be angered by my showing disinterest in his arati and puja, and would reduce the amount of time I spent at home, but if he was at school and I made excuses not to go, he would increase the hours of study.

There was one ray of light in this darkness. The school was close by so Kallu's old mother took me and my books there, and fetched me back too, and on the way, dogs fighting on the street, their wandering puppies, a cat sitting in a corner washing her face, a parrot hanging in a cage on a verandah practising human speech, flocks of ducks or quail, a performing monkey in a cap,

---

1 Bhabhi means 'brother's wife'. Hindi has different words for different types of sisters-in-law. A brother's wife is called bhabhi, and a husband's sister is called nanad. Mahadevi wonders here why she chose to call the older girl 'sister-in-law' rather than the more common 'older sister'.

and a female monkey in a veil or a dancing bear tempered the monotony of school.

I had never properly seen the old Seth-ji who sat at the shop that was decorated at one end with cotton and silk clothes, both white and coloured, and at the other end with shining brass vessels, but I was curious about the eyes that looked through a slit in the old sacking curtain on the back door of that house. I sometimes wanted to lift the curtain and peer behind it, but Kallu's mother was for me no less scary than that monster which is frequently invoked to frighten children. If I didn't obey her, she could hurt my pierced ear lobes while bathing me, pull my hair too tightly when plaiting it, get a narrow-necked frock caught in my eyes when putting it on, tell a lot of true and false tales about me at home and at school—in short, she had many ways of avenging herself on me.

But whether or not Kallu's mother liked the idea of my getting acquainted with the mistress of those eyes, she certainly enjoyed telling her story. She was an orphan and inauspiciously unfortunate too. The old Seth, despite everyone advising against it, got her married to his only son, who died the same year although he was not sick at all. Now the Seth-ji is fed up of her flighty ways. He doesn't let her go anywhere nor does he let anyone enter the house. Only on moonless nights, he allows her to give alms to a Brahmin woman who visits in his presence. The poor Seth is defamed in his community because of her, and look at her shamelessness—as soon as her father-in-law goes to the shop, she sticks herself to the curtain. There is no one in the house to supervise her. Her husband's married sister lives in the city and visits off and on, and then she gets a good hammering. Kallu's mother recounted all this in her own special vocabulary and in her own strange style.

But this information was for me much like my Nani's [maternal grandmother's] stories of Bela Rani. The only truth in Kallu's mother's story that troubled me was that this princess constantly gazed through the sacking curtain at the child who heard the story. This was discomfiting. Kallu's mother's stories, combined with the eyes peering through the slit in the curtain, taught me that if all the kings, queens, princes, princesses, and demons from stories looked at listeners in this way, the stories would cease to be enjoyable.

The black eyes stuck to the brown sacking would have remained an object of my imaginings had not heavy rain one day prevented Kallu's mother from showing up, and had I not set out alone for school as soon as the rain stopped and then slipped on the wet street right in front of that curtain. Children who fall down usually cry not from being hurt but from embarrassment. Perhaps this was the reason for my crying too, because I don't remember getting hurt.

I can't say when the mistress of those eyes emerged from behind the curtain and drew me into the yard, but the sudden surprise stopped my tears. A thin and pleasant-looking girl-like woman was wiping the muddy water from my hands and clothes with her sari when, from the verandah, the old Seth said, 'Arey, this is Varma Saheb's daughter.'

From that day, that house in which there was not a single window or skylight, where no servants or guests were ever seen, and where not a single animal or bird lived, became an attraction for me. In that tomb-like house, that teenage girl, like a flower within iron barricades, without any companion, without any form of amusement or entertainment, seemed devoted to practising how to grow old. The old man ate only once a day, and she was a widow. For her to eat twice a day would be enough to prove that she was bored with a widow's restraint-oriented life and was moving in some other direction.

Even my childish intelligence comprehended how much work she did despite her body being weakened by frequent fasting and by habitual under-eating. Just as I laughed at the way she squatted to sweep that ruin-like house and the long, broad yard, and the way she had to pause frequently while drawing water from the courtyard well for her own and her father-in-law's baths or while beating dirty clothes with a wooden baton to wash them since no washerman came around, so also a new kind of gloom welled up in my heart at the sound of coughing from the smoke-filled kitchen that was dark even in the day and lit up only by burning wood, or at the clash of pots falling from feeble fingers while polishing them with dry ashes until they shone like silver or gold (Marwaris rinse pots with water just before using them).

But however hard the work, however weak her body, I never saw any difference in the laughter that lit up her face and never saw her pause in her work. And that unfortunate girl's day stretched out like Draupadi's garment.[2] In the morning, she entered the dark kitchen only after bathing and worshipping the *tulsi* [holy basil], but by ten o'clock, after feeding her father-in-law, she was free to speak through the sacking curtain and invite me to come over in the evening. After she had finished cleaning, washing dishes, grinding, and pounding, there was still one watch of the day left. She was forbidden to go towards the shop so she spent her leisure near the sacking curtain, where she could see only the backs of some houses and one or two people walking along, but this was enough for her frivolity to be broadcast far and wide.

Today, I can understand the pitiful state of that nineteen-year-old girl, whose golden dreams had been carried away like dolls' houses in a flood and left her so alone that she could not even tell the story of those dreams. In that state, she gave all the affection of her companionless heart to an eight-year-old child,

---

2 When the villains in the epic Mahabharata try to strip the heroine Draupadi in public, she cries out to Krishna who saves her by miraculously lengthening her garment so that they cannot pull it off.

but because the child was incapable of entering her world, she embraced the world of dolls. The old man too was so glad to find such an innocent companion for his daughter-in-law that he himself made the effort to come and fetch me or take me home with much respect.

And Ma would turn her face away and wipe her eyes when she heard the story of that orphaned and widowed girl-child. One by one, my small doll, her shapeless husband, her lame mother-in-law, her sister-in-law who could not sit down, and her two children who had hands but no other features, all found their way to Bhabhi's room. All their household appurtenances, from the grinding stone to the palanquin and train, also moved into that ruin.

I had never seen Bhabhi wear anything but a white veil and a black skirt or a black veil and a brown skirt embroidered in white, but beautiful, colourful clothes were prepared for her husband's sister at every festival. Arrangements to preserve the dolls' modesty were made with some cloth-cuttings Bhabhi had gathered and some clothes that I brought from home. Bhabhi knew how to sew and she dressed my doll as a Marwari woman. I had learned at school to stitch loose pajamas and at home to stitch a gusseted kurta, so the male doll looked like a Lala.[3] A slit in a square piece of cloth sufficed to put it over the children's necks so they looked like offspring of some primaeval era.

Bhabhi was illiterate so she was greatly impressed by my scholarly abilities. I had astonished her by telling her the English names of most animals and by reading an English poem from a picture-book with much gusto, reduced her to tears by reading aloud Hindi stories like '*Mata ka Hriday*' [A Mother's Heart] and

---

3 'Lala' is an honorific for a male member of the trading and shopkeeping community.

'*Bhai ka Prem*' [A Brother's Love], and when I told her of a letter I was writing to my uncle, she was reminded of her paternal aunt who lived in a village near Bikaner. Sighing deeply, she would often say, 'I don't know her address or I would have had you write a letter to her.'

The hardest days were when the old man's fortunate married daughter visited her parental home. After she left, Bhabhi's fair hands would bear long, black burn marks and her feet blue bruises, but when I asked about them, she would distract me by getting me involved in one of the dolls' problems.

At that time, I was learning the art of embroidery at school and I embroidered large blue flowers on my green sari. Bhabhi loved colourful clothes so she was as amazed and charmed by the sari as if it was a beautiful painting. I still do not quite know why I insisted that my mother buy the same kind of cloth for me and why, without telling anyone, I secretly began embroidering blue flowers on a veil. Poor Bhabhi would send for me repeatedly, would show me new clothes for the dolls, and make new homes for them, but finding me unable to stay for long, would sadly see me off at the door.

Inscribed in my memory with hot iron is the day when I secretly took the veil to Bhabhi with the aim of plunging her into amazement. Perhaps it was Saavan ki Teej that day, because instead of wearing plain clothes to school, I had been allowed to wear a gold-bordered sari covered in wavy stripes, and instead of telling me to study in the morning, Ma had put *mehndi* on my hands.[4]

4 Saavan ki Teej is a monsoon festival celebrated by women. Rajasthani women wear clothes in wavy patterns that imitate the rain. Married women go to their parents' homes, worship the Goddess, wear new clothes, and enjoy themselves swinging and singing.

She was sitting on the verandah with her back to the door, cleaning some grain, so when I went up to her on tiptoe and put the veil on her head, she sat up, startled. She loved colours, and I had sat alone, far from my dolls and toys, embroidering such a large veil for her with my small hands. It is not surprising that for a moment she forgot her condition, in which she was forbidden to wear such coloured clothes, and like a little girl pleased with a new toy, she wrapped it around herself in a sort of oblivion, took hold of my chin, and laughed aloud.

And when she recollected herself, hearing someone's astonished, 'Daughter-in-law,' her father-in-law was holding on to the doorpost as if to stop himself from collapsing, and her sister-in-law, hard as an unsheathed sword, had stepped over the threshold, her eyes burning like coals. It certainly must have been Teej, because the old man had gone himself to fetch his daughter home.

What happened after that is too pitiful for me to endure even in memory. Never again have I seen such a display of cruelty. Perhaps it was because I had no way to save her that I began to cry loudly, but she was saved only when both her mind and her body lost consciousness. How the old man took me home and how many days I lay in a fever due to trepidation remain hidden from me in a heavy fog but when I saw her again after a long time, her childlike eyes were dyed in deep despair and the lips which once seemed to conceal laughter now trembled, as if tired of trying to hold back a wail. That one incident matured the child and turned the young woman into an old one.

We left Indore and only after many years was I able to try to find out more about her. I found that a huge mansion had long since replaced the small shop. The old man had passed on, leaving his daughter-in-law to the world's protection, but I still do not know how the harsh world protected her. I know what such a small bubble counts for in the large ocean of humanity but sometimes my heart longs to find again the one who forgot the emptiness of her life in arranging my dolls' household and adorning the world of my toys.

Even today, when someone curiously asks why I have no attraction to coloured clothing, that past becomes present to me. Can anyone understand how sad and withered the face is which gradually takes form before me amidst coloured clothing? Sometimes that face reflects itself in all the sad, weary faces I see and binds me to itself with an unbreakable bond.

I often think—when the old man closed his eyes never to open them again, where would she, whom he had not allowed the right to look at the world, have gone?

And then, in response to some unknown question, some malignant possibility, all the affection in my heart cries out in grief, No, No!

11 October 1933

Binda

With my eyes on that small, weak little girl with fearful eyes who seemed to shrink into herself, I returned the filled-out application to the gentleman sitting before me and said, 'You haven't put down her age correctly. Correct it, otherwise there will be problems later.' When he replied, 'No, she turned fourteen last Ashadh,'[1] I looked, amazed, at that prospective student who was devoid of a nine-year-old's playfulness but also unacquainted with the shy exuberance of a fourteen-year-old adolescent.

My curiosity with regard to her mother must have expressed itself in a question because I received a somewhat awkward reply, 'I have a second wife and you probably know…' Leaving his sentence half-unheard, my heart, placing a finger on the hazy picture of Binda, or Vindhyeshwari, overlaid with the dust of more than two eras in the art gallery of memory, said, 'I know, I definitely know.'

Binda was my childhood friend at a time when I did not know the ineradicable difference between life and death. When I heard that my maternal grandfather and paternal grandmother had gone

---

1 The month in the Hindu calendar corresponding to approximately mid-June to mid-July.

to heaven, I gravely informed the whole household that when my head began to touch the top of the clothes cupboard, I would go and visit them. No one wanted to oppose this auspicious decision of mine, nor did I understand the rule that once one dies one cannot return. How then could I imagine that a mother might leave her small children and depart? My experience of the world was also circumscribed. When the white dog who had been my companion from infancy became an alert guardian of her blind children who lay in the dark room under the stairs, her growls poured water over my friendship for her. The brown cat carried her helpless, mouse-like babies so gently in her sharp teeth that not a single tooth pierced them. I had also seen grains and insects being placed in the small, open beaks in the pigeons' nest in a corner of the roof and in the sparrows' nest behind a big picture. Nor was I unaware of our cow Shyama's distressed bellowing when her calf was moved away from her. The beggar woman who went door to door with a child clinging to her shoulder and another holding her finger begged for her children. So I clearly understood that all the business of the world was undertaken in order to feed children, put them to sleep, and so on, and the task of ensuring that no error occurred in this important duty was entrusted to the beings called mothers.

And Binda too had a mother, whom we called Panditayin Chachi and Binda called Nayi Amma.[2] Her fat, fair body tightly wrapped in a bright sari, she sat on a string-bed massaging Mohan, her plump-cheeked, flat-nosed baby who had eyes like blue glass buttons. I liked the thick line of vermilion between the two neatly arranged halves of her hair, the black string-like collyrium in her sleepy eyes, her shining earrings, necklace,

2 Panditayin: Wife of a Pandit (Brahmin). Chachi: Aunt (father's younger brother's wife). Nayi Amma: New mother.

gem-studded multicoloured bangles, and toe-rings with bells, because these adornments made her look like a doll.

All this was fine but her behaviour seemed strange. On winter days, when we were awakened after the sun rose, washed with warm water, dressed in socks, caps, and woollen clothes, and coaxed into drinking warm milk, our neighbour Panditayin Chachi's voice kept rising higher and higher. Had I been unable to understand the meaning of her roars, I could have thought them displays of affection like Shyama's bellows, but her vocabulary, because it was familiar, created confusion. Even my ignorant mind recognized the stream of harshness flowing through sentences like, 'Will you get up or shall I come?', 'Why are you staring at me with eyes like a bullock?', 'When will you heat up Mohan's milk?', 'You wretch, you don't even die.'

When I sometimes went up to the roof to understand the story of that house, I would see Binda, wrapped in a dirty sari, spinning like a top between courtyard and kitchen. Her sweeping, lighting the fire, filling water at the courtyard tap, giving a pitcher of milk to her new mother, seemed like a play to me, because all these tasks were impossible for me to do. But when Panditayin Chachi's harsh voice, ignoring these magical doings that amazed me, resounded, along with occasional rebukes from Pandit-ji, a shadow of sorrow seemed to surround me. I tried but failed to understand what that mischievous Binda could secretly be doing in her house since her good behaviour was held up as an example to halt my naughtiness. I did not do a single chore and raised a ruckus from dawn to dusk, yet mother neither ordered me to die nor threatened to gouge out my eyes. One day, I asked, 'Isn't Panditayin Chachi like you?' I don't know whether Ma understood my meaning but she simply said, 'She is,' which neither solved Binda's problem nor resolved my dilemma.

Binda must have been a little older than I was but she was short, as if someone had pressed her head down to make her small.

Her thin hands and feet, their thin skin revealing green veins, like the transparent covering of a two-pice tambourine, were always tremulous with some unknown fear. The way she started up, her whole body trembling, when Panditayin Chachi's voice was heard increased my amazement, transforming it to fear, and Binda's eyes reminded me of a caged bird.

Once, while we were counting stars, she pointed at a bright star and said, 'There is my Amma.' My astonishment knew no bounds. Did everyone have one Amma amongst the stars and another at home? When I asked, Binda gave me a few grains from her treasury of knowledge and I understood that an Amma who is called by God becomes a star and looks down at her children from above, while the one who comes into the house, highly decked-up, is called a new mother. My intellect did not accept defeat easily, so I thought about it and said, 'Why don't you call the new mother old mother, then she won't be new and won't scold you.' Binda did not like my idea because she had seen her old mother depart, lying down, in an open palanquin, and her new one arrive seated in a closed palanquin, so it was hard for her to change either's status.

But my heart was troubled by her story so I said pleadingly to Ma that night, 'Don't become a star, however bright a star God wants to turn you into.' Poor Ma, surprised by my strange mood, had not even managed to reply when I expressed my meaning plainly, 'Otherwise, a new mother like Panditayin Chachi will come in a palanquin to stop my milk, biscuits, and sweets, and I will have to become Binda.' What Ma replied I don't recall, but I remember that I managed to fall asleep that night only by grasping her *aanchal* tightly in my fist.[3]

---

3 *Aanchal* is the end of a sari that hangs loose and is used for many purposes, such as wiping a child's or one's own face. Idiomatically, it stands for the protection and nurturance a woman provides.

Binda's crimes remained unknown to me but I became familiar with all the punishments inflicted by Panditayin Chachi's courtroom. I had seen Binda standing for hours in summer afternoons on the burning floor of the courtyard, lifting by turns one bare foot and then the other; I had found her tied to a pillar in the kitchen all day long; and I had seen her, her face withered with hunger, fanning her new mother and Mohan in his cradle. She was punished not only for offences but also for lack of offences, so when a thick, black curly hair of Panditayin Chachi's was found in Pandit-ji's plate, Binda was punished. I liked the brownness and softness of her tangled, oil-free hair that she was not able to wash properly with her small hands. When Panditayin Chachi's scissors scattered it on the rubbish heap, replacing it with thin lines like the cat's black fur, I felt like crying but Binda sat still, as if both head and hair belonged to her new mother.

I remember another day too. Milk was boiling on the coal fire. Binda took the milk off with her small hands but it slipped from her fingers and fell. I was stunned when Binda stood at our door, crying, her feet burnt by the boiling milk. It was hard for me to understand why she did not tell Panditayin Chachi and get medication for her injuries. Things became even more mysterious when Binda put my hand on her thumping heart and explained to me the necessity of hiding her somewhere.

I pulled her into our house but I could not take her up to Ma or find a place to hide her. Then Panditayin Chachi's angry voice came over the wall, filling the air around us, so we tumbled into the small shed where grass was stored for the cow. The grass blades poked me and the darkness bothered me, but Binda sat, her feet hidden in the grass and her two cold hands clasping mine, as if the prickly grass was a silk coverlet. Perhaps I fell asleep because when the dairyman came to fetch grass and loudly announced this unprecedented event, I rubbed my eyes and asked, 'Is it morning?'

After Ma, having anointed Binda's feet with limestone water and sesame oil, sent her home with a special messenger, I don't know what became of her but I do know that Panditayin Chachi's justice had no place for forgiveness and no right of appeal.

For some days, I did not see Binda working in the house or yard. Ma had stopped me from going to visit her but she herself often went, taking some grapes or apples along. After much coaxing, the maid Rukiya told me that Maharani had come to that house.[4] 'Can't I meet her?' I asked, causing Rukiya to stuff a cloth into her mouth to stop her laughter. Since no one resolved my quandary, I secretly slipped into Binda's house one afternoon. Binda lay alone on a bed on the vacant ground floor of the house. Her eyes were sunken, her face distorted by pustules, and her body seemed indistinguishable from the dirty sheet with which it was covered. I didn't know that sickness was possible without a doctor, bottles of medicine, Ma stroking my head, and Babu-ji hovering around the bed, so I stood by the lonely Binda and looked around, mystified. Binda told me, partly in gestures and partly in unclear words, that new mother and Mohan were living on the first floor, perhaps from fear of smallpox. The maid Barauni came morning and evening to do what needed to be done.

After that, I was not able to see Binda because Ma was very upset by my having disobeyed orders. One morning, Rukiya said something to her, and she closed the Ramayana, wiped her eyes repeatedly, and went off to Binda's house. As she went, she did not forget to order me not to come out, so it became necessary to peer and peep out from wherever I could. Rukiya was no less than an omniscient reporter for me but she would not tell me anything unless I begged and pleaded, which was against my

---

4 Maharani means 'queen' and is used to refer to Sheetala Devi, Goddess of smallpox.

dignity. All I could see through the window was a crowd of men at Binda's door. I associated such crowds with weddings and the bridegroom's procession. Was someone getting married, and if so, who? Such questions tested my brain. Pandit-ji could marry only if his second wife, Panditayin Chachi, died and became a star, and Mohan, who could not even sit up, could not get married, so I concluded that Binda was getting married and had not invited me. Hurt by this unthinkable insult, I vowed, with all my dolls as witnesses, that I would not invite Binda for any auspicious event.

After gazing at Binda's house for many days, I asked Ma when she would come back from her in-laws' home, and I then found out that she had gone to join her sky-dwelling mother. After that, I often searched for Binda among the small stars around the brightly shining star, but how could she be identified at such a distance? Much time has passed since then, but the story of Binda and her new mother is not concluded. Who can say if it ever will be?

5 August 1934

Sabiya

Sabiya is not a short form of Shabnam or Shabraat. It is the local version of our ancient Savitri.[1] But, truth to tell, one would have to say either that our generous nobility kindly allowed the lowest among the Harijans to become pure in the shadow of this noun or else that her parents, conventionally in heaven but actually in hell, like clever pickpockets, clandestinely stole the wealth of this name and cut it to their own requirements in such a way that it is now hard to prove anyone's right over it.[2]

---

1 Savitri is the heroine of a famous story in the Mahabharata. She outwits Yama, God of Death, and wins back her dead husband Satyavan.

2 Although the word Harijan fell into disuse and was condemned by activists in the late twentieth century, and was adversely commented upon by the Supreme Court in 2017, these interdictions cannot apply with retrospective effect to 1935, when this essay was written. In 1935, Gandhi renamed the so-called 'untouchables' Harijans, which means 'people of God'. The term Harijan had earlier been widely used by devotional (bhakti) poets to refer to all devotees (bhaktas), especially worshippers of Vishnu, Rama, and Krishna. Gandhi's new use of the term was intended to emphasize their inherent dignity and to fight against untouchability and other forms of discrimination. In 1935, he founded the All India Anti-Untouchability League, which was later renamed Harijan Sewak Sangh. In 1935 and later, he worked on improving their social and economic conditions and showing Hindus

As if to oppose my rule of not changing servants, my old sweeper, without asking permission, set out on the great journey from which it is not possible to recall anyone, and then one day Sabiya appeared before me, with a month-old baby wrapped in a greasy cloth, and a five-year-old girl whose nakedness was veiled in dirt, holding her finger. Her face looked as if moulded from shiny black mud but every line was as finely drawn as one sees in plaster-of-Paris images. Her eyes were round instead of long and their gaze was civil but startled, like that of a child lost in a fairground. The heavy, dulled gilt circlets on her hands and feet seemed to put her in the position of a prisoner. The yellow glass spangle on her narrow forehead above her joined eyebrows looked like a yellow nightshade flower growing on a dust-heap. Wrapped in a sari that was once red but was now the colour of an old pitcher, Sabiya looked like a clay image carefully made by an unskilful sculptor, with its colours washed away and only its well-shaped lines binding the earth.

I learnt that her husband had gone away without telling her. She was in labour at the time and fell ill from grief, so another woman took her place at the bungalow where she worked. If I employed her, she would be able to raise her children. Looking doubtfully at the small bundle, I asked, despite her assurances that she would work with heart and soul, 'How

---

that untouchability had no sanction in Hindu scriptures. Mahadevi Varma was an ardent Gandhian, therefore she uses this term in a positive way. We cannot import twenty-first attitudes backwards in time to change her language and ideas. In this sentence, she both sarcastically condemns the hypocritical attitudes and behaviour of so-called higher jatis, and also points out that people like Sabiya's parents considered themselves as having equal rights over classical Hindu stories and names, such as Savitri. Mahadevi herself worked tirelessly for the welfare of the people Gandhi and Gandhians called Harijans, for example, in 'Gheesa' she devotes her weekends to teaching their children in a village.

will you work with him?' Sabiya stroked the feeble and dirty little girl's back, and nodding her head confidently, analysed her daughter's exceptional skill in looking after her brother, citing many examples that made me smile although I could not laugh. In truth, seeing the seriousness spread darkly in the little girl Bachiya's firefly-like eyes, it seemed cruel to laugh and unsympathetic to stay silent.

After I had explained the work to her and left the verandah for my room, old Bhaktin's curiosity broke the dam of her fear of me and many questions flowed out. Since she is a tireless storyteller, finding out everything about everyone is the primary principle of her life, and thanks to the greatest storyteller of all, God, the virtues of Yojanabahu's arms have been transferred to her tongue.[3] When a few scattered words from thousands of questions forced themselves into my ears, I could not ignore them because of the pathos of the answers.

I couldn't clearly hear the question relating to Sabiya's husband but the tone of her response, 'No, he couldn't have done anything, he was himself a married man,' indicated that the speaker was near tears. In answer to the statement, 'That woman must have been quite something,' Sabiya said in a tired voice, as if defending her, 'Mother, everyone has their own destiny.' I then absorbed myself in writing and the thread of the story was lost. Gradually I found out that Sabiya's husband was not only not a local version of Satyavan but was not even meaningless like his meaningless name Maiku. One day he disappeared with the new bride of another member of his community, and this at the time when Sabiya was laid up with her three-day-old baby. Sabiya had never stopped waiting for him but there was no news of him. The poor fellow

---

3 Yojanabahu was one of Ravana's warriors who had exceptionally long arms.

whose wife had run away proposed to marry Sabiya in order to take revenge and also to resettle his uprooted household, but she refused. Finally, following the idiom that a burnt child dreads the fire, he made his old, widowed sister-in-law the Lakshmi of his home and heaved a sigh of relief.[4]

Unsurprisingly, everyone began to call Sabiya eccentric.[5] But I did not see any eccentricity in her except an obsession with work. Early in the morning, she would spread a torn, dirty cloth under the neem tree and lay the baby down on it, seating Bachiya next to him to watch over him and drive away the flies. Then she would tie a ragged scarf tightly round her waist and pick up the broom. Then at one end of the courtyard Sabiya's dance would begin as she almost leapt in the air to the music of the broom, while at the other end, Bachiya, justifying her name, and seated sometimes in *virasana* and sometimes in *yogasana*, waved away the flies, or jumping sometimes on one foot and sometimes on both, shooed away the crows.[6] The mother's weak body had the flexibility of a green branch rather than the stiffness of dry wood, which spoke more of her life than her weakness, and the daughter's dried-up body had the unavailing mobility of a new shoot's bud unable to blossom due to frost rather than the playfulness of a new leaf, which spoke not of development but of stasis. The neem tree that was Bachiya's stage was directly opposite my window, and important spectators such as my bitch

---

4 Lakshmi is the Goddess of Prosperity. A wife, daughter or daughter-in-law is called the Lakshmi of the home, whose presence brings prosperity and happiness. Here, the man marries his widowed sister-in-law, thus making her the Lakshmi of his home.

5 In Sabiya's community, an abandoned or widowed young woman is expected to remarry.

6 Play on the child's name, Bachiya, which means 'little girl' and also means 'saved'.

and the cat from the girls' hostel were welcome there, as were visiting crows, unnamed birds, and the neighbouring squirrel who lived in the tree, but Bachiya's spontaneous watchfulness suggested that everyone, from the bitch to the birds and from the squirrel to the flies, was lying in wait to abduct her precious brother.[7] Perhaps it was to warn those disguised robbers that she spoke in many voices, from the cat's meowing to the birds' twittering, and always concluded by blowing a whistle, bought for a paisa, as if it were a conch shell.

When hunger pierced the fort of her duty, she would take out a piece of *roti* tied in a corner of the same dirty cloth and use it to contend with her hidden foe. But this was hard in the presence of so many spectators. Once, as soon as she tried to reproach a rebel crow with a rooster's voice, he snatched her only weapon against hunger and ran off with it. Finally, I performed the auspicious task of replacing a wooden dagger with a machine-gun by sending over some biscuits and a *besan laddu*. After that, Bachiya's requests reached me in the form of rooster-like crowing and whatever I sent in response was overlaid with Bhaktin's irritation.

Finishing all her work at ten, Sabiya would collect her creation like a conjuror and go off to bathe. By the time she returned with a well-scrubbed and shining brass plate, the long process of activities at lunch-hour in the hostel would be over. I could guess what bitter sarcasms from the woman cook, the woman Kahar and others, Sabiya must have received along with the *dal* and rice from the kitchen, given to her because of my strict but unconventional orders that the left-overs in plates not be dumped on the sweeper but be fed to the bullocks who drew

7 Mahadevi Varma was the principal of Prayag Mahila Vidyapeeth, a girls' residential school that developed into a college. Her house was on the premises and so was the students' hostel.

the school's carts.[8] Sabiya was as reluctant to complain about anyone as one would be if complaints produced burning blisters in the mouth.

Seeing Sabiya carry her meal in a *thali* with great difficulty, every morning and evening, while laden with the children, I suggested that she nurse the baby here and then eat here as well. She answered with great hesitation, as if she were acknowledging some unforgivable offence, 'Malkin, Bachiya has a blind grandmother![9] How can I eat without feeding her first?' It was useless to say any more; but my heart was enraged at Maiku who had dumped the burden of two children and his blind mother on a sorrowful and weak woman. Man is a strange being. For the smallest of pleasures, he gives woman the heaviest sorrows, and does it with great ease, as if he is giving her what is due to her. He wants all his duties to come in a sweet form, like quinine coated with sugar. As soon as he tastes bitterness, his first impulse is to throw down everything right there and run away.

Sabiya's nobility without a cause gave birth in me to affection with a good cause, so her time with me began to pass well. Then suddenly one day Bhaktin, as if working as a translator for Sabiya, who stood shrinking behind the door, told me that she wanted a nice sari. I gave permission to give her the khadi sari that was drying on the clothesline but Bhaktin pulled a face and said, 'A nicer one.' I got up and looked through the saris that could be placed in this uncertain category.

A blue silk sari faded from repeated washings, which was left over from the days when I had not given up wearing silk saris, came to hand, so I threw it to Bhaktin and went back to my work. I never want to know more about anyone than they tell

8 Kahar are a poor community of labourers and palanquin-bearers.

9 Malkin: Polite form of address for a woman employer.

me themselves so I did not ask about this untimely request for a sari, but Bhaktin cannot live without filling in this gap in my nature. However urgent the work I am doing, she sits within my auditory range and recounts stories about all the world as if talking to herself. I have scolded her many times for this but it makes no difference. Ever since she left eighteen mango and five mahua trees, a house of unbaked mud and 25 *bigha*s of land, and gave up her close attachment to three daughters, sons-in-law, and many grandchildren, to come and live with me, the possibility of returning to the village has never once entered her head.[10] Even if I don't pay her, she is not willing to leave; if I don't feed her, she will bring *sattu* and *gur* from the village to eat, but she will leave me only to go to heaven, and that too reluctantly.[11] Is it possible to reform such a person? Therefore, she continues to play the role of Sanjaya.[12] The only difference is that Sanjaya gives the blind Dhritarashtra news of the war when he asks for it, thus giving him the pleasures of vision, while I often have to suffer the grief of becoming deaf thanks to Bhaktin's unsolicited reports on the world.

Well, I found out from Bhaktin that Maiku had returned but with Genda, whom he had made a guest at the home of a sweeper at the railway station.[13] Poor Sabiya was crazy with joy, and immediately rushed off to make arrangements for the reading of

---

10 A *bigha* is a land measurement prevalent in north India. Twenty-five bighas are equivalent to 15.5 acres.

11 *Sattu* is a nutritious mix of roasted cereals and pulses ground to a powder.

12 One of the main narrators in the Mahabharata. He is the blind king Dhritarashtra's charioteer, and recounts the entire war, including the Bhagavad Gita, to him.

13 Genda means 'marigold' and is the name of the married woman with whom Maiku had eloped.

the Satyanarayan story.[14] When all was settled, Maiku kept sitting there, pulling a long face, and after much questioning, gave her the news about Genda and began pleading for Sabiya to fetch Genda home. And seeing Sabiya's silk sari, he said meekly, 'This doesn't look good with your black skin, Sabiya, give it to Genda, it will blossom on her.'

Without saying a word, Sabiya took off the blue sari, put it in Maiku's hands, put on her old sari, and despite her blind mother-in-law trying to stop her, went off to fetch Genda home. But it seems that her heart broke because she would sometimes lean on the neem tree and weep, and sometimes stop while sweeping to wipe her eyes. How long the poor thing had waited for him and repeated his name. Now that he had returned, he had brought Genda along, not bothered to ask how Sabiya was doing, and not even looked at the children, and believing Genda's tattling, was always quarrelling with Sabiya. Sabiya's burden had increased because Maiku had not found employment.

Then one day, Sabiya brought the impertinent, mischievous, wheat-complexioned, and round-faced Genda, wearing the blue sari I had given Sabiya, and said, 'The young one touches your feet, Malkin!' Great—what blessing was I supposed to give her? To wish for her happiness was to wish that she continue to harass Sabiya. So I said, 'May God give you the wisdom to live in harmony.'

Four or five days later, Sabiya appeared again. She wanted an advance of five months' salary, that is, fifty rupees at the rate of ten a month. Surprised, I asked why. It turned out that Genda's first husband and community members were making trouble. Only if the community leaders were feasted would they find the

---

14 Worship of Vishnu accompanied by recital of a story from the eighth-century *Skanda Purana*. Often performed in gratitude.

strength to deal with this constant Mahabharata warfare. If she did not reward the first husband for his continuing civility, she would neglect the principle of self-sacrifice. I did not want to starve Sabiya's children even for such an important endeavour, yet I had to give her some money. When I found out that she had arranged for the rest of the money by selling the last token of her dead mother, a heavy necklace made of coins, I repented. I should have known that this woman would never change her mind about a duty she had accepted.

Even when everyone had agreed to have Genda stay in that house, Sabiya's troubles did not diminish, because that woman kept quarrelling with her unremittingly. When, despite this, I saw Sabiya carrying home a big pitcher of dal, and roti and rice in a plate every day, I could not help feeling astonished. The veil of her parental kindness, despite being filled with burning coals, was able to shelter others. Just as she ignores her innocent children's mischief, she also ignores her husband's heartless ingratitude, her co-wife's improper sarcasms, and her mother-in-law's unreasonable reproaches. She seems to treat them all like children to whom she cannot be undutiful although they turn their backs on their duty.

Her short and simple response to detailed criticisms of Maiku's worthlessness is to ask what everyone would advise her to do if he had gone mad or had contracted some terrible disease. However illogical this argument may be, it shows Sabiya's heart. She is not among those ladies who can counterbalance their husbands' lightness with bungalows, cars, and other luxuries. Nor can she be counted among those whose torture houses are guarded by the harsh and alert guardians of religion or those over whose deluded heads society's naked sword hangs. In every way, she will be labelled the lowest of the low. How then to understand this mystical touchstone which can convert iron into gold?

In all these years, I have only once seen Sabiya in despair. Maiku and Genda had gone to some village to enjoy a fair when a theft occurred in a bungalow near her home. Who does not know that when such things happen, great people who have become rich by exploiting others hand over not only their servants but also the poor people living near them to wild beasts? Even if not a penny of their stolen wealth returns to them, they express their deranged anger by tearing to pieces and throwing away the few rags of honour that the lives of the poor retain.

When Sabiya, almost dead with fear of being entrapped, said to me, 'Now my honour won't survive, Malkin,' and wept silently, her grief touched my heart in a strange way. The value society has set on a woman's honour is not the only measure of that honour. The limits of her honour which are inscribed in a woman's heart are far vaster and more decided than society's. That is why the value of a true Sati can survive in the heart of a woman who trades her life with society's approval, while a Sati who practises religion because she is confined by society's prohibitions can construct the opposite of a true Sati with every tortured breath.[15]

Finally, the disaster that loomed over Sabiya was averted. How that happened is not part of this story. When a lawyer's wife of my acquaintance, referring to this modest and dutiful Sabiya, said to me, 'Why do you employ the wives of thieves?' my cold anger arose like the water which, along with fluidity, has the sharpness to cut through not only soil but even rocks. The words suddenly escaped me, 'If making another's wealth one's own by hook or by crook is theft, I would like to know which wealthy lady among us cannot be called the wife of a thief.' I was disturbed by the

---

15 Sati literally means a woman who adheres to truth. It came to be interpreted as a woman whose honour consists of her chastity and faithful service of her husband, and later also as one who burns herself on her husband's pyre.

blackness that overspread her face but the arrow had been loosed and had hit its mark.

The truth is that I find Sabiya similar to that womanhood of antiquity which extended the bounds of life to some unknown realm.[16] If that woman had to combat death for the sake of life, this one struggles with life in order not to die.

3 March 1935

16 The reference is to Savitri, who won her husband back from death by debating with and tricking the God of Death.

Bitto

Kulmani had not returned from the Mallital market. Sitting and waiting for him on a rock near the lake, I was getting bored and my vision was tired of bowing down along with the reflection of the swaying leafy canopy of boughs. Suddenly, I heard, 'Oh, it's Mahadevi', and turned around to see an old companion of mine standing in a strange posture as if performing exercise, trying to balance her somewhat stout body on the narrow, high heels of her *sandal*s.

The mountainous land that was my wet-nurse has now become my mother. Travelling for several hundred miles on foot, I have seen its peaceful loveliness and most of its life in different forms, but I have not been able to connect its unmoving beauty with the turmoil of the city. Leaving the bosom of my own dusty earth, I find rest at those snowy feet which have meditatively built vast forts from dust to keep her kindness secure for us. I have never enjoyed bundling up the tempests from here and opening them up there, so places like Nainital and Mussoorie have become for me like those unskilful actors who lose their own personalities but fail to play another's part well.

When doctors, worried by my fever, agreed that I should spend some months in the hills, I insisted on getting their permission to stay at Takula, which is three miles away from the turbulence of Nainital, but once a week I had to go to Nainital to consult my doctor, and while the servant was shopping for necessaries, I would wait for him on the somewhat deserted left side of the lake. But I was genuinely pleased to meet my childhood friend that day. I didn't even want to cook up an excuse to avoid going to the bungalow above, where she was staying with her two small children.

Who doesn't know how two people who meet after a long time try to relive their past moments together? We too spent some time placing the pictures of our lives before each other and comparing our experiences. Colouring in the faded memories of the past, my friend told me that an old gentleman, who was a mutual acquaintance of ours, had brought his third, newly-wed, wife to show her Nainital. Only my maturity prevented the surprise in my eyes from expressing itself in words. The old man had seen at least fifty-four springs and autumns.[1] Two wives, as if unable to keep pace with the swiftness of his life, had fallen behind. Of the two sons who were their gift to him, one was working in Calcutta and the other had become the treasure of his in-laws.[2] The old gentleman had two houses and some wealth, so he had felt the need to find a companion to make Vanaprastha Ashram enjoyable.[3]

In response to my silent curiosity, my friend said kindly, 'Don't worry. This time he has uplifted a thirty-five-year-old child widow.' The sarcastic smile on her lips matched the disbelief

---

1 In 1940, the average Indian life expectancy was twenty-seven years; today, it is seventy years. At the time, fifty-four was old.

2 A sarcastic way of saying that he did not work but lived with his in-laws instead of his father.

3 The third stage in the classical Hindu life scheme, from age fifty to seventy-five, when one should engage in social service.

in my, 'Impossible!' After some discussion, it was decided that she would introduce me to her on our way back.

The old man was staying with his wife in two rooms above a shop in Mallital. The woman who answered the door when we knocked, telling us that the old gentleman was out and humbly inviting us in, struck me as very weak and feeble, almost an invalid. A new gold chain confined by her protruding bones seemed to mock her wrinkled neck and bloodless skin as the old-fashioned earrings did her dried and hollow cheeks. Her eyes were big but looked as if they had been placed on top of her dry face under scanty lashes and would pop out if she blinked. Her two lower teeth were broken, perhaps from a fall, because one was invisible and the other half there.

This weak and exhausted-looking woman, who had spent thirty-five long years as a widow only to marry an old bridegroom who was virtually seated on a funeral pyre, was a source of wonder to me. There was neither beauty nor health, neither enthusiasm nor joy in this shrinking form wrapped in a mud-coloured tussore sari. For what reason had she decided to set up a new household? If that first meeting had been our last, there would be nothing else to report today, but as we descended the stairs, we met the old gentleman returning home with apricots tied up in a handkerchief. He repeatedly insisted that we improve our acquaintance with his newly-wed wife and that was how I was apprised of the sad fate of this strangely married woman.

The only sister of three brothers, she was pampered as a child. She was married and widowed in childhood. Neither was she excited by marriage nor was she depressed by widowhood. Because their son died the year he was married, her in-laws considered her inauspicious, and her sorrowful parents did not want to throw their beloved daughter, who had been protected like a doll of butter, into that fire. To make her misfortunes somewhat bearable, her parents immersed her in their love and did not let her want for anything, so she lived like a fairy princess, accursed but peacefully unconscious of the curse.

When her mother died, her father prevented any change in her condition. But as soon as he died, the value of everything in her world changed. When that one shield was destroyed, numberless attacks rained down on her, which she had known nothing of and therefore did not know how to protect herself from. Until then, her husband was to her like a deity who is beyond our senses but the basis of our unshakeable devotion and trust. Like an emotional devotee, she had surrounded her existence with a happy devotion without logical reasons. When her brothers' wives first blamed her for her husband's death and the neighbouring women sarcastically targeted her for the unknown lack in her life, her heart was startled into pain, like a sleeping person awakened by a burning spark.

New mental and physical torments began to be invented for her. The number of servants in the house was reduced; she was instructed, at first indirectly, then directly, and finally ordered to take on all the housework. Her sisters-in-law would say that her brothers belonged to the golden age, for who else would feed an idle person? These ideas were entirely new to her. She could not understand why she should always be drowning in a sea of gratitude because her siblings gave her food and clothing, in the house in which she had been born and raised, and in which she worked night and day. The oldest brother had a job, the other two managed the lands and property which had belonged to him who was her father too.

The poisonous environment gradually enfeebled her body and broke her spirit. She often developed a fever and fell unconscious. Some said these were early symptoms of tuberculosis, others that it was epilepsy. Both were aggressive diseases, so the poor sisters-in-law grew fearful about the welfare of their families. After consultations, the younger brother was made to write to her husband's younger brother, but the answer stated that they did not even recognize her, and that perhaps her family wanted to dump her on them because of some immorality on her part; if they did that, the in-laws would take the matter to court.

Desperate, the oldest sister-in-law said affectionately to her husband, 'Widows are getting remarried these days. What do you think of getting poor Bitto remarried?' When the brother asked whether Bitto wanted to remarry, the sister-in-law commented on his lack of understanding, saying that even a shameless girl would not express such a wish, while Bitto was an embodiment of modesty. Nevertheless, if she were not remarried, she would definitely pine away and die.

In a society where a sixty-four-year-old wants a fourteen-year-old bride, it was hard to find a groom for thirty-two-year-old Bitto. Thanks to her good fortune, a 150-year-old man was not to be found, and thanks to her merit accumulated over many lifetimes, our fifty-four-year-old gentleman took on the burden of uplifting her. When her sister-in-law told Bitto the good news, at first it failed to penetrate her large, vacant eyes and reach her heart, but when she finally understood after much effort, the result was the opposite of what was expected. Bitto wept bitterly and opposed the marriage, but the path of do-gooders cannot be blocked by oceans or mountains.

One explained to her the necessity of her brothers' and nephews' welfare, another drew her attention to the danger of her illness, and a third pointed out how useless her feeble body was. Perhaps it was because the old bridegroom was so near death that no one worried about his welfare. Finally, at an auspicious moment, Bitto, with burning but dry eyes, saluted her father's threshold for the last time and entered with slow steps a house that had been repeatedly uprooted and resettled, where, to display non-cooperation with her arrival, not a single being was present to welcome her.

Bitto told me this sad story, lacking an epilogue, in instalments over several meetings. The depth of her suffering made it imperceptible. It is hard to say whether our men would be able to understand even a part of it. Women keep disrupting poor men's continuous meditations and difficult asceticism, so men have written whole volumes analysing the nature of this enchanting gender.

Men have never been able to accept that when a woman makes asceticism her nature and some particular truth her spirit, men are no longer important to her and do not frighten her. Perhaps it is in order to forcibly give his defeat the name of victory that man tries to bind woman with many conditions of inequality and narrow-minded social and religious bonds. Normally, not only the appurtenances of grandeur but even a handful of grain outweighs a woman's whole existence. Even so, how can my heart accept that woman is defeated as long as a flame continues to burn in her heart despite its being crushed by circumstances?

One day, I had to bid farewell to that great woman, Bitto, when I saw her off on a bus, but her story had settled into my heart.[4] Therefore, I would sometimes write to my old friend, asking about her. Today, after about four years, I received unusual tidings of her. My friend wrote that the old man is seriously ill and is counting his last hours. Not his daughters-in-law but his sons have arrived and started the auspicious enterprise of acquiring the house, the money, and the property. These good

---

4 Mahadevi applies the epithet *mahiyasi* (a great woman) to Bitto; this is an epithet that was commonly applied to Mahadevi herself.

sons cannot stand their third stepmother, so poor Bitto's future is even darker than it was before.

I feel like writing a long discourse to my dim-witted friend. If one does not want to spend time in an infernal world by proving Manu's sayings untrue, one must admit that Bitto conceals in her heart the wish for a third marriage and that in this pure land of ours, there can never be a shortage of elderly well-wishers willing to uplift her. Where then is the need for such lamentations?

4 January 1935

The Child-Mother

How can I forget that golden twilight of Phagun's pink winter?[1] Birds, those happy musicians of the morning, were returning to their nests in harmonious flights. The sun's golden, sound-piercing arrows shot at them through the gaps between the clouds, got entangled in their frenzied pace, and missed their aim. I had just turned my head away from the festival of colours in the west when the servant entered and told me that an old gentleman, who would not give his name, had been standing outside for a long time, waiting to meet me. He would not listen to requests to come in the morning.

I had written only the first line of my poem so I felt irritated. What work could be more important than my work? What had compelled him to come without warning and turn my poem into a broken statue before life was breathed into it? My heart began to assert itself with pride around the words 'I am a poet' and I would perhaps not have risen had not the intellect ironically pierced me with, 'but not a human'. Somewhat irritably, somewhat harshly, I thrust my feet into one new and one old slipper, and hastily went out to the unwanted visitor, before whom I stood unmoving

1 Phalgun or Phagun is a month in the Hindu calendar which corresponds to the period from mid-February to mid-March.

and speechless. A painting of Rishi Kanva that I had seen as a child seemed to have come alive in the old man.[2] That face, with hair white as milk and beard white as milk foam, was covered with wrinkles that made it the abacus of time. The once sharp eyes now looked like a shining mirror on which someone had blown. Taking him in, in an instant, from white head to dusty feet, old black slippers to khadi cap with its thin overlay of sweat and dirt, I said, 'I'm afraid I don't recognize you.' He raised his eyes, bleary with experience but bright with tears, for a moment, and then his eyelashes, like the flowers of wild sugarcane, fell, perhaps from sorrow or perhaps from embarrassment.[3]

He said in a tired but quiet voice, 'What introduction can there be of one who comes with a request other than that he knows the name of the one to whose door he has come? My granddaughter is very anxious to meet you. I have been facing this quandary for two days. Today I plucked up courage to come. Perhaps this courage wouldn't have survived until tomorrow, which is why I insisted on meeting you today. But will you be able to endure the hardship of accompanying me today? I have a *tanga* waiting.'[4]

I stared at the old man in astonishment. Those who know me, and even those who do not know me, are aware that I do not easily agree to go roaming around. He perhaps was not from around here. I asked, 'Why can't she come here?' I could not understand why this plunged him into embarrassment. His lips moved but no sound emerged, and he turned his head aside to hide his wet eyes. Seeing his distress, I naturally asked whether she was ill. Looking

---

2 Kanva was a sage in antiquity who adopted baby Shakuntala and raised her as his daughter.

3 *Kans* grass, *saccharum spontaneum*, known as wild sugarcane, which grows up to three metres long, is covered with fluffy white flowers in autumn. The simile indicates that his eyelashes were white.

4 *Tanga:* Gig.

as if he was in despair, the old man nodded and explained in fragmented words that he had only one granddaughter whose parents died when she was eight and who was widowed when she was eleven.

There was no time for more arguments. I thought the old man's granddaughter was surely close to death. Poor unfortunate child! But I am no doctor, and people who invite poets on occasions such as the head-shaving or ear-piercing of a child have not yet learnt to invite one at the time of death as if they were reciters of the Gita. The old man was watching my face so intently that he seemed to compel me to say, 'Let's go then. I'll take someone along as it will grow dark by the time I return.'

That day, I became well-acquainted with the maze of alleys that pervade the city like veins, in which dirty water flows like polluted blood and dirty, naked children roam about like bacteria carrying disease. We climbed the stairs of a three-storeyed house. In the verandah, a woman sat on a dirty, torn mat, leaning against a pillar, holding in her lap a small being wrapped up in soiled clothes. The old man left me there, went through the room inside, and stood on the balcony on the far side, where the conflict of his tired body and broken heart looked like a silent but pathos-filled scene from an old, dim movie.

An apathetic voice said, 'Please come in.' I looked closely at the one making the request. It was surprising how much her face resembled the old man's. The same shape, the same shining but bedimmed eyes, and the same trembling lips. The hardness in her dry hair and dirty clothes was as pitiable as a sword dug out of the ground where it has lain buried for a long time. In a somewhat irritated voice, she said, 'Very kind of you to come. Only God knows how we have suffered for five months. Finally, we are freed from it, but look at the girl's obstinacy. She starts sobbing as soon as the orphanage is mentioned, and if we suggest giving it to someone she stops eating and drinking. We explained to her again and again that dragging someone we don't know at all into this mess is not proper, but she wouldn't listen. Poor Lala-ji was too ashamed to go but finally he was defeated and had to go. Now only you can save our lives.'

This long but meaningful introduction left me speechless, but when I gradually came back to myself, the situation began to become clear as objects on the shore become clear when one has been in the water for a while. It would be untrue to say that my body did not tremble, my feet did not freeze, and sweat did not break out on my brow. I have several times theoretically analysed social distortions, but this was my first encounter with this particular horror. Almost everyone in my family has shaken their heads in despair and told me, with regard to my reformist perspective, that my truthful art will not be able to withstand a gust of hot wind and my tender dreams nurtured in the shade of dedication will die in a smoke-laden atmosphere.[5] I have replied each time that muck cannot be washed away with muck but only with pure water. I have always believed that the infrangible purity of the lotus, which does not let even a pearl-like waterdrop stay on its petals, gives it the strength to stay rooted in the mire.

And then, feeling somewhat ashamed of myself, I moved aside the mud-coloured shawl and looked closely at him with regard to whom there was such an uproar within and without. The neglectful lap of that female embodiment of acrimony and the dirty coverings had left a mark of pathos on his tender face. The short, shiny black hair sticking to his forehead were like black letters of the alphabet and the closed lashes formed two semi-circles on his cheeks. The little mouth, like a red bud, was

---

5 'Dedication' translates *sadhana*, an untranslatable word for regular and consistent spiritual discipline aimed at achieving liberation from rebirth. Mahadevi here applies it to the artist's discipline.

open in sleep, and on it was a small, strange smile, as if he were having a beautiful dream. He had no idea how many full hearts had dried up, how many dry eyes had shed floods of tears, and how many had found it hard to continue living on account of his advent. What did this uninvited, unexpected guest know even of himself? His arrival did not bring his mother any respect, he was not welcomed with the distribution of sweets, no one sang welcoming songs, grandparents did not consider various names, aunts did not argue about presents, and his father did not see the reflection of himself in him. Even a mother's embrace, to which the child of the poorest, most anguished woman has a right, was not written in his fate.

When his mother, living hidden in the worst hell to escape society's cruel irony, obtained him, suffering torments all on her own, he became, as soon as he drew breath, a smouldering spark on an extinguished coal. No one cared how he would live. All they desired was the blessing of freeing him from life's burden without incurring the weight of murder. When this severe distress became unbearable, I stood up and asked to see the girl-child. Her aunt, in an uninterested manner, pointed to a dark, enclosed, small room to the left of the verandah. When I went in, I could not see anything but a sort of shadow rising from a bed with the rustle of clothing, but when, in a few moments, my eyes became accustomed to the darkness, I picked up and lit a match that lay next to the lamp in a niche.

I don't think I had ever seen such a sad sight before. It's impossible to give an adequate description of the pitiable figure I saw on the bed with its dirty rug, soiled and crushed sheet, and pillow covered in oil stains. She was no older than eighteen—weak and helpless-looking. Her eyes burnt in her dark but bloodless yellow face with its dry lips, like the wicks of a lamp without oil. Guessing her mental state from her unnatural stillness, I removed the pitcher from the stool near her head and sat down. And then for some unknown reason, the passive sadness in my heart began to change to hundreds of sparks of anger.

She cannot be blamed for her untimely widowhood nor is she responsible for the person who deceived her, but she alone is responsible for the part of herself, the fragment of her heart that lies before her. Will she refuse the child who is the truth of her life just because of the fake delusion that some man refused to make her his wife? Even if she does not obtain an epithet or identity in society, won't she be the proud mother of a child? Why is she arranging to reject this duty? Merely in order to return to that hypocritical society where she will continue the farce of bathing in Ganga, fasting, and worshipping as a true widow, and will find the means to make more mistakes or to be sold like an animal at a higher or lower rate at an auction in a widows' shelter or to drink poison drop by drop and give up her life?

A woman is not as fearless in any other situation as when she holds her child to her heart. She is never as ferocious a Goddess Chandi as when she protects her child. Perhaps it is because of this that the greedy world, before it entraps her in its snare and shoots arrows at her, arranges to snatch away this armour. If these women can hold their infants in their laps and bravely say, 'Barbarians, you have snatched away our womanhood and wifehood but we will not give you our motherhood,' their problems will be resolved right away. Will this society, which does not accept them with their heroic, courageous, and self-sacrificing motherhood, place them on a throne and worship them for their cowardice and victimhood? For ages, man has been punishing woman not for her strength, her *shakti*, but for her endurance.

I was so unsettled by the intensity of my feelings that I do not fully recall our conversation. But when she descended from the bed to the ground, embraced my feet with her weak arms, and hid her face in my knees, my heart was torn with remorse as I felt the silent tears pour from her eyes. Weaving unclear words into those soundless tears, she tried to tell me that she did not want to give up her child. If her grandfather would not agree, then could I make an arrangement for her to get two dry rotis once a day? She would wear my cast-off clothes and would have no other expenses. When the child grew up, she would do whatever work I told her to, and would spend her life doing it with heart and soul.

But as long as she did not commit any other offence, I should let her have a claim on me as she would if she were my daughter. She has no mother hence her abject state. If I can give her the affectionate protection of a mother, she and her child will be safe.

Putting my hand on the head of that child-mother, I thought—if only such a blessing could be obtained! In this autumnal era, flowers may not be obtainable from society, but this girl pleading for protection does not know the truth that there is no shortage of dust for any woman. At the age of twenty-seven, I had to accept the burden of an eighteen-year-old daughter and twenty-two-day-old grandson.

The old man wanted to return to his community that was devoid of sympathy, to spend the rest of his life in the fake atmosphere of a duplicitous society, and was eager to meet his sarcastic, cruel neighbours, but the high call of humanity had suppressed the weak voice of conditioning. Today he is in some unknown world. I have received only the perfume of affection from the treasure of the two flowers he gave to me, after he had drawn me into a thorny forest like a gust of sandalwood-bearing breeze. One of those flowers complains that I do not have enough time to hear her story and the other says I do not tell him stories about a prince.

21 November 1935

Gheesa

If it were easy to say what unknown inspiration in the present reiterates a forgotten story from the past with all its poignancy, I too would be able to say what the reason is for my suddenly remembering today that dusty, shy little student from a village who touched the shore of my life like a little wave with its tender moisture and then melted into the boundless ocean.

Perhaps it is because of my unreasonable attraction to the ruins of Jhunsi and the villages around it that people joke about my having an association with it from former births.[1] And it is strange indeed! The leisure hours that people spend with their friends, attending functions or other entertainments, I happily spend at these ruins and on the shore of Bhagirathi [Ganga] that plays at its wounded feet.

---

1 Jhunsi in Prayagraj district, near the confluence of rivers Ganga and Yamuna, is a place of historical importance, with neolithic sites and the earliest evidence of farming in the subcontinent. Fourth-century dramatist Kalidasa mentions it, and excavations have revealed many layers of civilization, including sixth-century BC items related to the major Hindu pilgrimage, the Kumbh Mela. It was known as Pratishthanpuram under a succession of Hindu rulers, but the name changed to Jhunsi (from *jhulasna*, to burn) due to its destruction by fire.

I am familiar now with the groups of women who emerge from some plastered and some dilapidated dolls' house-like homes, going with gleaming copper and brass or shining new red clay pots or old mud-coloured ones to fetch water from Ganga. Some of them are in embroidered red saris, others in white, and others in clothes that establish unity between dirt and thread. One has an inch-wide line of *sindoor* in her well-oiled hair parting, which shines in the setting sun, while another's dry locks, unacquainted even with mustard oil, hang around her face, highlighting its sadness. One has urban, studded glass bangles on her round, dusky wrist, which sparkle like diamonds, while the dirty yellow lac bangles on another's thin, black wrist look like thick, soiled lines of sandalwood on black stone. One seems to hide her hands, with their gilt bracelets, behind her pot, while another speaks only to the tune of her jingling silver bangles that hold her glass ones in place. One has lac rings in her ears which sometimes peep out of her sari, and another's shield-shaped earrings and long chain unite her neck and cheeks. Silver circlets on the tattooed wheat-coloured feet of one look like the circumference of shapeliness, while black anklets of tin and copper alloy, combined with another's spread-out toes and white heels, look like fetters of polished iron.

They first wash their hands and feet, then go a little way into the water to fill their pots. Then they put the pots on the shore, and while adjusting the cloth rings on their heads where they will place the pots, look at me, with dim or bright, sad or happy smiles. They know the distance between themselves and me, which they perhaps try to bridge with these smiles. The cowherd children run with their little sticks when they see cows and buffaloes straying towards me, the shepherd children pull any wayward goat or sheep back by its ears, and even the idle boys who spend their day playing *gilli-danda* don't forget to keep track of my movements.[2] Singing '*chunni ta rangauv lal majithi ho*' [Dye my veil crimson], the milkmen going to or returning from the city where they sell milk, the labourers going to the fort to work or returning home, the fishermen fastening or unfastening their boats, fall silent when their eyes fall on me. I get an occasional shy 'Namaskar' from those who pride themselves on being more cultured than the others.

I don't know when or how I thought of teaching those children something, but when without election by an administrative board, without selecting office-bearers, without a building, without an appeal for funds, and without one of those well-known inauguration functions, my students collected in the heavy shade of a pipal tree, it was hard for me to assume the proper solemnity of a guru. How to describe those seekers after learning? Some seemed a mix of town and village, with rings in their ears and bracelets on their arms, washed kurtas and high dhotis, some, wearing their older brothers' kurtas that reached their feet, looked like scarecrows, some with their protruding ribs, swollen stomachs, and weak, crooked legs could be defined as human children only by guesswork, and others with sad docility on their thin, dry, dirty faces and dull yellow eyes sat as if weighed down by the world's neglect. But Gheesa was alone amongst them, and even today is alone in my memory.

I have not forgotten that twilight. Night had scattered a fistful of collyrium on the vanishingly lit red and gold silken evening. My boatman was looking with some anxiety at the waves, and old Bhaktin had put my books, papers, and pens into the boat and was irritably muttering either about the gathering darkness or about the creator who had made me an eccentric. The poor

2 *Gilli-danda* (tipcat) is an ancient game dating back over two millennia. Its rules are somewhat similar to those of cricket and baseball.

thing has spent ten long years with me, and from a maid has started considering herself a type of guardian, but what has she obtained except the unfortunate consequences of my eccentricity? My heart suddenly overflowed with affection for her but my feet, proceeding towards the boat, stopped as I saw a woman coming towards me in the spreading darkness. Her thin, dark lips stood out in her long, dusky face. Her eyes were small but moist with pain. Her blouseless limbs were well covered by a soiled but thick sari, yet one got a sense of her well-shaped body. In the dusk, I could not clearly see the thin, half-naked child clinging to her, on whose shoulder her hand rested.

All I could gather from her mixture of broken words and gestures was that she had no husband, earned a livelihood by cleaning other people's houses, and her only son wandered around on his own. If I allowed him to sit with the other children, he could learn something too. The next Sunday, I saw him sitting alone, crouched down, behind everyone else. A wheat-coloured, well-shaped but dirty face, and two alert yellow eyes. The firmness of his tightly clenched, thin lips and the prickliness of the short, dry hairs standing upright on his head seemed at odds with the shy tenderness of his face. His yellow arms with their bloodless, dirty palms and crookedly cut nails hung from the bent shoulders that supported his neck with its protruding bones, as the two extra artificial arms hang on one who plays Vishnu in a drama.[3] In that

---

3 Here, Mahadevi comments on the near-starvation conditions in which Gheesa lives by pointing out that his arms look artificial. Second, she almost anticipates present-day activists, who replace the term *vikalang* (disabled limbs) with *divyang* (divine limbs), when she compares Gheesa to Vishnu. Later in the essay, it becomes clear that she sees divinity in Gheesa's extraordinary generosity, longing for knowledge, and devotion to his mother, his teacher, and even his puppy. Her choice of Vishnu rather than any other God is partly because Ramleela was and is the

flexible body, the weak legs seemed the strongest because of their constant running. That is how he was, with no room for poetic qualities in his name or his body.

But his alert eyes were full of curiosity. They were always wide open, like a clock, fixed on my face. As if their aim was to soak up all my knowledge and intelligence.

The other boys stayed away from him. Not because he was a Kori, but because their mothers, grandmothers, aunts had caught them by the ears and impressed on them the necessity of staying away from Gheesa. They also told them the secret of Gheesa's extra-ugly name, which means to drag. His father had died before he was born. Because there was no one in the house to look after him, his mother kept him stuck to her like a monkey's baby. When she laid him down on the ground while she was working as a labourer, he would drag himself along on his stomach, and thus, with his first experience of the world, acquired also the name appropriate to him.

His father was a Kori but was proud and wanted to become respectable.[4] Giving up the work of weaving baskets, he learnt some carpentry, and to top it all, he quietly brought a young bride from another village home, thus rejecting the beautiful girls of

---

most popular drama enacted every year, and Rama, a human, would appear with two arms, but Vishnu, of whom Rama is an incarnation, would appear with four arms.

4 This sentence indicates that in 1936, when this essay was written, Koris, classified as a scheduled caste, were not considered respectable. However, Gheesa's parents are self-respecting and determined to behave in a way that compels respect. Gheesa's father transgresses norms by giving up the conventional work of his local community and takes on building and painting, the work of another community. Likewise, his wife refuses to remarry as widows of her community do, and instead behaves like widows of so-called upper castes. The community resents this behaviour and slanders Gheesa's parents.

his own community in his village and dashing the hopes of their parents. Humans can put up with injustice, but the intolerance of God in such matters is well known. So, when he began to prosper by building fences and walls in the village and whitewashing the Thakur landlords' homes, he was suddenly called away by cholera to that place where neither intelligence nor pride can save one from going.

But his wife was no less proud than he. Several Kori widowers and bachelors from the kindness of their hearts offered to take responsibility for getting her boat across, but she flatly refused, and added salt and chillis to her refusal, saying, 'How can I, the wife of a lion, go to a jackal's house?' Then, when she started the farce of behaving like a high-class widow, crying without making a racket, opening up her hair, breaking her bangles, and wearing a borderless sari, the whole community was enraged. And then Gheesa was born after his father died. He was born just six months after, but what can be said of time since a moment can seem like a year and a year like a moment? How could the villagers be blamed for stretching the six months like a rubber band and making it a year?

This story was narrated to me too, with many derogatory interpolations, in order to change my mind, and my mind did change but, following some eternal principle, it changed in favour of the protagonists, not the storyteller, and Gheesa thus drew closer to me. He had probably not fully understood how his life was exceptional but what he did understand affected him greatly because he stayed away from everyone as if he had a contagious disease.

No one was as clever as he in reading, understanding what he read, remembering it when doing an exercise, not allowing a single smudge to appear on his book, keeping his slate shining, and earnestly fulfilling even his smallest responsibilities. I often felt like getting his mother's permission to take him away with me and make proper arrangements for his development but he was the only support of that derided yet dignified widow. I knew that she would not agree to leave her husband's home and also how hard her life would be without that child. And the dutiful nine-year-old Gheesa's devotion to his guru left no doubt about his devotion to his mother, so Gheesa remained in those harsh conditions, where cruel fate had placed him simply for its own amusement.

On Saturday, he would, with his small, feeble hands, plaster the ground under the pipal tree with a mix of cow dung and mud. On Sunday, as soon as his mother left for work, he would arrive with a thick roti and some salt or a few roasted chickpeas or a lump of gur, and sweep the ground under the pipal, and then come and sit on Ganga's shore, scanning the waves with his yellow but bright eyes, shading them with his dark hand. When he glimpsed my blue and white boat, he would run like an arrow on his thin legs and, saying 'Guru Saheb' to his classmates without taking their names, he would sit under the tree to once again go over the schedule that he had already read many times. Taking my cane mat kept on a low branch of the tree, he would dust it repeatedly and spread it out, extract the never-used black glass pot of dried-up ink and the brown-and-green pen with a broken nib from the tree hollow, keep them ready, and then this unique student and strange minister of a strange school would come forward to bow to me in welcome.

I could go there only four times a week, and sometimes due to excess of work would have to take a day off, but the knowledge I gained of that child's heart in that short time and those few days has remained ever-fresh like a photo album.

I cannot forget the day when, without providing clothes for them, I foolishly exhausted those poor children with my exhortations regarding the importance of cleanliness. The next Sunday, they all presented themselves as before except that some had washed their faces in Ganga-ji in such a way that the dirt had got divided up into several lines, some had scrubbed their hands and feet so thoroughly that they looked as if they had been separately joined on to soiled bodies, and some, following the idiom 'when there's no bamboo, there will be no flute' had left their torn, dirty kurtas at home and arrived in such skeletal forms that their retaining life seemed surprising. But Gheesa was not there. When I asked, the boys began to whisper and seemed anxious to collectively tell me the reason for his absence. Gheesa had been telling his mother all week to get him soap to wash his clothes. She had not received her wages and the shopkeeper refused to give her soap on credit. Last night, she was paid and she went first thing in the morning to get soap. She had just returned and Gheesa was washing his clothes because Guru Saheb had said they must bathe and wear clean clothes. And what clothes did that unfortunate child have? An old kurta with one sleeve half-missing, given by some kind woman, and a torn piece of cloth like a towel. When Gheesa, having bathed, stood before me like an offender, wrapped in the wet towel and a half-soaked kurta, not only my eyes but every part of me grew moist. At that moment, I understood how Dronacharya had got his Bhil pupil to cut off his thumb.[5]

One day, for some reason, I took 5-6 *ser* of *jalebi* for those students but partly due to the seller's cleverness in weighing them, partly due to my inability to bargain, and partly due to

---

5 In the Mahabharata, Arjuna's teacher Dronacharya suspects that a tribal prince, Eklavya, who has taught himself archery by building a statue of Dronacharya to inspire him, may outdo Arjuna. He therefore asks Eklavya to cut off his thumb as a gift to his guru. Eklavya does so, which diminishes his skill in archery.

the children's snatching and grabbing, each one could get no more than five sweets.[6] One said he had got less, another said his had been snatched away from him, a third wanted more for his younger brother who was asleep at home, and a fourth remembered someone else. In this racket, no one could say where Gheesa had slipped off to, with his share. One mischievous child said to his companion, 'The wretch has kept a pup, he must have gone to feed it,' but seeing my eye on him, he fell silent and just then Gheesa returned. His calculations were perfect. He had wrapped two jalebis up and hidden them in the thatch for his mother, had fed his motherless puppy one, and had himself eaten two. When I asked if he wanted more, he dropped his eyes shyly and his lips moved. He said that the puppy had got less than he had. If Guru Saheb could give more, she should give one more for the puppy.

An event from before Holi is inscribed in such deep colours in my memory that it will not easily be washed away. Hindu-Muslim animosity was gradually increasing in those days and seemed likely to boil over soon. Gheesa had been lying sick of a fever for two weeks. I used to send over medicine but there was no proper arrangement for taking care of him. His mother sat with him for a couple of days. Then she went back to work and asked a blind old woman to sit with him.

Bidding farewell to the children on Sunday evening, I went to see Gheesa but when I had taken fifty steps from the pipal tree, I was upset to see him coming towards me with faltering steps. He had not risen from bed for a fortnight so I was afraid that he had contracted scrub typhus. Liquid electricity seemed to flow through his dried-up body, his eyes were even brighter than

---

6 A *ser* or seer was differently measured in different parts of India. In United Provinces, now Uttar Pradesh, where Mahadevi lived, it was approximately 933 grams.

usual, and his face was like a piece of iron gradually reddening on a slow fire.

But more worrisome than his illness was his state of mind. He had woken up, thirsty, but there was no water near him, and not wanting to ask Maniya's blind grandmother, who had been deputed to sit with him, he silently bore the discomfort. Just then, Mullu's uncle, returning from across the river, told the blind woman from the door that riots had broken out in the city. And then he remembered Guru Saheb. As soon as Mullu's uncle left, he got up so quietly that the old woman did not hear him, and ran this way, supporting himself by holding on to walls and trees. Now he would hold on to Guru Saheb's feet and lie here but would not let her cross the river.

This complicated the problem. I had to cross the river but I also had to explain it to Gheesa in a way that would not worsen his condition. I could not find the usual shy, mild, and obedient Gheesa in this determined and stubborn child. The year before, he had seen two fishermen wounded in just such circumstances and perhaps that sight had assumed larger proportions in his brain disturbed by illness, which deepened my quandary. Trying to explain the situation to him, I touched a chord which was new to me. As soon as he heard that many students, who had come to me from far away in trains and who met their mothers only once a year, would be upset and alone if I did not return, Gheesa's obstinate opposition melted away. Who had such powers of reasoning as Gheesa! Guru Saheb must go to those children who could not go to their mothers every evening. Gheesa's Bhagvan-ji would be angry with him if he stopped her.[7] It is he, who, seeing Gheesa wandering around with

7 The term Bhagvan-ji has more intimacy in it than the term God because ji is attached to the names of honoured older people, such as parents and teachers.

nothing to do, sends Guru Saheb here. Remembering his many reasons makes my heart overflow even today but that day, when I returned from taking Gheesa back to the broken string-bed he had left, dragging his weak body, burning with fever, in order to save me from danger, I was filled more with astonishment than anything else.

Gheesa recovered and fought daily battles with the summer that roamed around like a mad person carrying dust and dried leaves. Growing vocal through the burning rustling of the wind that called the dry leaves, covering the school with a sheet of dust and brown, yellow, and some green leaves, entwining herself in the skeletal branches, she would tease that deluded child in his attempts to clean it. I decided to change the school hours to late afternoon and evening, but I found that Gheesa, rubbing his eyes that were troubled by the dust, and constantly brushing dust off his book, sat under the tree all day, as if he were a homeless, celibate ascetic from a bygone age dedicated to meditation, whose endeavours the hot, dusty wind kept trying to disturb with its gusts.

Going on in this way, when time, like a child running to touch the finish line in a race, leapt forward and touched the day I was to leave all of them, my heart lost its equilibrium. Some children were sad, others happy at the vacation commencing. Some wanted to know whether the vacation days should be counted with drops of lime or by drawing lines with coal. Some were confronted with the question of preserving their eight-page book in houses that dripped through the monsoon, others wanted a strategy to preserve paper from attacks by rats. Gheesa seemed to consider his presence unnecessary in such important hubbubs so, as usual, I could not find him. When I set out, somewhat worried, my heart felt heavy and a fog was before my eyes. In truth, the doctors suspected an ulcer in my stomach and thought they might have to operate. When would I return or would I return at all? So thinking, I looked around with moist eyes which remained entangled with those familiar places.

In the dimness spreading like earth's exhalation, those mud houses were lost in her throat—only the mud-coloured straw and brown- and black-tiled roofs were visible like old boats in Ganga's muddy waters swollen by rains. The watermelon and muskmelon fields spreading far out in the alluvium reminded one of some primaeval island because of their protective grass nets and huts. A couple of lamps had been lit in them, and far off I saw a small, black blot advancing. It must be Gheesa, I realized even from afar. I had no doubt that his little heart was experiencing with all its strength of feeling the fact that today he must bid farewell to his Guru Saheb. But I did not yet know what simple affinity with me and what grief at parting from me there was in that neglected child's heart.

As he came close, I saw in the twilight that the unclothed Gheesa, looking like a black picture on brown paper, was carrying a big watermelon in both hands, from a cut-out portion of which the red interior gleamed through the green around it like a half-closed pink flower. Gheesa had neither money nor land—had he stolen this? The question in my mind found expression and then I came to know that the God who had made that soiled body was no different from the old man who is freed from anxiety after he hides his gold coin in the clay of his mud wall.

Gheesa considers lying to Guru Saheb the same as lying to Bhagvan-ji. He had chosen this watermelon several days ago. His mother was late in returning from work so he had to go alone. The field owner's son was there, who had long had his eye on Gheesa's new kurta. He often used to tauntingly say that those who serve food to one who can satisfy his hunger with others' leavings must be crazy. He said, 'If you don't have money, give me your kurta.' And if Gheesa had not taken the watermelon today, what would he do with it tomorrow? So he gave his kurta away, but Guru Saheb need not worry because he doesn't wear a kurta in the summer and the old one would be fine if he had to go anywhere. He had to get the watermelon cut to check whether it was ripe and had to scoop some out with his finger to check its sweetness.

If Guru Saheb did not take it, Gheesa would cry all night, and cry throughout the vacation. If she took it, he would bathe every day, sit under the tree, and keep repeating his lessons, and after the vacation he would be able to show her the entire book written out on a slate.

With my hand on the head of that child, eloquent in his affection, I stood, motionless from excess of emotion. I am not sure whether any earlier guru ever received such an offering from a student on that shore but all the giving and taking in the world up to now pales before it.[8]

Having made special arrangements for Gheesa's comfort, I left, and did not return for several months. I received no news of him in the interval. When I found time to return, Gheesa's Bhagvan-ji had given him the leisure to study forever. I do not have the strength today to tell that story, but perhaps once today becomes tomorrow, tomorrow some more days, more days become more months, and more months more years, I may, like a philosopher, be able to calmly recount the neglected end of that little life. For now, it is enough for me to keep searching for his reflection in other soiled faces.

17 August 1936

8 The word translated as offering is *dakshina*, a gift given to a guru.

An Unfortunate Woman

Lightning had been extinguished in the sky like a lamp covered with a heavy lid. All evening the wind had been busy piling up layers of clouds and they were now so thick that, appropriately for night's shadows, they had become an unbroken roof of moist black stone from which water slowly dripped.

My heart too was heavy. Laying my head on the table in my small, outside study, I was unsuccessfully trying to forget my pain. The face of a girl from the distant south, who lay sick with typhoid in the girls' hostel, kept growing before my closed eyes like the enlargement of a photo. How could her parents, with their average income, afford to come and visit her? As I grew increasingly worried about her, my annoyance with myself too grew.

My body was so useless that it was hard for me to stay awake with the girls in their joys and sorrows for even a few nights. Why then had I drawn these girls so far away from their mothers? Since my work to become fully human was not complete, how had I undertaken to build these girls into humans? Such arrogance was unforgivable. Suddenly, someone's footsteps on the verandah broke my train of thought.

After waiting a couple of minutes for someone to call out, I had to ask, 'Who's there?' In answer, a fair, well-shaped hand shook the curtain. A frightened female voice hesitantly asked, 'Can I come in?' Perhaps because my voice sounded polite but indifferent as I said, 'Come in,' the visitor's feet halted for a moment, but the next moment she stood like a colourful picture against the background of the blue curtain.

Unable to soak into her dark green shawl of thin wool, raindrops lay studded on it, shining like diamond fragments. When she took off her shawl and, following my eyes, sat on the chair opposite me, I sought, with surprise and curiosity, some wordless answer in the lines of her face. Waterdrops quivering in the small curls near her eyes looked like mercury. Her face, framed by a white sari with a somewhat blotched purple border, seemed withered. The redness at the tip of her nose indicated recently wiped away tears and the corners of her eyes were swollen too, making her grief seem deeper. Her lips were so dry that every effort to moisten them showed a new fatigue even in its monotony. I too was very tired so I waited for her to speak. But when she bent her head even lower and a tear shone in the light like a bright line, I realized that this woman sitting before me had come to tell of some sorrow. That she had left home despite the heavy clouds and light rain was evidence that her need could not be postponed even to the next morning.

In a sleepy way, I asked an over-familiar question that I had asked countless times, but I awoke and grew alert when she replied, 'Please give me some work.' Asking about her skills seemed heartless but was necessary. She solved my problem herself, saying she knew Hindi. Before she added, 'Singing too…' her whole body grew embarrassed but relaxed after she had said it, as if she had completed an onerous task.

The story advanced. Her husband had been ill for one and a half years, and all their resources had been expended on his treatment. The only thing she had left by way of jewellery was a gold ring; the thought of selling it distressed her because it was the only gift from her husband and even if she did sell it, how long would the money last? If she could not find work, she wasn't afraid of starving to death but … she choked up. She was experienced in stopping tears that welled up at the corners of her eyes from spilling over. Therefore, just a little more restraint than the energy that had caused her body to shake like a cane plant prevented the watery stillness of her eyes from melting.

I couldn't find appropriate words to express my sympathy so I asked about her parents and parents-in-law in order to hide my feelings. Her body shrank again as before and her lightly trembling words startled me. Her in-laws were angry—they were not willing to let her enter their house and her husband refused to go without her. After her marriage, she had had no relationship with her mother. It would be better to die than to take money from her.

This comment helped me understand the essence of the story. She is the daughter of a mother who is called a fallen woman and she wants to enter the temple of respectable women without an entry ticket from society. She does not know that only women touched by society's magic wand can be called Sati. Those who have been kept outside the line of family brides must consider it their life's blessing to remain forever outside with all their descendants. And society has given them no small task! They have the right to worship man's vast form as one worships the Lord's vast form, but when they unwisely break this discipline, their crime is unforgivable. They should know that the one who has created the high celestial world has also created the infernal world below. If all the denizens of the infernal world rush to the celestial world, the creation will not survive for a day. It is necessary, indeed compulsory, for them to be punished for creating disorder in society by trying to change their lives, otherwise society has nothing to do with them. Who doesn't love one's own creation? Society has been explaining to them for ages that they are simply women, liberated from the triple titles of mother, daughter, and wife, and this liberation is tied up with society's welfare. If, despite this, they abandon their important duties and steal the relationships of wifehood and motherhood, must society accept their claim to the stolen titles and falsify its constitution?

This ignorant woman had certainly failed to understand society's complex principles, which is why her eyes, fixed on my face, seemed to ask with pathos-filled curiosity, 'Am I not pure?' On the one hand is this woman whose mother was not given the right to be a mother, and on the other hand am I whose mother, maternal grandmother, and great-grandmother, paternal grandmother and great-grandmother, and their ancestresses, taking the water of their husbands' feet and some of them crossing the path of fire while still alive, have procured the certificate of purity not only for themselves but for me too. I have been addressed as 'worshipped mother' and 'respected sister' by many, but who would become impure by calling this unfortunate woman 'mother' or 'sister'? And she wants to know the reason for her being called impure. Even if she were to burn herself to death with her rebellious husband, the impure inheritance pervading each drop of her blood would not be washed away. Her devotion to purity arising from her own conduct is like the meditation of that Shudra that destroyed society's varna system and to behead whom Maryada Purushottam himself came running.[1]

When I returned from the gate, having made arrangements to send her home, my feet were heavy like iron drawn to the magnetic earth. I remained absorbed in that problem late into the night but could not find a solution. From concern for her

1 Refers to the story of Rama and Shambuka.

husband's dignity and her own self-respect, she would not accept charity and I could not help laughing ironically at the thought of finding work for her. Little does she know what ruin her presence can precipitate!

I tried for two days to make arrangements for her and failed, and what I did next shows my own ignorance of psychology. I gave her essays to copy of which I had no need. I had her write letters that went straight into the dustbin, but when her eyes drooped even lower with the burden of shame and her throat grew even more choked, I realized that she knew this work was a sham. She well knew that I didn't need her work and I could not summon the courage to keep up the pretence any longer.

I had no news of her for some days. Perhaps her husband's illness had grown more severe. Only once during this time did she request help, from which I understood that she had accepted my sympathy as true.

Days turned into weeks and weeks into months until a woman of my acquaintance told me the epilogue to this sad story. This will be called hearsay but the event touched me as no other has. The solitary devotion of that unfortunate woman could not save her husband. His father came to see his son's face in his last moments but did not make the mistake of looking at the daughter-in-law weakened by lack of food and many sleepless nights. Perhaps he felt that his son had died because of this wicked woman.

By the time the neighbours brought her back to consciousness, her husband had been cremated. She sat unmoving all night but came back to her senses next morning when her father-in-law began preparations to leave. Wiping her eyes, she asked from behind the door, 'What time are we leaving?' He reacted as if lightning had hit him. When he recovered the power of speech, he hit back with cruelty, saying, 'Take whatever you brought from your mother's house and return quietly there, otherwise we will have to teach you a lesson. Aren't you satisfied with having stained our family?'

She was not angered by the insult. Begging for a hand's breadth of space in the home where she had the legal right to reside, she pleadingly said, 'There are many servants in your house. I need only two fistfuls of flour. I will serve you as they do.' But the father-in-law's answer would put shame itself to shame.

This news reached me much later. I searched for her, and was told that she may have gone to a widows' refuge or may have returned to her mother. Time gradually dimmed the memory of her when a dirty, crushed envelope revived it. She was well and had not forgotten me but did not want to trouble me further. She earns a pittance by sewing and knitting. If she is in need, she will not hesitate to ask me. She also asked when I would open the shelter that I wanted to establish, for women like her to learn the means of earning a living.

And I keep asking myself, 'Do you still believe in the certificates of virtue and wickedness given by society?'

6 September 1937

Alopi

A scientist might be able to say whether or not there is even an atom of usefulness in blind Alopi's eventless life. To me, his story seems like a link in a sad song, quivering in the shadow of a tearful gaze. The way I first met him is also a story sad in its strangeness.

Vaishakh, like a new singer, was trying to astonish the world with one long note after another on its instrument of fire.[1] My small house was like a potter's rustic furnace but also created the illusion of a modern factory because of the noisy way windows and doors kept blowing open and slamming shut in the wind. I was engaged in a task suited to this loud heat; in order to determine the value of the elements of knowledge, I was heating with intellect the compound of knowledge and ignorance crammed helter-skelter into answer-books.

We are strange people. When artificial means, such as ice, cooling straw mats, and electric fans fail to stop our brains from melting, we set ourselves to examine others' knowledge.[2] If our intelligence was functioning well, we would perhaps not be so

1 Vaishakh is the Hindu month that corresponds to the period from mid-April to mid-May.

2 The reference is to holding final exams in the heat of summer.

unjust in order to do justice. The afternoon progressed slowly like an exhausted traveller, and the contest between my hand and eyes racing across the pages continued. At such times, anyone's arrival adds an element of annoyance to our impatience but it's even worse if we detect from the visitor's voice that he is a beggar. All the servants had deepened the unnatural darkness of their rooms and of their own will were enjoying the pleasure of becoming owls. I considered not getting up. The one calling out should be penalized for coming at the wrong time. But my conditioning with regard to beggars has become illogical enough to be not far from a blind belief.

From childhood until I grew up, Ma had explained in many discourses and commentaries the principle of conduct whereby our civility is measured not by how we treat an important guest who graces our house but by how we treat a beggar who, tossed hither and thither, stands at the door and asks for a drop of kindness. There must have been many occasions during Ma's lifetime when I forgot the lesson she had taught but ever since I have moved away, beyond the bounds of her displeasure, I have begun to remember everything I had forgotten, along with the subtlest analyses.

I was more alive to my civility being tested than to the beggar's needs. I had no choice but to get up. After calling out many times, the two callers had sought shelter under the neem tree that was poor in leaves. Hearing me call out, they returned, and my curiosity increased with each step they took. An eleven- or twelve-year-old, whose long, torn kurta was like a second prison for the skeleton rebelling against its covering of skin, walked in front holding a stick, and, supported by the other end of the stick, a blind man, his skeletal form almost liberated in a high dhoti and dirty jacket, picked his way after him.

Shaking his head like a pitcher on a stick in a field, the mature child placed the old youth ahead of him and told him something which caused him to lift his face and salute me as if saluting the date palm. For the first time in my life, I found no words to frame a question and became dumb before the blind man.

His clothes and feet were covered in dust, but the layer of dust on his short hair, his flat forehead, the thick lashes on his weak eyelids, the scattered eyebrows, dry thin lips, and somewhat turned-up chin, was so firmly settled that he looked like nothing so much as a half-dried clay model. The small eyes, devoid of the lustre of sight, were dull like dirty balls of raw glass, strengthening the delusion of the lifelessness of that body. Perhaps it was for this reason that his voice startled me with unexpected emotion.

The lives of this class are like an open book so it is easy for them to recount their whole story from start to finish on any occasion. In contrast, our ever-more complicated world and artificial existence create a condition like that of a stork which derives its external whiteness from the rotting fishes within.[3] For this reason, it becomes increasingly difficult to recount our incommensurable stories, and the simple poignancy of joys and sorrows is lost. We are not able to tell our complicated stories in a simple manner. When we try to tell these stories, each imagined footnote creates the illusion of many colliding truths.

There were neither psychological complexes nor a maze of problems in Alopi's story. His sad eloquence showed that his tongue had filled the gap left by the absence of sight so that the balance of knowledge obtained by the five senses had not been lost, although the balance was unequal.

His father was the chief of his Kaachhi clan, but having waited a long time for his heir, he was compelled to approach Goddess

---

3 A metaphor derived from the Hindi idiom of the stork who lures fishes by pretending to be a meditating sage.

Alopi as a petitioner.[4] Goddess Alopi was like that generous rain which bestows itself not to fulfil the petitioner's need but for its own fame. She could not even produce a complete man. She gave him only one son and that son was eyeless. The parents were not so ungrateful as to throw at her feet the child she had given them, but in order to warn other petitioners of her miserliness, they named him Alopidin [given by Alopi].

That Alopidin is now twenty-three years old, and his father, having paid, in the form of his blind son, only the interest on his debt to the ancestors, has gone to the court of his forefathers to pay the principal by his service. His mother does the rounds, selling vegetables, but her son does not think it right for the old woman to kill herself earning a living while a young man sits at home so, having heard from his father's older brother, a vegetable vendor, about this place, he has come here in search of work.

I had never encountered such a wonder. There is no shortage of ignorant youths who aggressively demand the comforts of life from mothers whose fingers have become like sieves from doing needlework. Nor is there any shortage of young men who swallow their tears like well-bred brides but whose manhood does not shrink from robbing the little that their poor fathers have and does not dwindle when they take to begging. There is no shortage of men who consider their failure victory, and who spend at cinemas the money their wives earn by working all day, leaving their small children untended.

The manhood of men today consists mainly in lamentation. The more ways they can lament their hopeless lives, in many

4 The Kaachhis are peasants and vegetable vendors. The temple of Alopi Devi is near the confluence of Ganga and Yamuna in Prayag. The name Alopi means both 'concealed' and 'revealed'. The Goddess is remarkable for having no image. An empty seat is worshipped in the temple.

tones and with many gesticulations, the more praiseworthy they are and the more deserving of the name of man. Alopi, who casts his blind eyes to the heavens in order to protect his manhood, deserves nothing but a death sentence in the court that runs on such traditions.

Trying to sound natural, I asked, 'What kind of work can you do here?' Alopi had it all thought out. He would bring inexpensive and good vegetables straight from the fields for me and for the girls in the student residence. Without giving me the opportunity to ask how he would fulfil this duty in the darkness that overspread his existence, Alopi pointed to his cousin Raghu and explained that their joint industry had made possible many difficult enterprises.

The proposal was unprecedented but I am pretty outlandish myself so Raghu and Alopi went home, having taken a burdensome duty on to their weak shoulders. The next morning, holding the end of Raghu's stick with one hand and a big basket on his head with the other, Alopi began shouting, 'Maalik ho! Maalik ho!'[5]

When he insisted on finding out what I liked, I found myself in a quandary. Doctors have removed some vegetables from my diet and it has always been a rule that for the rest, I accept whatever Bhaktin decides to cook. And one who has to spend some months of the year eating curds, other months eating fruit, and others eating *khichri* and porridge, becomes detached from the idea of dietary preferences.[6] But in order not to disappoint Alopi, I took everything he had brought for me. When I was paying him, Alopi

---

5 Literally 'owner', 'maalik' refers to the house-owner but is also a polite way of addressing an employer.

6 *Khichri*, literally, a mixture, is an ancient dish made of rice and lentils, to which vegetables may also be added.

said he would take payment at the end of each month. I started explaining that I am forgetful and not good at keeping accounts, but he explained with much confidence that his knowledgeable uncle, who knew multiplication tables up to ten and had studied the first primer, would help him keep my accounts straight. The matron would maintain the accounts for the student residence.

The appearance of these two at the student residence had created an amusing sensation there, which could best be described as 'the voice has no eyes and the eyes have no voice',[7] but in a few days' time Alopi had become dear to everyone. He could take liberties that none of the other servants could. He sat with legs spread out in one corner of the courtyard and weighed in the big balances the already weighed vegetables that he brought for the mess. His sense of touch was so advanced that he could tell the weight of bottle gourds, pumpkins, and jackfruit just by holding them in his hands. While weighing the vegetables, he would give information about them and about the fields to the cook, the leaf-plate preparer, and others.

The small girls, chirping like little birds, usually gathered around him. He began to bring guavas and berries for them, the price of which seemed to be undetermined. One day, the fruit vendor who supplied the college complained that the blind man distributing fruit to the children harmed his trade, so I asked Alopi about it. He caught the tip of his tongue between his teeth, shook his head, and replied, suggesting that he received the price. Also, he did not come during school hours so how could he cause the fruit vendor any loss?

The little girls could not make Alopi a liar nor could they lie in my presence so they stayed quiet. In response to my speech about

---

7 This is a famous line from Tulsidas's epic *Ramcharitmanas*, '*gira anayan nayan binu baani*'.

the appropriate and the inappropriate, Alopi wipes his foggy eyes with his dirty scarf and says that his eight- or nine-year-old cousin-sister [father's younger brother's daughter] has died. These little girls' voices create the illusion of his sister's voice, which is why he brings what he can in his poverty—a few guavas, berries, rose-apple fruit. In his village, these things are free so how could he have known that in the city it is considered bad to give them away? Had he bought them, it might be proper to sell them. But he gets them for free with the vegetables he buys. His heart feels uneasy at the thought of making money from them. The emotion on his face made me angry with myself for the arrogant stupidity of my long speeches on propriety. It scarcely needs to be said that Alopi was not required to modify his principles.

Perhaps because he did not have eyes, Alopi was neither afraid of nature's fearful forms nor distracted by her beauty. When torrential rain created the illusion of a snowstorm, lightning flared up like a fountain, and the mountains seemed to speak in the clouds' roaring, Raghu would hide his eyes as he walked, but Alopi, like a drenched rag doll, ignored the water dripping down his nose and walked along, clasping the slippery stick with soaked fingers and the basket that looked like a green field, as if today was the day that he must attain complete knowledge of the earth. If his foot ever fell into mire, Raghu suffered for it because Alopi considered it unforgivable for a sighted person to make such a mistake. When winter drew a circle of snowy stars and wind blew like the breathing of a stroke victim, Raghu's teeth chattered and his body shook in his thin kurta like an epileptic's, but Alopi, holding his trembling lips shut with all his strength, advanced his feet, blue-nailed and stiff-toed in the cold, in measured steps. When the dust of summer rose as if someone was pounding the earth into fragments and the hot wind, shrieking like a person on fire, ran from one corner to the other, Raghu, sheltering his eyes with his hand, would lift his feet fast like grain dancing in a furnace. But Alopi, holding the darkness of his eyes with shut lids, placed each foot as carefully on the burning earth as if he were measuring the heat of its heart. Alopi never altered his routine, whether it was Basant or Holi, Dashehra or Diwali.

Once, when our Hindu and Muslim brothers, ashamed of their long inactivity, were busy participating in a heroic contest, Alopi arrived by a deserted path, carrying a basket twice the usual size while Raghu had a large bundle on his back. I was annoyed rather than surprised by his daring. In reply to my welcome speeches, such as 'Is your heart blind as well? You won't get to heaven by giving up your life in those dark alleys', he drew out eggplants and bottle gourds. Having constructed a hill of vegetables in my courtyard, he silently set off to the student residence. By the time he returned, wiping his dry eyes with some uncertainty, my anger had evaporated and my heart was moistened by affection.

Recognizing the reassurance in my voice, he hesitatingly explained that he had brought vegetables for two days. The matron had told him that the pickles in the pantry were used up and the dried lentil dumplings had grown a fungus. Only a person like Alopi could eat roti with just dal, so he had bought all these vegetables in the village and come here, selling them along the way. No one would harass a blind man, he thought, but since I had forbidden him to come, he would not set foot outside his house. He had brought provisions for two days and after that the conflict would be over. It was not possible to stop Alopi from returning home because it was his responsibility to protect his old mother.

Alopi could not see whether or not I was on the verandah but he never passed to or fro without saluting in that direction. I had often seen Alopi sitting under the neem tree with his empty basket, deep in conversation with Bhaktin on such grave matters as whether I preferred bitter gourd or jackfruit, drumsticks or mountain ebony blossoms, spinach or fenugreek leaves, and whether sweet limes are more nutritious than oranges.

One incident that seems trivial is important to me. I was sick with a fever. Having saluted the verandah for many days, Alopi said to Raghu, 'It seems Guru-ji is very angry. She doesn't talk to me as she used to.' When he discovered that I could not come out because of illness, he grew very worried.

The next day I received the message that Alopi wanted to see me. I could not keep myself from laughing even in my distress. Even if given permission numberless times, how could the blind Alopi see me? But Alopi came in with a *namaskar*, groped around, and seated himself near the threshold. Wiping the moisture from his dim, empty eyes with his sleeve, he opened a knot in his scarf and told me, as if he had committed an offence, that he had visited Alopi Devi himself and brought her sacred ash. A pinch on the tongue and on the forehead would remove all sicknesses and problems. I felt like saying, what can that Goddess do for me who could not do anything for you? But the solemnity with which he gave his gift prevented the words from rising to my lips. Alopidin's heart, like iron in doing its duty and like wax in its affection, should suffice to prove Alopi Devi's divinity. Such sympathy for a person whose familiarity with him could extend no farther than words is indeed unforgettable.

Alopi had been coming to us for three years. His somewhat sturdier form was clad in a kurta, a turban sometimes ornamented his head, and the high dhoti had descended a little. In a month, we purchased about seventy rupees' worth of vegetables and greens. Having paid the sellers as well as Raghu, Alopi made enough to live in some comfort with his mother. And one day, Raghu laughingly told me that his older brother's mother had begun to bury some rupees as savings.

Providence had made arrangements for the epilogue of Alopi's life to be no less dark than its beginnings. One day, Bhaktin, sitting near me and talking to herself about the world, said that Alopi was going to set up his own household. I was so surprised that forgetting my usual indifference to Bhaktin's stories, I exclaimed 'What!', at which Bhaktin looked at me with as much pleasure as Bhishma must have looked at Krishna running towards him with a chariot wheel.[8] I found that what she said was the unalloyed truth.

A Kaachhi woman, who had seen off two husbands to liberation, wanted to set up a paradise for the blind man, but Alopi's mother would not agree to give away the son she had received as a blessing. Returning after the summer vacation, I heard that Alopi's mother now lived on her own and his new wife had taken over his house. I got the opportunity to see her on one occasion. She was a sturdy, middle-aged woman of medium height. She was ordinary to look at but there was an elasticity in her voice and a pleasing invitation in her tones that could not fail to attract anyone, and also a cunning harshness gleaming in her eyes that made it difficult, if not impossible, to trust her. Perhaps Alopi was able to trust her because he knew only her voice.

Raghu was an informer in that household, so everyone soon knew that his new sister-in-law had no interest in talking about

---

8 In one of the most moving episodes of the Mahabharata, Krishna, who has sworn to be a non-combatant, gets fed up with the endless warfare, and in a rage runs towards Bhishma to kill him with a wheel that has broken off a chariot. Bhishma, delighted at the prospect of being killed by Vishnu (whose weapon is a wheel), calls out to Krishna, asking him to kill him, as there could be no greater honour for him than to be killed by the flawless, lotus-eyed God of Gods whose slave he is. Krishna does not kill him.

anything but money. Sometimes she wanted to know whether or not Alopi had saved up for a rainy day, and at other times she asked in which corner she should bury her bracelets and earrings. Alopi managed to live in this tottering paradise for six months. Then we heard that the clever wife had taken everything and liberated him forever from the bonds of her enchantment.

For several days, the poor fellow could not believe what had happened. He would touch the dug-up place and then sit at the door waiting for her. When the benevolent neighbours dug mines and blew up the buildings of belief he had erected, he fell ill. But when discussions started about giving the good news to the ever-efficient police, he said with the steady calmness of despair, 'Only a base man would write a report against his wife and have her arrested.'

When he began to recover, he started coming once more but he had lost his former vigour. He dragged his feet and lost his grip on the stick. One day, while saluting in the direction of my verandah, he let the basket fall. One betrayal by the world had swallowed up all Alopi's courage, all his enthusiasm, and all his self-confidence—this is true but still seems phantasmic to me.

The blind man's sorrow was mute, so his comforters could not find a path to his heart. My saying a word about it caused him to shrink with shame as if hail was pelting him from all sides, so I thought it best not to heighten his pain and embarrassment by talking too much. But I was alarmed by the darkness that had gathered around Alopi who was like a child unaware of his fault and stunned into silence by being harshly punished for no reason. His mother had forgotten all the offences of the blind son she had obtained after so much waiting but the obstinate son could not forgive himself, therefore, their sad but sweet past could not be revived.

I spent the Dashehra break at home. One day, after delivering vegetables, Alopi sat in the mess until evening. He touched the balances with great affection, tenderly stroked the cat's bow-shaped back, and had fun teasing the little girls. He gave my dog Flora some puffed rice from his scarf, fed the doe Sona with radish leaves, and bowed to my verandah before he left, never to return. Three days later, Raghu, eyes swollen with weeping, informed us that his blind older brother, without taking him along, had set off on the great journey to an unknown world. I believe that he will reach his destination without fail, just as he had arrived here without warning.

Having made arrangements for other work for the child Raghu, I have let the curtain of forgetfulness shroud the other memorials of Alopi, but even today when I look at the threshold, my vision begins to crystallize around a shadowy figure. The shadow's face gradually swims into view. Lightless eyes like balls of raw glass become visible and a line of tears drying on hollow cheeks. Then I rub my eyes and think—will Alopi, who obtained his life from an irony of fate and his death from the world's betrayal, keep hovering like a ghost in search of my affection?

20 February 1938

Badlu

Badlu was the unremitting creator of shapeless pots and also the carefree progenitor of children formed like Ashtavakra.[1] The living asymmetry of lifeless mud failed to draw his attention and the lifeless ugliness of living flesh and blood could not disturb his *samadhi*.[2]

I always saw him hedged in by a heap of raw or baked, broken or completed pots on one side, and a crowd of dirty, untidy, naked, feeble children on the other. Just as the clay pots kept breaking in the course of being dried, baked and piled up, so also the children kept dying, some as soon as they were born, others when they had learnt to crawl, and others when they began to totter along on crooked legs, helping their parents in their work. But I never saw Badlu happy or sad in relation to their births or deaths. It is not easy to sketch Badlu, because he was framed on such unconventional lines that emphasizing one line would render another invisible.

---

1 Ashtavakra was a sage born bent in eight places, due to his father's curse.

2 *Samadhi* in Hinduism is a state of profound absorption in ultimate reality. It is the culmination of yogic practice, and the practitioner is oblivious to the external world, including pain and pleasure. Mahadevi applies this to absorption in work or art.

His face was dark and pleasant but the protruding cheekbones revolting against his hollow cheeks made him look skeletal. His long, thin body must have once been well-shaped but the uncertainty of livelihood had bent him over with untimely age. His small, bright eyes were shy like those of a woman, but because of their lack of enthusiasm, they looked like small coins pressed into wet black mud images to form eyes. The cough rising from his trembling lips startled the hearer as the sound of a conch emitted by a flute would.

Badlu was a man of few words and he also did not know how much a city-dweller like me would want to hear so I had few opportunities to converse with him. Whenever I was passing by and briefly stopped to look at the creative process of his steady-seeming fingers on the revolving wheel, he would grow uneasy. To hide the unease, he would repeatedly clear his throat and call in a rasping voice to Khedan, Dukhiya, and Nathu to fetch a string-stool. While the children competed to bring the sieve-like stool with its three and a half legs from the dark room, I would consider it best to take my leave. My sitting on it seemed likely to endanger the stool itself and also jeopardize the future of the pots and pitchers.

Badlu's home was on my regular route so I was always either in a hurry to reach somewhere or to return. It was hard to spend time there without inconveniencing those who were waiting for me. Yet it became necessary, even unavoidable, to stop for a while whenever I saw Radhiya sifting mud at her door or doing some other household chore. I liked to hear the story of her mono-toned life, told sometimes with overflowing eyes and sometimes with laughing lips. Her eyes, lips, hands, and feet all seemed eager to tell their stories, so it was little that she needed to put into words, but that little was so touching that the listener found it difficult to remain self-contained. Like some sad tune, her story churned the other's heart as much as her own, so that on many occasions I had difficulty hiding my emotion from that potter's wife.

Radhiya was poverty embodied. Her dry, tangled hair, tied up with the dirty edge of an old sari, did get washed with black mud on festive occasions but was unacquainted with the softening touch of mustard oil. Her sari was united by dust with its border, and such was its raggedness that when she pulled the end over her face, the border alone was drawn down by her fingers to her nose. Sorrow becomes a type of ornament, which is why faces of sad persons hold the viewer's vision.

Grief seemed to be the attraction of Radhiya's face. She had an unusually broad face. Her nose drew a sharp line between her eyes and grew rounded above her lips. Her eyes, encircled by deep black hollows, looked as if someone had pressed them with a finger into a pit of collyrium. Her lips were shrunken as if constantly touching a cup of bitter medicine. The attraction that connected these disparate elements must certainly have arisen from Radhiya's pain-melted heart. Life's pleasure had been wrung out of her but, heavy from being drenched in sorrow, she had neither that hollowness which fails to hold the viewer nor that lightness which fails to touch the heart.

Radhiya had no acquaintance with any ornament other than copper bracelets that were rubbed down from roundness to flatness and lac bangles that had lost their form in dirt, but she did not seem upset by this. That woman's shapely body and full limbs had been reduced to a skeletal frame because of an uninterrupted series of offspring and the unbroken shadow of poverty, so that one was almost surprised when she moved and walked.

Radhiya completely lacked the harsh cleverness often found in women of her class. Perhaps it was for this reason that my indifference was inevitably transformed into curiosity and curiosity into respect. Her affection for Badlu was deep and therefore quiet. He never seemed to be the least bit anxious about the house, the children, or her, and no one ever had the good fortune of hearing Radhiya criticize her foolish husband. Radhiya believed that her husband was the crest-jewel of potters and a good artist although people did not understand his greatness.

Radhiya's hard duties began in the morning, when she ground up maize or millet or barley, and concluded when, by the dim light of a twinkling oil-lamp or reeds that flare up and die down in a second like a sparkler, she distributed left-overs from the morning to the drowsy, whimpering children. There were five living children but when she says how many there are, Radhiya cannot help counting those who are now merely memories. The three dead children are mentioned along with the living in such a way that the listener is bound to consider them alive. The difference is simply that the dead children, like protagonists of a story, were alive in an aerial form suitable to be talked about, while the living were dying as they helped their artisan father and labourer mother. Their feeble, naked bodies engaged in as much work as was needed to prevent their lives from leaving those bodies. The work ranged from digging up mud to carrying pots to market. One could neither laugh nor weep when the youngest one, four- or five-year-old Nathu, putting on his head a pot ten times larger than his swollen stomach, staggered on his crooked, dried-up feet to show his enthusiasm for going to market.

Radhiya, seeing that the inherited trade of selling pots was insufficient to solve the problem of a livelihood, went to work in the nearby fields. Sometimes, by the time she returned from the fields and Badlu from market, the small creatures had fallen asleep on the clay platform outside the hut or below it in the dust. Radhiya would carry them in and lay them in a row on an old dirty sari. Anyone who woke up in this process was given a piece of thick roti from the pot that hung on a hook above, while those who stayed asleep had to pass the night on the strength of affectionate patting.

Badlu too had a right to the offerings from the pot, but it would be hard to know when the Annapurna of this limited treasure was able to break her fast rather than fulfilling it in sleep.[3] Those two were strange beings. The husband could not provide food or clothing and never worried about the children's future or present, while the wife saw no fault in him and found no cause for discontent.

There was no particular upheaval when Radhiya gave birth. I had seen Radhiya filling a heavy pot with water in the evening before little Lakkhi was born at night. Setting down the pot, she brought out the well-known three-and-a-half-legged string-stool for me. Balancing myself on it with care, I began chatting with the children while Radhiya sharpened her blunt curved knife on a piece of stone beneath the platform and then washed it. Half-laughing and half-surprised, I asked, 'Why do you need this at night? Are you going to cut someone's throat?' In response, Radhiya gave me a humourless smile.

The next day was Somavati Amavasya so I had a holiday and was able to go there again. Badlu's wheel was turning with its usual indifference but the children were raising a racket at the door. Not looking at the embarrassed Badlu, I asked Dukhiya about her mother. Being the most talkative of the children, she told me several stories in one breath. She had a new brother. Mother did not let them call Chamarin Kaki to help because she

---

3 Offerings translates *prasad*, the sacred food offered to a God or Goddess and then distributed to worshippers. Radhiya is poignantly compared to Annapurna, Goddess of Food, symbolic of the earth, whose store never runs out.

demanded one rupee.[4] Mother cut the cord with her knife and it is buried in a corner of the verandah. Brother is lying like a lapwing, his legs curled up and eyes closed.[5] Father has given mother roti made of pearl millet. I obtained these and other important bits of information in a few seconds. I then tried to peer into the room, which was futile because the dark-complexioned Radhiya wrapped in dirty clothes had blended into the darkness of the dusty walls. On receiving an invitation to come closer and see the future potter, I stepped in.

The mingled odour of smoke and tobacco in the room weighed down my breath. The walls, smeared with yellow soil but marked as if with smallpox by white ants, seemed ready to sit down in order to recover from the fatigue of trying to hold up the thatched roof. In the corner closest to the mud stove, mud-coloured and black pots for storing grain along with shining pitchers and plates were like A-class and B-class prisoners in jail. The length of the hammock-like cot in the middle of the house that was meant for the head of the household's use refused to accommodate his feet. A long-neglected dusty oil-lamp in a hollowed-out niche in the wall seemed to have preserved its name by retaining an inch-long wick and two drops of oil.

In the empty western corner of this house, Radhiya was introducing her newborn baby to life and to poverty at the same time. Lying with eyes closed, he looked like a wingless baby that had just emerged from some big bird's egg. There was swelling and some congealed blood at the spot where the cord had been cut. She told me that the Chamarin was not willing to come for

---

4 A woman of the leather-working Chamar community who would work as a midwife for a fee. Kaki is a particular type of aunt, a father's younger brother's wife.

5 There is a local belief that the red-wattled lapwing (*titihari*) sleeps on its back with its legs pointing upwards.

less than a rupee, so she had managed on her own in order to avoid unnecessary expenditure. Pain prevented her from getting up so she had cut the cord with a knife while lying down and it was not cut properly, but there was nothing to worry about because she would apply oil and it would dry up in a few days. With astonishment, I looked at the calm and pleasant expression on the face of this strange mother.

Hearing that I was going to send her milk and *harira*, she smiled even more pathetically and said that this would go on all her life and how long could I keep making such arrangements.[6] When I told Badlu, who was sitting unconcerned by his wheel, to fetch gur, ghee, dried ginger, and other stuff from the grocer, he seemed to fall to earth from the skies. He said that his Dukhiya's mother felt nauseous when she saw gur and her stomach ached when she ate ghee, which is why he contented himself with feeding her pearl millet roti.

Looking at Badlu's simple face, I glanced at Radhiya who was, as it were, shrinking under the burden of her lies, and then I felt no need to ask the couple any more questions. It didn't take me long to understand that whatever Badlu could not provide turned out to be harmful for Radhiya. But hiding this divine knowledge of mine, I said calmly that Dukhiya's mother would have to eat what all women eat, even if it caused nausea or pain.

Death came to that house without clamour just as birth occurred without fanfare. Muliya roamed around with a high fever. When pox pustules appeared, her brother made her lie on the broken bed in a dark corner of the house. Radhiya did not fail to sweep the house with a lock of her hair, offer water to the neem tree in the name of the Goddess, and do whatever else was compassed by her beliefs and abilities, but on the fourth day the child departed

---

6 *Harira* is a strengthening mix of nuts and spices fed to new mothers.

for the ultimate resting-place. Badlu was especially fond of this girl, so when he returned from immersing her in Yamuna's grave waters, Radhiya, understanding the grief concealed in his peaceful silence, invented the story of a dream. The Mother Goddess had come to her in a dream and said, 'I sent this girl for a short while, please return her to me.' A simpleton like Badlu was bound to be impressed by the dream. Since the Mother Goddess herself was eager to take Muliya with her, it was good that they had not had her treated by a doctor. The girl could not have been saved by medication and they would also have had to endure the Goddess's anger. And what better fortune could the girl have than to be summoned by the Mother herself?

Once I did give Radhiya a profound sermon about telling falsehoods but her answer, given as she wiped her eyes with the end of her torn, dirty sari, was no less profound. Her husband was very innocent. His heart was so tender that he was disturbed by even small injuries. The state of their home was such that they couldn't even procure food twice a day for so many beings, so she concealed her own and the children's small sorrows. God might punish her in the next world but she did not lie in order to grab what belonged to anyone else. Radhiya's answer became a question for me. How could her untruth be called untruth, and yet what else could it be called?

I explained to Badlu several times that if he could make beautiful, well-carved goblets and pitchers instead of his shapeless pots, they could be sold even in the city. But the answer he gave in his hoarse voice, with his eyes fixed on the wheel, was that his father, grandfather, and great-grandfather had all made pots like these, and he was a rustic potter who could not make urban-style vessels. I decided it was useless to say more.

One day I took some pictures along to explain Puranic stories to the children who were my pupils. The pictures were not artistic but they were somewhat better than the unsuccessful replicas of Shiva, Parvati, and Saraswati sold in the market. Of Badlu's children, only Dukhiya was able to come and study. Perhaps it was she who gave her father the information. But I was astonished beyond measure when Badlu, forgetting all his gravity, came running to us. I showed him all the pictures and explained their meaning as simply as I could, yet Badlu kept sitting among the children. Seeing his eyes fixed on Saraswati's picture, I had to ask, 'Do you want to keep this picture with you?' Badlu hung back—how could he ask for such a beautiful picture? Understanding his emotion, I gave him the picture, and excess of joy made him as excited as a child. Many days later, I saw the picture stuck with paste on the rickety wall of Badlu's dark house, and to tell the truth, I felt sorry for the picture's misfortune.

I like to buy many clay toys for Diwali. This is the festival when clay sculptors are in demand, and the encouragement they receive on this day helps them develop their art throughout the year. The modern era has not only stolen our enthusiasm for our festivals but also stopped the development of these sculptors. As I, deep in thought, entered my big room to decorate it with toys, I heard Badlu clear his throat outside. He had never before come to see me so I was surprised and also worried. Had someone fallen ill in his house or had some calamity struck them? I came out on the verandah and saw Badlu standing shyly in his dirty clothes, holding a broken basket.

When he came forward, put the basket in front of me, and removed the torn rag that covered it, I was left speechless. Badlu had brought an image of Saraswati—depicted in white and gold colours. The peaceful expression of the icon was made more charming by her white clothes, golden hair, golden veena, and the white swan with its red beak and feet. The sculptor must have been highly skilled to render each lock of her hair with such art.

I asked, 'By whom did you get this made?' but was not at all prepared for the answer. Badlu dropped his eyes modestly and spreading out his dry, shapeless hands, said that he had made it with his own hands. This was hard to believe so I kept looking at the image and at him. Was this the same potter who a year ago had declared himself incapable of making a beautiful pot? I couldn't help saying, 'You are a rustic potter from a village. How could you imagine making an image like this when you thought it impossible to make a carved pot?'

The truth gradually emerged. As he had kept gazing at the picture of Saraswati, the desire to become an artist had awoken in Badlu's heart. He had put all his energy into embodying that pictured beauty in clay. He failed many times, but after continuous practice, he managed today to make a statue of Saraswati which was worth presenting to me.

Since then, many Diwalis have come and gone, and Badlu has made many beautiful images, of which several now adorn the homes of the prosperous. Simple Radhiya seemed to have lived only to make her husband an artist. As soon as beautiful statues took the place of his shapeless pots, Radhiya gathered up all her affections and departed for an unknown world.

Badlu was left like one of a pair of *chakva-chakvi* birds.[7] From morning to evening, he kept waiting for Radhiya to return. Waiting is always sad but when a living person waits for a dead one who will never return, it becomes extremely sad. The place that the lying Radhiya had left empty in that seemingly indifferent rustic's life became apparent when he hit a man on the head with a pot for suggesting that he marry again.

---

7 *Chakva* or Brahminy duck is a vegetarian migratory bird. According to tradition, the male and female birds are together in the daytime but are separated at night, and they wait for dawn to reunite. In Indian literature, they are symbols of enduring love.

A mother's form in woman is Satya or true; motherly love is Shiva or auspicious; and motherly attachment is Sundar or beautiful.[8] When she is established in a man's life with these three characteristics, filling her place is, if not impossible, certainly difficult. Finally, the thirteen-year-old Dukhiya spread out her small aanchal to provide shade to her father and siblings.[9] Becoming a replica of Radhiya, she began, like her, to melt herself away while making arrangements for the others to grow.

Two years later, Badlu's maternal cousin, charmed by his art, took the family away to Faizabad, but Badlu never forgets to show up on Diwali with some image or other. This year, the routine was broken because Diwali came and went, but Badlu did not bring an icon. Perhaps he has departed in search of Radhiya, but the Buddha, Krishna, Saraswati, and others set up in every corner of my house remind me of the rural potter who made shapeless pots on an old wheel, and they say to me—art is not just your patrimony, imagination is not your purchased slave.

17 December 1936

---

8 Satyam Shivam Sundaram are the three epithets of Shiva, which Mahadevi here adapts to women.

9 Aanchal is the sari-end, symbolizing the protection and nurture provided by a woman. It is here poignantly adapted to a little girl whose mother's death forces her to grow up.

Lacchma[1]

With her old black skirt faded from repeated washings and tucked up in a strange manner, her torn and dust-stained veil wrapped tightly round her waist, and a large sickle in her hand, Lacchma leapt down on to a heap of grass and leaves that lay below, and burst out laughing. In a mixture of Pahari and Hindi, she said, 'Why do you worry about me? Do you think I'm a human being like you? I'm an animal! Look at my hands and feet? Look at the work I do!' I don't know why I am so fond of this young hill woman who overflows with spontaneous laughter.

Her suntanned face is like an unripe apple roasted in the fire. Her eyes, liquid beneath their dry lids, look as if they are swimming in fathomless depths of unshed tears but have been dried out on the surface by the sunshine of laughter. Her teeth are white and even but her lips have turned blue with continual exposure to cold. Her soles have grown hard from climbing over rocks day and night, her hands rough from cutting grass and breaking sticks. Damp mud and cow dung are the only softeners they know.

Like a mole on the breast of a mountain, Lacchma's small grass hut stands perched on a rock. Her father's eyes are weak,

1 This is an updated version of a translation that first appeared in *Manushi* 21 (1984), 40–44.

her mother's arm is broken. Her niece and nephew have lost their mother to death and their father—Lacchma's brother—to asceticism. Lacchma is the only one strong enough to support these helpless beings.

In this wilderness, what work can Lacchma find to keep so many people alive? That is her perennial problem. They have one buffalo, a memorial of better days. Lacchma gathers grass and leaves for it. She does the milking, sets curds, and churns whey. In summer, she grows a few potatoes around the hut. But this does not make up for the lack of grain nor does it solve the problem of clothing.

Lacchma's life-story is so wet and heavy with tears that even the most tireless storyteller and the most patient listener would find it difficult to recount or to listen to. She was married into a village that lies sixty miles away from the abodes of civilization. Her in-laws were thriving cultivators with plenty of land and many cows, buffaloes, and oxen. Her husband could not be called insane but his mental development was no greater than that of a child. Parents-in-law may grow fond of a mentally delayed son's intelligent and hardworking wife, but to her brothers-in-law she can only be a nuisance. Her presence means that they must give their brother a share in the property; in addition, they have to restrain themselves from laying hands on her.

When all the tortures inflicted on her failed to make Lacchma relinquish her rights, she was beaten so severely that she fell unconscious. Thinking she was dead, they threw her into a pit. It would be hard to describe how she returned to consciousness and, though suffering unbearable pain, managed to drag herself across the valley to the next village. Not a word escaped her lips about what she had suffered because she thought that to talk of it would entail a loss of family honour. Also, how could Lacchma, self-respecting as she is, say that she had been beaten nearly to death? The story she invented, of having suddenly fallen from a high rock, bore testimony to a courage that one would not have found in the brutal story of how she had been beaten.

On the way home, she had no food for three days. Laughing, Lacchma says, 'When I felt very hungry, I would make a ball of yellow mud, put it in my mouth, close my eyes, and tell myself, "I have eaten a laddu, I have eaten a laddu." Then I would drink lots of water and everything would be all right.' When her family saw Lacchma returned from the mouth of death, they wanted to teach her husband's family a lesson, but she insisted they should not, and thus managed to avert an epic battle.

Sorrow seems to have taken up permanent residence in the shadow of this unfortunate woman. As soon as she reached home, her brother's wife died, leaving behind a little girl and a month-old baby boy to be cared for by Lacchma. Her body may be broken with toil and her fate harsh, but Lacchma has a whole and healthy heart on the strength of which she took up this bittersweet duty. But what did she know of childcare? There was no nursing mother to be found in the vicinity and the baby was not yet able to drink milk from a cup. Lacchma had an idea. She managed to beg an empty oil bottle from somebody and loosely tied a cloth around its mouth like the wick of a lamp. With this, she fed the baby watered-down buffalo milk.

Every bone in Lacchma's body is enfeebled by the tortures she suffered at her husband's house. If she sits still for a while, her spine begins to ache unbearably; if she remains standing, her knees begin to hurt. Yet, waking by night and toiling by day, she continues, singlehanded, to fulfil her sister-in-law's trust. Today, that baby is old enough to follow his aunt around like a pet animal, mutely imitating her every act.

When I first met Lacchma, I considered taking her to Prayag and educating her there. When I made the proposal, Lacchma merely looked towards her fragile hut and then bowed her head. In whose care could she leave those beings? There was still hope at that time that her brother, who had been severely shaken by his wife's death, might return and do his duty. But even when that hope proved vain, Lacchma's radiant laughter remained unshadowed by despair.

With an unforced smile, she says that reading and writing are of no use in the forest. Here, one must know how to climb trees, pluck leaves, and chop wood. When her old parents are no more and the children grow up, why should God keep her in this world any longer? Her next birth will definitely allow her to stay with me and to study without neglecting her duty. To educate her, I must wait at least until the next birth—if this strange statement did not speak of such dedication to duty and such simple trust in life, how could one keep from laughing at Lacchma's peculiar madness?

If friendship is defined as the free exchange of joy and sorrow on a plane of equality, I lack friends. I express my joy not only in art but also in the company of birds and animals, trees and plants. Sharing my gladness with them satisfies me completely. As for the expression of sorrow, I do not like to burden others with even a fragment of my sorrow. When someone is happy, I feel a kind of freedom from anxiety about that person, so I stay at a distance, and my relationship to the grief-stricken is one of tenderness.

But my primary feeling for Lacchma, with her bramble-torn hands, her stone-bruised feet, and her radiant laughter, is one of respectful friendship. She is not so unstable in her distress or so lightweight as to require my support. On many occasions, I have found her far wiser and greater than I am. Lacchma, too, unlike other hill women, behaves as my equal. She fills the gap between us with her simple sense of equality, so I do not have to make any effort to reach her.

She knows that I can afford to eat choice dishes, yet she goes out of her way to bring me foodstuffs that are found in the forest. One day, she came running with some fresh honey in a waxy piece of honeycomb and insisted that I eat it at once. I am not fond of sweet things, and the sight of honey always calls up a vision of bees that takes away my appetite, but to satisfy Lacchma I had to taste it.

Many people keep bees and trade in honey, but Lacchma could not buy a wooden hive, nor were the walls of her house built to accommodate bees. When I asked, she told me that one wall of the hut had a split in it. Lacchma wanted to rear bees in the crack. But why should bees consider it worth their while to take up residence there? Tired of waiting for them, Lacchma began to catch bees and transport them to the crack. Several times they stung her and her hands became swollen; several times they rejected the narrow crack and flew away. Finally, some generous bees obliged Lacchma by settling down there. It was the first honey from their hive that she had brought me.

Similarly, one day, when I was leaving, she wandered far and wide to procure a bunch of black grapes as a parting gift for me. When the buffalo yields milk, Lacchma comes running with milk in a wooden cup, curd in a leaf-cup or butter on a leaf, and making muddy pictures on the dry floor with her wet feet, she reaches my kitchen and insists that I eat a little.

Throughout my student days, I lived in a hostel. When I went home during vacations, my mother used to feed me with special care. But her care always seemed an exception to the rule, so I did not get used to expecting it from others. As soon as I completed my studies, I accepted the duty of caring for a number of students, so I have not had anyone insisting that I eat. Lacchma's insistence does away with my alleged and imagined adulthood, and carries me back to the easy and natural state of childhood.

She is simple in her motherly love. Irritated by constant interruptions to my work, one day I said to Lacchma, 'Next time I come here, I will make a hut on that lonely mountaintop and live there, where nobody will be able to disturb me.' Through constant worry about feeding everyone, she has come to realize that the problem of food is not easily solved, yet without solving it, no work can be done in this world. Fearing that I too might be beset by this problem in the wilderness, she made a proposal that was truly characteristic of her.

Lacchma suggests that I go and live on the high mountaintop only when her two-year-old buffalo calf turns four and starts giving milk. Then the milk of one buffalo will suffice for the old people and the children and the milk of the other for me. She will come every day and bring me a ser of milk, a ser of curd, a couple of potatoes, some wood, and water. She will not speak a word; she will not even look at me. She will just leave the things at the door and come away. Then, when I have finished writing my fat book and when I tire of staying alone, I will just have to call out, 'Lacchma!' and she will immediately come up and carry all the stuff down, even the thatched roof of the hut.

When Lacchma made this weighty proposal, looking at me with pleading gravity, I was too taken aback to say a word. Solitude and quiet can easily be obtained, nor is it difficult to write fat books, but one would have to look far and wide to find a helper as inexplicably loving and caring as Lacchma.

Lacchma is not far from the truth when she says that she lacks good fortune, not good understanding. One day, as she watched me painting a picture of the Himalayas, she suddenly said, 'If I had the materials, I would paint the snow exactly as it appears.' Jokingly, I asked, 'What materials would you want?' With a strange combination of gestures and words, she explained that she wanted a big, blue paper and some white and green colours. Then she would climb a very high mountain, spread her blue paper on a flat rock, and sit there all day, drawing the mountains, some of them upright as a wall, some spread out like thatch, and some domed like a temple. The blue paper would be the sky, the white colour the snow, and the green would be for the deodar trees.[2] I was amazed at this vast proof of little Lacchma's intelligence. The sight of my struggles to paint a blue sky on white paper must have led her to think of blue paper.

When I enquired, I found out that though Lacchma had never been taught the art, she was so fond of drawing flowers and leaves, plants and creepers, that she had covered the walls not only of her own but also of her neighbours' houses with *geru* and rice-powder colours.[3] Her pictures may not hold much meaning but the unskilled labour of the artist's fingers and the lack of resources are clearly visible. In the same way, by watching others she has learned to knit, but since she did not have wool and needles, she could not knit the sweater she wanted for her old father. When I heard about this, I got her the materials, but I am convinced she would have run away, leaving them behind, had the question of protecting her father from cold not been involved. She has a great deal of affection for me, but she would never think of using that affection to fulfil even the smallest of her own desires.

In general, the numberless discomforts and hardships of hill life bring selfishness to the fore, but I found Lacchma's life exceptional in this regard. I have to look for the tears hidden beneath her natural laughter and then search for the causes hidden beneath those tears. And, finally, Lacchma never fails to foil my efforts by saying, 'Oh, I am just a jungle woman, what do I need?'

---

2 Deodar is Himalayan cedar.

3 *Geru* is red mud.

Lacchma, whose heart is so clean, is forced to remain unclean in outward appearance. Sometimes, she gets annoyed by her own uncleanliness and says, 'How dirty I am! Don't let me come inside the house. Stop me at the door. See how the whole house gets spoiled when I come in.' These outbursts are addressed to herself, because she immediately starts exonerating herself to me: 'I scrubbed and washed my feet this morning, but when I was halfway here, I had to turn back to give the buffalo grass. I beat my skirt on a stone and washed it yesterday, but the children wiped their muddy hands on it. The day before yesterday, I washed my veil in the stream and dried it, but I had to tie the bundle of grass with it because the rope suddenly snapped.'

In some distant past, Lacchma possessed a wooden comb. Ever since she lost it, she does her hair by washing it in the stream and then pulling out the more tangled parts. The gift of an old black comb was a great event in her life. Having tucked it in her waistband along with her knife, she would perform her toilet in the forest, bathing in mountain rivulets. Her strange happiness at being able to do her hair could only bring tears to one's eyes.

What name should one give to the misfortune of a woman for whom such a minor object is a rarity, even in the twentieth century with its countless unprecedented beauty aids?

The other women once told me that Lacchma was in the habit of burning incense and wishing ill on their children. When I asked her, she said that she wished ill not on children but on the eyes of certain people. There is an old moth-eaten picture of Durga in her house. Morning and evening, she puts lighted coals and fragrant dry leaves before it, and prays that the eyes of those who look on her with evil intent may be burned to ashes.

I did not find it easy to explain to her the truth that purity cannot be protected by wishing ill on anyone's eyes because the test of true purity is that the most impure vision is cleansed by contact with it, but Lacchma had no difficulty in understanding the subtlety of what I was trying to say. Ever since, she prays only for well-being—her own as well as that of others.

This daughter of the mountains is as determined as she is fearless. Just as she finds her way through the darkest night with the help of her sickle, so also she stands resolute and unmoved in the face of the fiercest opposition.

Some years ago, some of her in-laws' relatives heard that she was alive, so they brought her unknowing husband along and asked Lacchma to go back with them. She asked her childlike husband to hand over everything to his brothers and stay with her. She would sleep in the buffalo's shelter but would provide a clean hut for him. Even if she had to lie on dirty, foul-smelling grass, she would procure a string-bed from the villagers for him. Even if she went hungry, she would labour night and day to provide food for him. She told him that since she was married to him, she was willing to stay with him all her life long. But she was not willing to go to his house because his people would kill her, and then her parents, nephew, and niece would die of hunger.

Her husband's relatives refused to leave him there because they did not trust the good faith of this magical woman who had risen from the grave. A wave of discontent with Lacchma's behaviour swept through the surrounding areas, and she became the target of all kinds of gossip. The psychology of society is the same in the hills as it is on the plains. If they so much as imagine that injustice is being done to a man, all men rise up to take revenge on the woman concerned, but even after seeing clear evidence of cruel injustice done to a woman, women are ready to add to her unjustified punishment.

Thus, a woman who does not solicit male help at every step is in a strange position. As she moves beyond their reach, men get increasingly exasperated, and their exasperation usually expresses itself in false accusations. This is natural, because we find satisfaction in asserting our possession of that which we cannot possess, whereas we feel no need to declare our hold over that which we have.

If they who are standing upright keep being denounced for having fallen, is it surprising that they may begin to consider their efforts to stand futile? Until a woman becomes strong enough to remain unperturbed by false accusations, her situation remains insecure.

I saw in Lacchma the strength to remain unperturbed and also the generosity to forgive her accusers. Neither does she demean herself by criticizing others nor does she diminish her self-confidence by justifying herself. Her heart, like a mirror, is evidence of its own purity. Once, while a certain gentleman was sitting in my house and enumerating to me her various imaginary faults, she was standing outside the door and pulling faces at him like a small child.

Even when the wickedest men in the village are mentioned, she only says in her simple way, '*Apne aap rahega*.' In the vocabulary she has framed, this means, 'Let it go; he will be what he is.'

She is not angered when respectable people pass her on the road as if they see no difference between her and the buffalo she is grazing. She justifies their behaviour, saying, 'I am not like a human being. They are very good. How can they talk to me? I don't talk to them either. You talk to me—that is not very good. But you talk nicely to me, that is why I don't leave you alone.' It is not easy to grasp all the implications of Lacchma's broken sentences, but one can understand that she has no place for ill feeling towards anyone in her heart, which has shrunk into itself at the thought of her own smallness.

The day I leave is a painful day for Lacchma. She comes running to see me after milking the buffalo. She comes again after filling water and once again after feeding the children. As my packing proceeds, each joint in her body seems to shrink and shrivel.

She always walks the first mile with me. When we reach the second milestone and I tell her to go back, she stands, looking lost, wiping her eyes, and watches me proceed. Hill paths are not broad and straight like our roads. They turn and twist; sometimes a tree blocks the way, sometimes a rock. Long after she has disappeared from view, I hear her tearful voice calling after me, 'Go carefully. Come back soon, all right.'

These days, Lacchma does not have to face the prospect of starvation. The apple orchards are heavy with fruit. The unripe and sour apples lying beneath the trees wither or rot there, so no one is forbidden to gather them. These days, Lacchma sits down under any tree and eats a half or three-quarter ser of sour, inedible apples. Then she works two days without eating anything.

But gradually winter approaches, when snow will lie three feet deep like a burden of sorrow on earth's heart, when people will sit around the fire at home telling old stories after a new fashion, when the rich and the poor will live on their stored-up grain and mock nature's cruel game, when some animals will be sent to the warmer villages below while others will be secured in their shelters and fed on dry grass. What then will Lacchma do with the disabled old people, the small children, and the unsheltered animals?

It is true and yet not true that I get no news of her. When I tell her that if she were literate she could write me letters, Lacchma, with strange gestures, says in her broken language, 'I write in my own way. I sit on a rock and think, "I have written this, I have written that, that should not have been written." When I think that the letter has been sent, I get up happily and cut grass or chop wood. All that I write—does it not reach you?'

Who can help laughing at the idea of a letter written without paper, ink, pen or alphabet, and sent without the help of a post office?

But when suddenly, in winter, I am seized by the desire to leave my warm room and go to those mountains lying buried in snow, or when in summer I disregard all the fashionable, beautiful hill resorts in my eagerness to reach that silent, anguished corner of the mountains, who can say that I do not receive unlettered Lacchma's letters?

28 August 1939

LINES OF MEMORY

Smriti ki Rekhayen
(1943)*

* This collection was published in 1943. Some individual essays in it are undated.

Bhaktin

An era has passed since Bhaktin, small and thin, with firm resolve and unusual good sense in her narrow eyes, first showed up on my doorstep. But whenever someone asks her about it, she half-closes her eyes and lifting her chin as if to think about it, says with confidence, 'What can I tell you? We have lived together for about fifty years.' Bhaktin doesn't realize that this would mean I am seventy-five years old and she over a hundred. Even if she did realize it, she probably wouldn't want to even slightly reduce the time she has spent with me. I am beginning to be convinced that after a few years, she will increase our time together to a hundred years, even if this results in my having to carry the impossible weight of 150 years.

Although she rivals Hanuman-ji in devotion, Bhaktin is the daughter not of Anjana—Hanuman's mother—but of an anonymous cowherd woman, and her name is Lacchmin, that is, Lakshmi. But just as it is hard for me to carry the magnificence of my name, so also Lakshmi's prosperity could not be contained in the shrunken contours of Bhaktin's head. Most people have to live with the paradoxes generated by their names, but Bhaktin, being very sensible, does not tell anyone her prosperity-related name. When she came in search of a job, she did tell me her name along with the rest of her history but requested that I never use that name. Little did this rustic know that had I had the gift of inventing pseudonyms, I would have used it on myself first of all, so when I gave her a new name based on the sacred necklace she wore, she was delighted with the unpoetic name Bhaktin, which means 'devotee'.

It would be hard to even partially, let alone fully, understand Bhaktin's nature without knowing her history. She was the only daughter of an Ahir [cowherd] well-known in his village in historical Jhunsi and was raised in the shadow of a stepmother's legendary maternal love. Her father earned fame for staying two steps ahead of the scriptures by getting her married to the youngest son of a wealthy cowherd in Handiya village, and her stepmother earned the merit of a moneylender who returns a debtor's wealth without being asked, when she sent the nine-year-old girl to her marital home.[1]

Because her father loved her very much, her jealous stepmother, eager to protect the property, sent her the news of his fatal illness only when it had already become the news of death. To avoid inauspicious wailing and crying, her mother-in-law hid the truth from her. She told her to visit her parents since she had not visited them for a long time, and dispatched her. This unexpected kindness gave her feet wings, which fell off as soon as she reached the village. Murmurings of 'Oh, Lacchmin has finally come' and sympathetic looks accompanied her home. But there she found no sign of her father and no symptom of civility in her stepmother's behaviour. Weak with grief and enraged by the disrespect, she left the house without pausing to drink water and returned to her in-laws. She relieved her anger at her stepmother by rebuking her mother-in-law and expressed

1 Girls married as children are customarily sent to the marital home only after they reach puberty, not at the age of nine.

her sorrow at eternal separation from her father by throwing her jewels, one after the other, at her husband.

There was more sorrow than happiness in the next phase of her life too. When she produced two more editions of her wheat-coloured, pebble-faced first daughter, her mother-in-law and older sisters-in-law made their displeasure evident. This was only proper because her mother-in-law, the creator of three earning heroes, was ensconced on a string-bed as progenitrix, while her two sisters-in-law, having created a string of sons black as Kakbhushundi, the sage crow, were candidates for the position. The youngest daughter-in-law had to be punished for going her own way.

The sisters-in-law sat discussing the world and their coal-hued sons ran wild, while she churned buttermilk, pounded grain, ground spices, and cooked, and her little daughters gathered cow dung and made dung-cakes for fuel. The sisters-in-law poured molasses and thickened milk on their rice, and skimmed cream off boiling milk for their sons. Buttermilk and black jaggery fell to her share while her daughters chewed on boiled millet and chickpeas.

There was no provision in this penal code whereby a husband could be alienated from a wife who minted false coins. All the complaints and reproaches got transformed into his loving her even more. The sisters-in-law were regularly beaten but her husband never laid a finger on her. He recognized in her the noble daughter of a noble father. He must have deeply loved this hardworking, bright, and utterly loyal wife, because it was on the strength of his love that she managed to set up a separate household, defying his family. Since she did all the work, it was she who knew all about the cows, buffaloes, fields, sheds, granaries, and mango orchards. She carefully selected the best for their share, pretending to be dissatisfied but inwardly delighted, and the hardworking couple's efforts turned everything into gold.

After getting their oldest daughter married with much pomp, the husband left the burden of two little girls, still playing with dolls, and the freshly established household to his twenty-nine-year-old wife and took leave of the world. He must have been barely thirty-six when he died but his wife remembers him as the old man. Bhaktin thinks that because she has grown old, he too has grown old in God's house, and it would be an insult not to call him the old man.

Her husband's brothers and their sons naturally envied Bhaktin's flourishing fields, sturdy cattle and buffaloes, and fruit-laden trees. They could lay their hands on all of this if she agreed to remarry, but Bhaktin, false coin that she was, refused the lure. She stamped her feet in rage, setting the courtyard trembling, and declared, 'I'm no cat or dog. I'll stay right here and rule here, so get used to it.'

She would not give them a needle-point's worth of the land accumulated by her father-in-law, grandfather-in-law, and many earlier generations. She performed rituals with her guru, sacrificed her hair, slick with ghee, to her husband, and vowed never to remarry. To protect the property, she got her younger daughters married and sent them off to their in-laws, but kept her oldest son-in-law, whom her husband had chosen, at home with her.[2] Thus began the third phase of her life.

Bhaktin's misfortune was as stubborn as she was; her oldest daughter was widowed in her late teens. The brothers-in-law who had failed to thwart their sister-in-law, and their sons who were waiting to defeat their aunt saw a ray of hope. Her oldest cousin proposed that she marry his wife's brother who was an afficionado of pheasant-fighting and would therefore let them control the

---

2 *Ghar-jamai*: A man who stays with his wife's parents instead of his own parents. Generally used in a derogatory way, but used positively here.

property. Bhaktin's daughter was sensible, like her mother, and refused the match. The cousins did not want an unknown man to marry her so the proposal went nowhere. Mother and daughter worked with might and main to improve their property while the supporters of the would-be groom hatched a plot to confer on him the authority of a husband.

One day, in the mother's absence, the prospective groom entered the daughter's room and bolted the door from inside while his supporters summoned the villagers. When the Ahir girl beat up the dacoit groom and opened the door, the village elders were perplexed. The pheasant-fighting youth said she had invited him in, while the girl asked them to read her invitation in the marks of her five fingers on his face. A panchayat was called, and all the elders nodded their heads and said the *Kali Yug* was the cause of the problem.[3] The unappealable judgement issued was that whether one was truthful or both were lying, since they had issued from one room, only their living as husband and wife could remedy the fault produced by this dark era. The insulted girl, biting her lips, drew blood, and the mother looked with flaming eyes at the son-in-law with whom she was saddled. The marriage was not a happy one, because the son-in-law now spent all his time on pheasant-fighting while the girl was aflame with helpless rage. The cattle and fields nurtured with such care soon withered in the family conflict, with the result that it was hard to pay the land revenue. Finally, the landlord summoned Bhaktin and made her stand all day in the fierce heat. This was a huge stain on her reputation for hard work, so the very next day she came to the city in search of earnings.

---

3 *Kali Yug*: In Hinduism, the present era (which began at the time of the Mahabharata) is considered the last and worst of four eras.

When Bhaktin was initiated into my service, her shaved head covered with a thick, dirty cotton sari and one ear poking out of the cloth as if to hear everything, the fourth and possibly the final phase of her life began, the end of which is far away. Observing the mixture of householder and ascetic in her appearance, I asked, doubtfully, 'Do you know how to cook?' In reply, she wrinkled her upper lip, pulled back her lower, and said reassuringly, 'What's so hard about that? I know how to make roti, I can cook dal, and fry up vegetables. What else is there to do?'

At dawn the next day, she poured several pitchers of water on her head, purified my clean cotton sari by sprinkling water on it, and worshipped with two pitchers of water the sun and the pipal tree, emerging respectively from the darkness of the east and from my wall. After holding her nose closed and reciting a mantra for two minutes, she established herself in the kitchen, drawing a thick coal line to demarcate the borders of her empire, but I realized that this server's companionship was a mixed blessing. Although I am not particular about food, I am renowned in my family for being a good cook, and anyone skilled in culinary arts cannot help finding fault with another's cooking. But when I recalled that people who insist on the purity of the kitchen will go on a fast to protest an infringement and when I experienced the prohibition in Bhaktin's suspicious glance, the coal line became as difficult to cross as the line drawn by Lakshman's bow.[4] I could do nothing but lie on my bed, hold a book above my nose, and

4 *Lakshman Rekha*: In the Ramayana, Lakshman draws a magical line around the house to protect his sister-in-law Sita. Disobeying instructions, she steps over the line and is abducted by Ravana. Mahadevi uses the proverbial term in an unusual way. Here, a woman draws her own line.

try to forget the unauthorized person enthroned on the stool in the kitchen.

At mealtime, when, according to my predetermined role, I seated myself as directed, Bhaktin, smiling with self-satisfaction, her eyes overflowing with pleasure, placed four rotis, each plump as a finger and covered in dark black spots, on my pewter plate, tilting it to spoon thick dal in. But when I asked tearfully, pouring frosty water on her enthusiasm, 'What's this you've made?' she was perplexed.

The rotis had become a little too crisp in her attempts to cook them thoroughly but they were good. There were vegetables but what was the point of cooking them when there was dal? In the evening, she would cook vegetables and no dal. I didn't like milk and ghee, otherwise it would all have been fine. Should she grind some *chatni* out of mango powder and red chillies? Or she could give me some gur from the bundle she had brought from home, and did city folks like to eat the beaten silver that was put on sweets? She was no uncouth amateur, not she. Her father-in-law, grandfather-in-law, grandmother-in-law, and others had all bestowed on her numerous oral certifications of her skill in cookery.

The consequence of Bhaktin's profound lecture was that because of my dislike of sweets and aversion to ghee, I ate one thick roti with dry dal and proceeded to the university, where, while I studied the Nyaya Sutra, I continued to think about this difference between urban and rural life. I had had to make separate dining arrangements for myself because of my failing health and my family's anxiety about it, but this arrangement I had made precluded the question of remedial eating. This rustic old woman had so awakened me to the simplicity of life that I began to hide the inconveniences I experienced; organizing conveniences was out of the question.

Bhaktin's nature had been so shaped that she wanted to mould people to suit her ideas but she could not imagine any change in herself. That is why I am more rustic today but she is untouched by the winds of the city. Pounded maize porridge cooked at night is fragrant in the morning if mixed with buttermilk. Puffed millet bread with sesame seeds tastes less good when hot. The green grains of roasted ears of sorghum make a tasty khichri. A dessert made of *mahua* berry juice can put the whole world's *halwa*s to shame. All this she keeps teaching me with practical demonstrations but never has a *rasagulla* from here obtained the good fortune of entering Bhaktin's toothless mouth. Despite my expressing annoyance night and day, she refuses to wear a clean cotton sari, and on the pretext of folding the clothes that I wash myself and spread out to dry, she wrinkles them all over. She has had me memorize several folk tales from her language but has not learnt the civility to respond, when called, with 'Ji' instead of 'Oye'.

It would be hard to call Bhaktin good because she does not lack bad qualities. She cannot become a truth-telling Harishchandra but neither does she believe in the equivocation of 'whether man or elephant'.[5] Bhaktin alone knows the secret of how my stray cash, lying around the house, finds its way into some jar or other in the pantry. But if anyone makes an insinuation about this, she challenges them to a debate which even a master logician cannot

---

5 In the Mahabharata, Krishna, in order to help the Pandavas demoralize and defeat the invincible Dronacharya, advises Yudhishthira to tell him that his son Ashwathama is dead, which is not true. Bhima kills an elephant, who is also named Ashwathama (subduer of horses). Yudhishthira, renowned for always telling the truth, says to Dronacharya, 'Ashwathama is dead,' and adds in a low voice, 'whether man or elephant, I do not know.' This is a famous example of equivocation.

win. This is her own house—is it theft for her to put away safely money that she finds lying around? The main duty in her life is to keep me happy—is it a lie for her to tell me in a roundabout way things that will annoy me? Even the Lord of Dharma would tell that sort of lie or commit that sort of theft, or else how could he please God and run the world?

Bhaktin explains the scriptures too to her satisfaction. I don't like women shaving their heads so I told her not to do so. She confidently said that it's written in the scriptures. Out of curiosity, I asked, 'What is written?' Pat came the answer, 'The liberated one went on pilgrimage and shaved.' It was impossible for me to find out from which scripture this mysterious verse was derived. I accepted defeat and fell silent, and Bhaktin's head continued to be shaved every Thursday by a low-income barber whose razor was washed in Ganga water.

However, it would be untrue to say that she is foolish or does not understand the importance of knowledge. She makes up for her lack of education by taking pride in my reading and writing. Once, when I told her my rule that everyone who worked for me had to learn to sign their name instead of making a thumb impression, Bhaktin was in a quandary because she didn't want to take the trouble to learn to read and also because she considered it insulting at her age to have to sit and learn with the drivers and maids. So, she said, 'My employer is buried in books night and day. Now if I start studying too, who will look after the house?'

This logic made such an impression on both students and teachers that Bhaktin obtained the right to roam around in the classrooms like an inspector, making observations about one person's way of writing 'a' or 'e', another's slow pace of writing, and a third one's dull intellect. Since she didn't need to make a thumb impression to get her salary, she became the guru of the students even though she was uneducated. She is skilled at finding evidence not only for her logic but for her lack of logic. She wants to make her mistress out to be extraordinary in order to enhance her own importance, but for this too she has to find evidence.

Once when I was busy with the answer-books and paintings, Bhaktin went around telling everyone, 'That poor thing is bent over her work day and night, and you girls roam about doing nothing. Come on, help her out a bit.' Everyone knew that they could not help out with this work so they expressed their helplessness in the matter. This provided evidence for her hyperboles to multiply—no one could do the work her madam did, that was why no one dared lend a hand even when called upon to do so.

It would be below her dignity, though, to acknowledge that she too can't help, so she sits in the doorway repeatedly insisting that I give her some work to do. Bhaktin demonstrates her intellectual superiority to the others by tying the answer-books into bundles, putting half-done paintings in corners, washing paint-cups, and dusting off the rug with her sari-end. She knows that while the others cannot imagine helping me, she gives practical shape to her wish to help, so whenever a book of mine is published, her face lights up with pleasure just as the hidden radiance in a bulb does when the switch is turned on. Touching it repeatedly when alone, peering closely at it, and carrying it around, she seems to search for the imprint of her help, and the self-satisfaction in her expression says that she does not fail to find it. This is natural too. When I'm immersed in finishing a painting and don't get up to eat even after being repeatedly summoned, she brings me a yoghurt drink or tulsi tea to stave off the pangs of hunger.

By the time the day's work is done and I sit down to finish an essay or capture an emotion in metre, the hostel's lights are out, my doe Sona settles on the floor at the foot of the bed and stops chewing the cud, the dog Vasant on the cane stool puts his head between his paws and closes his eyes, while the cat Godhuli curls up to sleep on my pillow.

But Bhaktin, not wanting to leave me alone in the silence of the night, takes up her position on a rug in a corner and stays awake calmly, blinking in the dazzling electric light. She doesn't doze off, because as soon as I raise my head her dimming vision follows my eyes. If I look towards the rack kept near the head of the bed, she gets up and asks the colour of the book I need, if I put down my pen she brings the ink, and if I push the papers aside, she picks up the next file. Even when I go to sleep late, I wake up early and Bhaktin has to get up even earlier—Sona is desperate to leap and run around outside, Vasant wants the door to be opened so that he can get on with his daily routine, and Godhuli hears a call to the hunt in the twitterings of birds.

Bhaktin has also been my sole travel companion. She has insisted on walking ahead of me on the steep and narrow mountain roads to places like Badrinath and Kedarnath, and also on following me down dusty village paths. Whenever and under whatever conditions I decide to go anywhere, I find Bhaktin accompanying me like a shadow.

When people grew afraid that a border war was about to erupt in the country, Bhaktin's daughter, son-in-law, and grandson came to take her home but she resisted all their arguments and refused to go.[6] She visits everyone and sends them money but to live with them she would have to leave me, which perhaps Bhaktin will not agree to do until the end of her life. Last year, when the spectre of war awakened a tendency to flight rather

6 We do not know when this essay was written but the book in which it appeared was published in 1943. There was nothing like a 'border war' in 1942. Perhaps this is an odd way of referring to the impending Partition.

than to courage, Bhaktin for the first time assumed the humble attitude of a servitor to coax me into going with her to her village. She will spread her new dhoti in the loft where wood is stored and keep my clothes on it, she will hammer nails into the walls and put planks on them for my books, and make a bed for me out of rice straw and a blanket. She will put my paints and inks into new mud pots and preserve my papers in a net suspended from the ceiling.

'I don't have the money to go and live there,' I said in order to dismiss her proposal, but the result astounded me. As if revealing a profound secret, Bhaktin brought her toothless mouth to my ear and whispered that she had five twenty-rupee notes and five one-rupee notes kept by. She would make all the arrangements with this money. And the war would not last forever. When it ended, we would return here. Bhaktin's miserliness had assumed mountainous proportions with her accumulation of capital, but the dynamite of her generosity blew it up in a moment. The money she had was so little as to be negligible but her love of money was so well known that her willingness to sacrifice it for me was of boundless importance.

It is hard to say that the relationship between Bhaktin and me is that of employer and employee, because there is no employer who cannot get rid of an employee, nor has any employee been heard of who laughs contemptuously when dismissed by the employer. Calling Bhaktin a servant is as absurd as considering the darkness and light that come and go in one's house or the roses and mangoes that blossom in one's courtyard one's servants. Just as these give us sorrow or joy in order to manifest the meaning of their own existence, so also Bhaktin's independent individuality surrounds my life to express its own development.

From the oddities that have developed in her temperament because of family and circumstances, a light of affection and sympathy keeps bursting out, in which anyone who comes in contact with her experiences the natural poignancy of life. A girl from the student hostel sits in a corner of her kitchen to drink tea, another sits on the threshold to have her thicken some milk, a third standing outside tastes the snack made for me and analyses its flavour. As soon as I step out, they fly away like birds, and when I come back inside, they again take their accustomed places. Perhaps it is to avoid any obstacles to their coming that Bhaktin cooks her two meals in the morning and keeps them in a high-up niche, and when she eats, compromises with the eternal rules of purity by washing a corner of the kitchen.[7]

Bhaktin knows all my acquaintances and literary colleagues but her respect and good-will for them is in proportion to my respect and good-will for each one. Bhaktin's common sense in this regard surprises me. She refers to some by their appearance and way of dressing and others by a distorted form of their name. Her knowledge of poets and poetry has increased but not her respect for them. Observing one's long hair and disorderly dress, she asks, 'Does he know how to write poems?' and follows this up with the dismissive remark: 'So he doesn't do anything, just wanders in alleys singing and playing.'

But everyone's sorrow has an impact on her. When one of the students goes to prison, Bhaktin tires everyone out with her comments, 'Sending little boys to jail is *kaljug* but now the end of the world is near. Their mothers need to fight for them right up to the big Lat.'[8] Bhaktin has the same sort of sympathy for everyone who goes to jail, from Bapu to an ordinary person.

---

7 Eternal is an inadequate translation of *sanatan*, without beginning or end, which refers to Hinduism.

8 This sentence incorporates Bhaktin's colloquial speech. She pronounces Kali Yug *kaljug*. The boys are sent to prison for nationalist activities. 'Lat' (for Lord) probably refers to the Governor-General. 'The end of

Bhaktin's *samskara* are such that she fears prison as if it were the abode of the God of Death.[9] She almost faints when she sees those high walls. This weakness of hers is so well known that people tease her with the possibility of my going to jail. It would be untrue to say that she has no fear, but greater than fear is the importance of being with me. She quietly asks me which dhoti of hers she should wash with soap so as not to embarrass me there and what stuff she should pack to save me from inconvenience there. That no one has the right to accompany anyone on that journey does not bother Bhaktin. Even more than her pleasure at the idea that I will not go there is her indignation at the possibility that she will not be able to accompany me. How extremely unfair! Where the mistress is, there the servant is—it is not as unjust to lock up the mistress as it is to leave the servant alone. If such enormous injustice is perpetrated, Bhaktin will have to fight all the way up to the big Lat. The mothers of jailed boys may not fight all the way to the big Lat but Bhaktin will certainly do so.

It is hard to imagine such unequal contestants.

Often I wonder: when that summons comes, which will allow no time to wash dhotis or pack stuff, when Bhaktin will not be allowed to stay nor I to stop her, what will this old rustic woman do in those final moments of the eternal farewell, and what will I do?

Bhaktin's story is unfinished, but I don't want to complete it by losing her.

---

the world' translates *pralay* (Sanskrit *pralaya*), which follows the last of four eras or Kali Yug. It ends this cosmic cycle and dissolves this universe, after which another will begin.

9 *Samskara* are the patterns inherited from ancestors and also from one's upbringing. 'The abode of the God of Death' translates 'Yamlok', the underworld ruled by Yama, God of Death.

The Chinese Vendor

I do not find much memorable variety among the Chinese. Their flat faces seem to me to be cast in the same mould, and the noses, which, like a pleat in clothing, dispel uniformity, also seem not very different. The liquid lines of their slanted, half-open eyes, brown eyebrows far apart, delude me into thinking that they are all cut with the same sharp knife to the same measurements. Their natural yellow complexion becomes like a dry, red leaf in the footprints of the heat overlaid with dust. Their looks and dress give the form of mechanical puppets to these inhabitants of a distant land, so that even having seen one Chinese vendor several times, I find it difficult to distinguish him from another.

But today I recall the moist bluish eyes of a face that stands out in the crowd, saying to me silently: We are not carbon copies. We each have a story. If your eyes are not illiterate in life's alphabet, read and see.

Many years ago, I alighted from a tanga and was entering the house when a Chinese vendor emerged from the gate, holding a brown cloth bundle on his left shoulder and swinging an iron yard-measure in his right hand. Perhaps he was leaving, having found my house locked. 'Will you take something, Memsaheb?' asked the unfortunate Chinese man.[1] How was he to know that

1 Memsaheb is a form of Ma'am Saheb, used to address European women.

this form of address arouses a wave of intense anger in me? I am used to many forms of address, such as Maiya, Mata, Jiji, Didiya, Bitiya, and I like all of them, but this foreign address seems to snatch away my identities and leave me standing in a gown. To not go away disappointed after addressing me thus was, if not impossible, at least difficult.

I replied with indifference, 'I don't buy foreign stuff.'

'I am phoren? I'm from China,' he said, with astonishment as well as hurt arising from my disinterest. This time, I had to stop and look properly at the speaker. Standing there, short and thin, without beard or moustache, in pajamas that seemed a compound of pants and pajamas, and a coat stitched on the basis of the oneness of kurta and coat, his forehead half-covered with a hat whose frayed borders declared its age, and his small feet hidden in white canvas shoes caked with dust, he seemed an eternal embodiment of a Chinese person. For the first time in my life, the question of seeing him apart from the others arose.

Realizing that my indifference had hurt that foreigner, I tried to make my 'No' gentler and said, 'I don't want anything, brother!' The Chinese man turned out to be rather strange. 'You've called me brother, you will definitely buy something, won't you?' Reminded of the idiom about burning one's hands while making an offering to the fire, I was forced to say, 'Let's see what you have.' Putting his bundle down in the verandah, he said, 'Very nice silk I bring, sister. China silk, crepe.' After much discussion, it became necessary to buy two tablecloths. I thought, well, I got off easy. Having sold so little here, he won't make the mistake of coming this way again.

But after about a fortnight, I found him sitting on his bundle in the verandah and humming a tune, keeping time on the floor with his measuring stick. Without giving him a chance to speak, I hastily said, 'I won't buy any more, understand?' He stood up, took something out of his pocket, and said delightedly, 'I've brought *hankie* for sister—very *best*, all the rest have been sold. I hid these in my pocket for you.'

The handkerchiefs' edges were embroidered in light blue and every petal of the tiny flowers of the same colour in the corners testified to the artistry of Chinese women's tender fingers and told the sad story of life's deprivations. Addressing my negative expression, he opened and closed his blue, line-like eyes and repeated in one breath, 'Brought them for sister, brought them for sister.'

I thought—this is a fine brother I've acquired. In my childhood, people would tease me by calling me Chinese. I began to wonder if there was some basis for that teasing. Otherwise, why would this genuine Chinese man pick me out as his sister from all of Allahabad! But from that day, he acquired the special right to drop in whenever he liked. Observing his refined taste, I realized that even an ordinary person in China has a special taste for art.

A Chinese person has as much understanding of which colours in a picture will look good on a blue wall, what kind of birds should be embroidered on a green cushion, and what sort of flowers and leaves should adorn the corners of a white curtain, as any artist would. Their intense familiarity with colour makes me believe that they could recognize a colour by touch even while blindfolded.

Chinese clothing and pictures are so colourful that they create the illusion that every speck of dust in their country must be drenched in colour. When I expressed a desire to see China, the blue line of his eyes lighted up with pleasure and he said, 'I'll go along with sister.'

He was eager to tell his story but there was a deep gulf between speaker and listener. He knew Chinese and Burmese, in relation to which, despite all my learning, I embodied the idiom, 'a blind person named Nainsukh'.[2] All the nuances of the story could not be conveyed in the strange language made by mixing verb-free nouns of English with the noun-free verbs of Hindustani, but a story that breaks the heart's dam and flows out to give itself to others is usually sad and the wordless language of sadness is eloquent. The Chinese vendor's story was no exception.

Before his birth, his parents had moved to Mandalay and opened a small teashop. He cherished an unbroken devotion to the mother he had never seen, who died in childbirth, leaving him in the care of his seven-year-old sister. Perhaps it is only a mother whom a person remembers without having ever seen. This is natural too. A mother is the creator who links a human to the world. One can easily disown her if one disowns the world, but if one accepts the world, it is impossible not to acknowledge her.

The harsh story of those two motherless children's torture began when their father enthroned a Burmese-Chinese woman as the new mistress of the household. Fate was not content with this, for as he approached the age of five, his father died in an accident.

Like other innocent children, he too adjusted to the circumstances, but the increasing hostility between his sister and stepmother with regard to some proposal rendered the adjustment ever more poisonous. Both the adolescent girl and her young brother suffered for her disobedience. Many times, he forgot his hunger by putting his hand in his shivering sister's trembling fingers, hiding his tearful face in her soiled clothing, and shrinking into her small lap. Often, in the morning, he would try in vain to warm up his frozen fingers in his sister's wet hair

---

2 *Nainsukh* means 'delight of the eyes'.

as she sat against the wall outside the closed door and would ask her how they could go to their father. Upset by the large tear that rolled down his silent sister's faded cheek, he would hurriedly say that he didn't want tea, he only wanted to see his father.

Several times, his sister washed the neighbours' dishes and obtained rice in exchange to feed him. How could the child know what final torment broke his sister's little heart? But one night as he lay in bed, waiting for his sister, he half-opened an eye and saw his stepmother, like a skilled magician, transforming his dirty and untidy sister. The stepmother spread redness on the girl's dry lips with her thick fingers, rubbed a mix of white and pink on her cheeks with her broad palm, dressed her untended hair with her harsh hands, and then, having dressed her in new, colourful clothes, more or less dragged her out into the dark night.

The child's surprise turned to fear and he cried himself to sleep, and woke only when his sister, holding back her sobs, put her face on his brow. That day he got good food, the next day clothes, and the third day toys, but every day his sister's fading lips needed darker colouring and her withering cheeks more powder.

The child noticed that his sister's body was dwindling and her strength declining but he did not know what to do or whom to tell. The only thought that came to him was that if he could find his father, all would be well. He had no memory of his mother but the vague memory of his father assured him of affection. Every day he would decide to ask all who came to the shop where his father was, so that he could quietly go and fetch him home. How scared his stepmother would be and how happy his sister!

The teashop was now owned by another but he was sympathetic to the old owner's son, so the child stood in a corner and stuttered as he asked each customer about his father. Some looked at him in astonishment, others smiled, but one or two said something to the shopkeeper which caused him to take the child's hand and put him out of the shop, threatening to tell his stepmother if he repeated this mistake. That was the end of his quest.

The routine of his sister being transformed each evening, returning home with reluctant steps after midnight, the huge-bodied stepmother leaping out of bed lightly like a jungle cat to snatch the purse from the girl's feeble hands, and the girl lying as if stunned with her face on her brother's brow continued.

But one day his sister did not return. Seeing his stepmother search for her next morning with some anxiety, the child was seized by an unknown fear. His sister—his only support. He had not found his father and now his sister too was lost. He set out to roam through the alleys every day and night, looking for her. It was hard to recognize her in her nightly garb, so whenever he saw a well-dressed person, he would run across the road to them. Sometimes he would knock into someone and barely escape falling down, and people would curse at him or sometimes ask him a kind question, wondering whether such a small child had gone mad.

Wandering around in this way, he was captured by a gang of pickpockets and thus began his re-education. As people train dogs to sit up, stand with their necks stretched out, salute, and so on, they locked him in a room full of tobacco smoke, stinking breath, torn rags, broken pots, and dirty bodies, and began teaching him certain special gestures and ways of laughing and crying. Like a puppy, he would stand on all fours and practise different ways of laughing and crying. The springs of laughter had dried up in him so that he often made mistakes in his acting and was beaten. But tears so surged within him that as soon as he twisted his face, two round drops would run down his face, making parallel lines on both sides of his nose, touching both sides of his mouth and flowing down his chin. Considering this the fruit of his excellent teaching, his teacher, who had a yellow scarf tied round his hairy black stomach, would leap with joy and reward him with a kick.

The gang was a mixture of Burmese, Chinese, and Siamese men, and each group was highly suspicious of the others. He had patrons but their antagonists were suspicious of him and would beat him up. Whenever someone lost something, he would be suspected and would start trembling like a thief although he was not one, and would be beaten so badly that remembering it even today, his eyes burn with pain and indignation. The left-overs from everyone's plates would be put in a twisted-up enamel vessel, kept covered with a paper burnt by cigarettes, and would be shared by him and the green-eyed black cat.

Late into the night, his co-residents in this hell would keep coming in, one by one, and pass on, stumbling over the child who lay huddled next to the brazier. He could read their footsteps. He who trod lightly and fast had made quite a bit of money; he who dragged his feet was empty-handed; he who staggered along, leaning on the wall, had spent all he had on liquor; and he who stumbled at the threshold and stomped his way in had got into a fight.

Shortly after his initiation was complete and he had just been inaugurated into using his skills, he ran into a Chinese trader who knew his father. Had that not happened it is hard to say what the end would have been of the knowledge he had obtained from his labours. But destiny changed his life's direction so that he began to learn the art of selling clothes in a store.

To pick up and display the oldest cloth first while praising it to the skies, to measure in such a way that not the tiniest bit of extra cloth was cut off even if this meant measuring a finger's width less, to examine every note and coin received with great care, and to specially ring old, fake coins when giving change—all these were the mysteries of the trade. He ate with the owner so he no longer had to share left-overs with a cat, yet he slept in the store so he was still compelled to lie near the brazier and be stumbled over. From a young age, he had understood that all the arts of acquiring wealth are alike, but one can practise some respectably while others have to be hidden.

When he grew up, he made great efforts to find his unfortunate sister but was unsuccessful. The life of such girls is beset with dangers. Sometimes they are bought and sometimes abducted. Sometimes they commit suicide in despair and sometimes drunkards liberate them from life. The stepmother who held the key to this mystery had perhaps remarried and moved away to bestow happiness on another. That channel of enquiry was thus shut down.

His employer sent him to Rangoon, then to Calcutta for two years, and then here with his companions. He stayed in the city with a Chinese shoemaker and went on his sales rounds in two shifts, from eight to twelve in the morning and two to six.

He had two desires—to be honest and to find his sister. The fulfilment of the first was in his own hands and for the second he prayed to Lord Buddha every day. He would often go out of town for months, but on returning he would appear with some stuff, saying, 'I've brought this for sister.' I was so used to this that one day when he said 'for sister' and seemed to grope for words, I did not understand his difficulty and burst out laughing. Gradually he revealed that he had been summoned to China to fight. How could he sell all the cloth so fast? Yet, not to sell it would be dishonesty, because his master would suffer a loss. If I could buy all his cloth, he would settle accounts with his master and set out at once for his country.

Once he had stuttered while trying to find his father, now he was stuttering again from embarrassment. To gain time to think,

I asked, 'You have no one of your own—who has summoned you?' His eyes grew wide with astonishment: 'When did I say that China is not my own? When did I say that, sister?' I felt ashamed of my question—all of China was his, how could he be alone?

I rarely have any money; where could I find so much? But I dredged out some and took loans to make arrangements for him to leave. When he set out, light-footed, having said his final farewells to me, I called out, 'Take this measuring rod.' With a slight smile he turned and said, 'For sister.' The rest of his words were lost in stutters.

Many years have passed. There is no likelihood of meeting him again and I have no acquaintance with his sister, but for some reason that brother and sister are inscribed in my memory.

I have used up many rolls of his fabric, making shirts for my rural children, but I still have three rolls in my cupboard and the iron measuring rod stands in a corner. One sister, a devotee of khadi, who saw the rolls in my cupboard, said sharply, 'Our country doesn't prosper because even those who seem to be pure wearers of khadi buy and keep rolls of foreign silk.' With great difficulty, I held back my laughter.

There is no evidence that that Chinese man, sorrowful from birth, motherless, fatherless, and separated from his sister, has known the satisfaction of reaching China, the one focus of all his affection, but my heart says that he has.

Jang Bahadur the Porter

When I turned away from the porters' Chitragupta, that is, the contractor, and, clutching a receipt written on an old almond-coloured piece of paper, came out into the dusk that looked like a lamp flaring up just before it goes out, he had to end his description of the many souls under his command and of his own greatness.[1] Since his repeated coughing failed to pierce this listener's indifference, he tucked away his bent, stained pen, grasped with crooked fingers his coverless inkpot filled with watery ink, and slowly descended the stairs. As soon as his back was turned, a crowd of porters gathered in front of my room.

The porters who come from Nepal and Bhutan are known as Dotiyals. Their value is measured only by their ability to carry loads. Even the smallest among them can usually carry one and a half or two *maund*s up steep mountains for miles.[2] They look like

---

1 Chitragupta, the divine accountant of the Gods, keeps records of the actions of every living being. He is said to be the progenitor of the Kayastha community, since they were traditionally accountants and book-keepers.

2 A *maund* is the equivalent of 37 kilograms.

the participants in Shiva's wedding procession, except that those were ugly, not poor, and these are poor but not ugly.[3]

One, clad in strange pajamas made of sacking and a kurta that looked like a quilt-cover made from a torn, black, rough blanket, seemed like a bear. Another, in a loincloth and a ragged cotton coat, with a thick rope for tying burdens around his waist, scratches his upstanding dry hair and looks like a porcupine. The feet of one, with their hard heels and stiff, spread-out toes, compete with instruments for pounding the road, while another's feet, tied into self-made, rough grass slippers, create the illusion of paws.

One, sitting in the sun and picking lice out of his clothes, reminds me of a monkey, while another, face, hands, and feet rubbed with oil begged from a shopkeeper, shines like a water-animal emerging from the water. We know from experience that they are human, not from seeing the human form in them.

Seeing this crowd of various strange forms, my aunt sat, shrinking, in a corner, while Bhaktin, standing on the threshold, surveyed them with astonishment, because such a mixture of poverty and strangeness is not to be found even in our villages. I said in neutral tones, 'You all can go. Our porter is Jang Bahadur, send him over.'

They looked at one another and an especially brave one said, 'Mai-ji, this is Jangiya.' I didn't recognize Jang Bahadur by this name so I repeated, 'Call Jang Bahadur.' They began to nudge one another in surprise, then one pushed a person forward and said to another, 'He's called Jangiya.' Not finding any element of the importance necessary to my porter in the person they had

---

3 Shiva's unusual wedding procession is described in the Shiva Purana. Since Shiva is an ascetic, his companions include various ghoulish-looking beings who appear deformed and distorted.

pushed forward, I doubtfully asked, 'What's your name?' He replied, 'Jang Bahadur Singh.'[4]

The name required me to look closely at the possessor of the name. Nails broken by the stones of mountain paths and grass slippers forming a shield between wounded toes seemed to laugh at the God who had turned a human into an animal but not given him hooves. Pajamas made of woollen and cotton patches, ending two hand-spans above the feet, were like a parody of human modesty. His old coat, donated by someone long ago, showed its lining through many holes, and had frayed borders like a fringe, making its wearer look like an insect. Dry hair sticking out through the holes in a cap of unclear colour and shape reminded one of water grass sticking out here and there in muddy water.

Under thick brows, his face was broad and his nose round. Lips always open in laughter spread to his ears, hiding the gap between ears and cheeks. A small, scanty moustache, like a black thread hanging on both sides of his mouth, contradicted the childhood visible in his small teeth. Small eyes, looking tear-smudged in his broad face bordered by a narrow forehead and a small, round chin, shone like water in a desert. His wheatish colour had become coppery in places and wrinkled in others due to his constantly being out in the sun. One end of the rope for tying burdens hung round his neck and off his shoulder like a necklace, the other end tied round his waist was semi-visible through his rough coat. Such was Jang Bahadur Singh aka Jangiya. He and his brother Dhan Singh were to carry my luggage via Kedarnath to Badrikanathpuri and bring it back to Srinagar.[5] Their wages were fixed at a rupee each a day, of which one quarter of a rupee was the contractor's commission.

---

4 Jang Bahadur means Brave in Battle.

5 Dhan means wealth. Badrikanathpuri is an older variation on the name.

As soon as I asked, 'Where's your brother?' the cry of 'Dhaniya, O Dhaniya' went up on all sides, but I knew without being told that he who stood firmly behind his brother despite being constantly jostled was Dhan Singh. Also, Dhan Bahadur's face, always alert to his own junior status, reminded me of some younger brother of antiquity. The plump and sturdy-bodied Dhaniya's form was like his nature. The simple line of his scanty brown eyebrows and the sharp end of his small nose spoke both of his simplicity and of his energy. The outer corners of his lips were a bit drawn up, which made his face seem always smiley. His clear complexion and smooth skin showed that he had not yet suffered all the hardships of a porter's life. His old pajamas of sacking and his torn cotton coat gave him the look of a defeated soldier, which was not in consonance with his face.

The knowledge that I had to entrust my life and my companions' lives to them, and that they would be dependent on me for all conveniences on the road, produced an unsought maternal feeling towards the two porters. I said, 'Take a look at the baggage. If it seems too much, a third porter will be engaged.' Startling my aunt and Bhaktin, they stepped into the room, Jangiya in front and Dhaniya behind, and began to lift each bundle to estimate its weight.

I have made long mountain journeys on foot, in which the basic recipe for success involves taking along the minimum of baggage, so I don't make mistakes in that regard. I also don't think that on those journeys where food is available on the way, one needs to carry cans of ghee and dozens of biscuit tins along. I don't understand eating Polson's butter and Huntley Palmers' biscuits in the shadow of beautiful snow-capped peaks, but I know well the pleasure of roasting potatoes and thick bread-cakes on wood and dung gathered in the forest. My aunt wanted to carry more luggage than was needed but she is used to valuing even my smallest wish. I am taking her on pilgrimages where her sons cannot take her, so she has no doubt that I am greater than all sons and my wisdom is always to be relied on.

Thus, we had with us a few clothes for each person, bedding, a first-aid kit, detergent, and other such necessities. Jang Bahadur said they could carry everything, so our journey began next morning. On such a journey, we see life like a movie, in which we learn a lot about a community, which cannot be learnt in any other way.

At home, people can hide and fake their treatment of servants and dependents but it is hard to do this on a journey. A person's selfishness, folly, unkindness, and intolerance all become evident every step of the way. People's character can be judged by the way they pay the porter's wages, take into account his need for rest and food, and take opportunities to help their companions and pay attention to their comfort.

One feels less pleasure and more sadness when one observes the life moving among the mountain ranges, which look like petals of a white lotus, some open, some closed, some clear, some invisible, the meadows spreading like green leaves, and the waterfalls like melted silver. A fat man sitting in a palanquin calls '*Sarpa-sarpa*' to the panting men carrying him, in order to make them run faster, a sight which reminds one of Nahusha who could not become divine even when he became ruler of heaven.[6] In another palanquin, a decked-up and made-up woman from a wealthy family ignores the mountains' beauty and lies sleeping. In yet another, an old woman with shaved head, a body like a

6 Nahusha was made king of the celestial world during Indra's absence. He decided to seduce Indra's wife and forced the seven sages to carry him in a palanquin to Indra's house. He spurred them on, crying '*Sarpa, sarpa,*' meaning 'move on'. Sage Agastya punishes him by turning him into a serpent (*sarpa*).

dry stick, and an expression suggestive of just having swallowed a bitter drink, goes along, shaking and rocking, her eyes fixed on the path. An elderly man, not wealthy, goes by, legs dangling from a sedan chair, and gazes pleadingly up at the skies. A hero ensconced on a pony forbids the horseman to walk behind, holding the tail, because this scares him. The head of a monastery sits on deerskin spread in a palanquin and, watching his disciples walk along with conchs and cymbals, experiences the happiness of being in heaven while still in the body.

Apart from this large group of people in palanquins and sedan chairs and on ponies, there is also a large group composed mostly of the poor. Most of them, due to lack of money, are skilled in completing the railway part of the journey without tickets. Then they set out, with five annas or five rupees tied in their waistcloths and a bundle of parched grain, flour made of parched grain, and jaggery. Not having the resources to ensure their return, they say a final farewell to everyone before they leave. When they fall ill along the way, their companions leave them behind. They are afraid that if they stay with them for a few days, they will use up all their food and money, and none of them will manage to make it to the destination. Before they set out, they all agree on this procedure, because if one person fails to reach the goal it's their individual demerit, but if others fail to reach because of them, the demerit of having prevented them will also fall to their account.

At each halting place, one or two fall ill; some die too. Their companions beg from other pilgrims in order to complete the funeral rites. If they fail, the deep ravine is a natural tomb.

One also meets tourists among the pedestrians. They are well-equipped travellers, who walk just for pleasure because they usually have ponies with them who walk either ahead or behind them, as desired. Neither those in palanquins nor these fashionable tourists speak to the poor pedestrian pilgrims.

Death is not unknown among the cavalcades of palanquins but it is confined to the porters. Sometimes a porter contracts cholera or develops a fever or suffers a serious injury. Another porter is immediately engaged and the journey continues uninterrupted. The sick porter is left to his fate. If he survives, he returns to the starting point and finds another traveller; if he dies, there is no problem throwing his body away.

The palanquins are accompanied by porters who carry luggage, who have to run to keep up with the palanquins. A traveller is a lot like a horse-cart owner. He buys a pony for twelve rupees and works it day and night in order to make thirty-six rupees in as short a time as possible. When the exhausted pony dies, he makes a profit even after buying another for twelve rupees. Travellers buy a porter for a rupee a day and, in order to make a profit, they naturally wish to cover three days' distance in one day, otherwise they lose money.

The passengers doze on the way, and carry snacks and dried fruit with them so there is no question of their being hungry or tired, but they keep cutting into the porters' meal times and rest times. In the morning, they say that twenty miles must be covered in a day. Do it as you wish but if you don't cover that ground your wages will be cut. The poor human animals run on, gasping and foaming at the mouth. The irony is that they are the ones with the power. If even one of them were to look askance at his rider and then look meaningfully at the ravine which is hundreds of feet deep, the rider would fall unconscious. But how can the porters ever get angry?

We had to make our way through the death hidden in the heart of this paradise and the sickness that dwells in its purity. I do not sit in palanquins and the others too walked. Nothing is as easy to communicate as human emotion, so the porters became our affectionate companions, and I consider my memory of them the merit I gained from the pilgrimage. They had two pieces of sacking and a torn black blanket, which was not broad enough to cover oneself with and which left either one's feet or one's head uncovered when used lengthwise.

Despite their dirty, unwashed clothes, the two brothers had not lost their knowledge of cleanliness. At the campsite they would find a remote, dark corner, where they would remove their clothes and cook in the state of a loincloth-clad ascetic, even in extremely cold weather. I tried to explain to them that this solution to the problem of not cooking in dirty clothes was an invitation to pneumonia, but I could not convince them.

Each of them had an iron pan, in one of which they cooked rice and in the other dal. Sometimes to avoid the expense of buying dal, they gathered a wild vegetable called *liguna* from the shores of streams and enjoyed eating it with half-baked roti.[7] On this path, no vegetable is available except potatoes, yet travellers were not willing to eat this local vegetable, considering it a poisonous grass suitable only for savages. On their insistence, I agreed to try this vegetable as their guest, after which they always kept a share of it for me, and then it acquired an important place on our menu.

On the road, we walked behind them and because their bodies were hidden by the loads, all I could see were their feet. Dhan Singh was too shy to raise his eyes but his feet rose firmly to keep pace with his brother's. As we climbed, when the weight of his feet would begin to fall on his heels and the foot placed in front seemed to slip, I knew without looking at his face that he was getting tired. But when I asked, 'Jang Bahadur, are you tired?' I would get the usual response couched in strange

---

7 *Liguna*: A type of fiddle-headed fern that grows in the Himalayas, known variously as *linguna, linguana, lingdi,* and *linguda,* from the Latin *lingua* maidenhair fern.

accents, 'I'm fine, Ma! No problem.' The seriousness of his voice prevented me from laughing at the accent.

From a young age, I have received the gift of being addressed as mother and the affection that goes along with it, but I have rarely found elsewhere the tenderness that these sons of the mountains put into the word and their simple acceptance of motherly affection.

Dhaniya was too shy to raise his head but Jangiya would often turn as he walked to take note of our needs and fatigue. Finally, one day he said, as if he were asking for an invaluable gift, 'Ma, it would be good if you walked ahead of us. I keep looking back and it's hard to turn my neck while carrying a load. If you are ahead, I can look at you while keeping my head erect—ah there is Ma, there she goes—and my feet will move faster.' From that time, we started walking ahead of them.

When we reached Adi Badri, Dhan Singh lay down in a corner of the campsite and his temperature rose rapidly. I took out some medicine from my box of homeopathic medicines, demonstrating the proverb, 'where there are no trees, a bush is a tree', and Bhaktin felt like a skilled nurse when she offered him tea. I told Jang Bahadur to press the invalid's feet, but he replied with his usual shyness, 'I am older, Ma! He will feel ashamed, how can I?'

I was naturally surprised by this etiquette. An old mother in a respectable family has told me that her son hits her at times, and when she invokes motherhood, he says, 'That era is over when you all had your children worship your feet. You gave birth because you wanted to. Should we spend our lives offering you sandalwood and rice just because of that?'

When people have become so polite to her who gave them life, it would be useless to expect courtesy between siblings. But Jang Bahadur's younger brother has not managed to become so progressive, therefore it is not surprising that he thinks his older brother pressing his feet would be opposed to courtesy.

Travellers don't wait when a porter falls ill. They employ another porter from the campsite or a nearby village and carry on. The simple, spontaneous affection between the two brothers that became evident due to this practice would not have shown itself under other circumstances.

Jang Bahadur knew he could take another porter instead of his younger brother but if he left him behind, what would he tell his mother? Dhaniya was too sick to go back, nor could he recover if he lay alone at the campsite. If they both stayed behind, their money would soon be used up and they might not find another client. In such a situation, the older brother would violate his duty if he left him alone, so he decided to find two new porters and stay back to look after Dhaniya.

Although he did not tell Dhaniya this, Dhaniya understood. He was sure his brother would not be able to leave him and would thus lose his own wages too. The little money they had earned would be spent while he was ill—then it would be hard to wait for another client and also hard to return. He decided that he would somehow carry on walking.

The next morning, when I returned from washing my hands and face in the stream, I found Jang Bahadur waiting in the lower campsite with two new porters and Dhan Singh wrapping a cloth around his head in preparation for lifting a load. 'Have you recovered?' I asked, and he, wiping the sweat caused by exhaustion, answered that he would be able to carry on. If he did not, his brother would also suffer a loss.

For a moment, the affection between the two cousins silenced me.[8] The surprise that dawned on their faces when they heard that I would wait there for two or three days and then continue the journey with both of them made me feel guilty and also distressed.

---

8 Cousins are called brothers (or sisters) in most north Indian languages. This is the first time Mahadevi reveals that the two men are the sons of two brothers.

Humans have made their mistreatment of other humans seem so natural that the lack of it creates surprise and the continuation of it seems normal. Dhan Singh recovered on the third day and we set out on the fourth.

Their sympathy and conduct towards each other created in me an affectionate respect for them which kept increasing. My books, first-aid box, vessels, and a few other things were heavy, so each would try to put them in his own load to spare the other. Each would try to get up earlier than the other in the morning in order to secure all the heavier items. If someone gave even a small sugar-candy to one, he would run to find the other to share it with him. When one of them saw an interesting sight, he would start calling out to the other. They were like two children whom someone had touched with a magic wand and made big.

They were also sensitive and sympathetic to other porters on the road. Once, a cow came sliding down the mountain so fast that her hoof wounded a porter's foot. Jang Bahadur put Dhan Singh in charge of the baggage and then carried the injured porter on his back to the stream. After we had bound up his foot, he carried him one and a half miles to the next campsite and also carried both their loads there. Then, shivering in the darkness, he had to wash the bloodstains off his torn clothes. But whenever one asked, he always replied, 'No problem, I am fine.'

Dhan Singh was too shy to talk much but Jang Bahadur would sometimes sit and tell us sad and happy stories about his parents, village, and home. He was the youngest son of parents who lived in a small village in Nepal. Since there was no other livelihood available, he began to traverse this road, along with other porters, while he was still a child. They come at the beginning of summer and return at the onset of winter. Some have to go to Kailash, some to Pindari, and others to Badri and Kedar. The contractor has all their names and numbers. If a porter does not return and there is no news of him, he is considered dead. When one does not return home at the end of the season or send a message through his companions, his family think that he has set out on the greatest of pilgrimages and they try to perform the rituals required to render his path easy.

Jang Bahadur has often fallen into difficulties because, in his eagerness to earn more, he makes not only long journeys but several of them in one season. Because of his unsettled life, fathers of marriageable daughters thought him unfit to be a son-in-law, but two years ago he had been freed of the curse of singleness. His adult bride had no parents. Her relatives thought that whether her groom found a tomb of snow on a mountaintop or returned as Kuber, God of Wealth, the girl would at least stay with her in-laws and free her unfortunate guardians from their duty.

Last year, Jang Bahadur did not go to work, this year the crops failed, and his wife gave him the gift of a jewel of a son. Now the question of earning had acquired new urgency. When he set out from home, his son was two months old but so small and weak that the father could not summon up the courage to hold him. Now he was saving all his earnings except for what he had to spend on food. With his savings and what he gets in tips he hopes to get a kurta and cap made for his son. With tears in her eyes, his young wife had begged him to accompany decent people and not to climb with a load more than once. His father had put one hand on his back and looked up at the sky with dim eyes, as if surrendering him to God.

His weeping mother went with him to the boundary of the village. Even after repeated reassurances, she refused to turn back and stood there, supported by a weak old tree, trying in vain to hold her son with a thread of tears as he went out of her field of vision. This was an age-old way of bidding farewell, but this year his agitated wife and silent son had joined the ritual. Knowing Jang Bahadur's superior abilities, his widowed paternal aunt had sent her son with him. That was why he always looked for travellers who would take both of them together.

This was my second pilgrimage to Badrinath so I thought it best to leave the path to Kedar and try to reach Alkapuri on the banks of Alaknanda river as soon as possible. But when we reached Rudra Prayag on the way back, which, on the shore of the wildly dancing waves of Alaknanda, reminded one of a flower pausing for a moment in a storm, my regret at not having gone to Kedar deepened.

Only one who has seen Mount Kedar, encircled by five streams, meditating in white snow, from its feet hidden in many-coloured flowers to its brow manifest in the blue void, can understand its attraction. From miles away, that radiant peak is clearly visible like a wordless invitation. As we approach it, it expands in breadth, and its contours, pulsating like lines of silver lightning, become ever clearer. On the way back, the moment when it disappears from our sight plunges us into a strange aloneness.

When we reached Rudra Prayag, some of my companions were so tired that they could not summon the courage to make the long climb. Badrinath's peak is only two and a half *kos* from Kedar's peak but it takes nine days to cover the distance.[9] Perhaps this is the origin of the saying, 'walked two and a half kos in nine days'.

When I decided to make the journey, those of my companions who were especially tired decided to wait and rest in Rudra Prayag, thus demonstrating the proverb, 'one path, two tasks'. One porter was enough for those who were going on this journey,

---

9 A *kos* is a traditional measurement. According to the *Arthashastra*, it is the equivalent of 3,000 metres, so 2.5 kos would be a little over 7 kilometres.

so we had to solve the problem of what to do with the second porter. My personal desire was for the second porter to rest with those staying behind and to return with us after eighteen days.

But how could Jang Bahadur take Ma-ji's eighteen rupees for free? He said something, with much modesty and as if asking a favour, which meant that he now knew Ma-ji and could safely leave Dhan Singh with her. He would go to Srinagar and find another traveller, and wait there for his brother. When everyone returned, he would travel with Dhaniya.

Perhaps no epic will be written on the self-sacrifice of this hero in battle [*jang-vir*] but his memory is a tender poem in my heart. When I ordered Jang-Vir to accompany me and Dhan Singh to rest in Rudra Prayag, it is hard to say whether his eyes were moister or his throat more choked up. It had required all his courage to propose returning but it was hard for him to endure separation from all of us. After many days, he told me in his broken Hindi, 'I didn't cry here because of shame and politeness, but I went far away and cried very loudly, thinking Ma-ji is going and my insides are churning.'

That journey too ended, and then came the day when the two brothers put us on the bus and stood outside, looking lost. Trying to hold back his tears, Jang-Vir said, 'Live long, Ma-ji, and come again. Send a letter to Jangiya.' Dhaniya stood looking at the earth as usual, saying farewell with his falling tears. I cannot say where those two sons of the mountains are now, but it is also not easy to convey in words the dignity I obtained by being their Ma-ji.

Munnu's Mother

When I first saw a concrete but broken building among the ruins at Arail, I asked a woman who was busy covering its unplastered wall with cow-dung cakes, 'Whose house is this?'[1]

Making her harsh voice drier, she responded, 'What have you to do with that? Have city women nothing better to do than to roam around anywhere and everywhere?'

Dubri's wife is renowned for her harshness. A few locks of dry and dirty hair stick to her scabbed lips. Her dark body is hidden by so many layers of dust that her mud-coloured dhoti seems part of her body. Each finger of her hands, which are always decked with cow dung in place of henna, hides many meaningful gestures of war. Her basic formula for friendship is 'Content yourself with battling me', because she considers it beneath her to talk to anyone who has not defeated her in a battle of words. One who refuses her challenge to battle is undeserving of her friendship.

At that time, I was unaware of these important details of her temperament. Also, I was not unused to such questions, because

---

1 Arail is an ancient settlement on the right bank of Yamuna near its confluence with Ganga. It is located opposite the fort in Prayag.

irritable temperaments are natural in villages replete with poverty and numberless scarcities. And Arail is considered the home of criminals. Few people go there expecting courtesy or even decency. I knew that a sharp retort would have the effect on her of an iron arrow shot at a stone, so it took me a few moments to think about how to propose a truce.

But Bhaktin thinks silence in response to such a volley is as despicable as turning one's back in battle, so she immediately said, 'It's rumoured in the city that the queens of this village pick bits of dried cow dung and make cakes of them, so we have come running to meet them—what else?'

As if to prevent the verbal explosion that would follow this pungent retort, a weak, thin woman of medium height emerged from a mud house near a small temple on the nearby hillock. With her dhoti, which was once red but now competed with the colour of earthenware tiles, pulled down to her brows, she asked in a sweet, mild, and shy voice, 'What do you want to know, Maji? From which city have you come to see Arail?'

I was strangely situated between these two sets of questions. As a pendulum pulled in one direction swings back and hits the other side, Dubri's wife's question sent me to the plastered platform outside Munnu's mother's house.

It would be untrue to call Munnu's mother beautiful but hard to call her ugly. Her beauty resided not in lineaments but in emotions, therefore eyes cannot see it but the heart involuntarily experiences it. Her face that looks long because of her colourless, dusky cheeks is not remarkable. Had not her nose indicated sharpness, its smallness would indicate foolishness. Eyes neither big nor small but irradiated by an unusual light. A glimpse of white teeth between thin lips expresses pleasure for no reason, but when the lips close, a nameless sorrow overspreads them. Small hands and feet that are hard, in contrast to her face. Her body is flexible but straight as an arrow, which she somewhat conceals by keeping her head bent.

The copper anklets on her small feet covered with cracks are flat and tight, showing that they have not been changed since she was a child. The grimy, worn-down bangles on her wrists seem to have been born with her horny hands.

Munnu's mother is soft-spoken, modest, and devoted, like wives in respectable families of the village, but her life in that desolate place blossoms neglected and unknown like a flower in the wilderness. Munnu's mother introduced me to the elderly lady from a distant region and her old brother, who are now members of my family. She plastered Patel Baba's battered old terrace and made it so beautiful that now that mud house without doors or windows has become more precious to me than a hundred bungalows. Even today, she runs around that ruin like its last remaining breath.

Looking at the child Munnu, one feels that he is a fragment of his mother's fading dream, which she has preserved in her bosom. His round face, round eyes, and round nose make him strangely attractive. His five years do not match his wisdom and ability to converse, but my heart aches to think that it will be hard for his abilities to find any sphere other than crime in which to flourish.

Poverty has put ordinary clothes into the list of rare goods. His mother patches together a long, ill-fitting kurta out of cheap, rough cloth, and gives him so many lectures about not getting it dirty that the child considers the kurta more valuable than his body. In rain or shine, he removes the kurta and keeps it in a safe spot before playing with his companions. And when he returns home from play, naked, with the kurta under his arm, he appears like a doll made of Yamuna's black mud, walking by some magic spell.

There are two more beings in the house—Munnu's father and old grandfather. Munnu's father is of medium height, wheat-complexioned, and lean. Short hairs stand upright on his head. Black rings round his eyes and wrinkles on his cheeks, and pimples embodying the idiom 'eczema in leprosy'.[2] It is hard to say what is misshapen in his face but everything seems misshapen. His face lacks the placidity that reflects beautiful emotions.

When he wakes up in the morning, he sits under the pipal tree by the hillock and smokes tobacco while he feeds his partridges.[3] At ten o'clock, he takes a cup of mustard oil from a niche covered in cobwebs in his dark room and massages his body with it. Then he takes a long bath in Yamuna, and when he returns, accepts in exchange for scolding and rebukes some chickpeas or whatever else is available. Then if he manages to coax either his wife or his old father into giving him some money, he takes it, or else sets out penniless to look for his gambler friends.

His returning late at night signifies winnings and returning as the sun sets indicates losses. In the former case, he does not bother about food but in the latter, he eats whatever is available as if he is bestowing a great favour on his wife, lies down on the broken straw-woven cot, turns over, and sleeps until morning. This has always been his daily routine. His mother was freed from her duties while he was a child but his father raised him by hand, which is evident from his name Hathai.[4]

That his father's indulgence resulted in the development of his negative tendencies can only be the fault of fate.

---

2 One trouble on top of another.

3 The grey francolin or grey partridge, native to India and Iran, which men keep as fighting birds to bet on.

4 Raised by hand translates *hathon haath paala*, idiomatic for raising with love.

Finally, considering it cowardice to bear on his own the curse of the consequences of his actions, the father found a simple, hardworking, and orphaned daughter-in-law. The old man is an ornament to his Brahmin family and considers all those who do not believe in 'Alms alone are the Brahmin's wealth' unprincipled products of this dark era. Every morning he sits with his pitcher and dirty, torn towel on Yamuna's shore, in front of the confluence of the rivers, and recounts his sad story to passers-by with his quavering voice, trembling hands or with his wrinkled face alone.

His listeners are absorbed in their own pitiable stories so, instead of listening to his story, they grasp its essence. Just as at the end of a story narrated on festive occasions, listeners throw the unbroken flowers held in their hands, so also, to purchase merit, they put into the old man's towel a handful of rice, chickpeas or barley from the cheap grains they have brought with them, and get going. One braveheart leaves him a small coin, and another who is in a hurry throws him a somewhat larger one by mistake. Observing their haste, one feels that they do not fully believe their demerits will be submerged even if they take several dips at the border of the deep confluence of rivers, where the depth is unfathomed. On the contrary, they know in a confused manner that their faults are chasing them down and, as soon as they pause, will again mount on their heads. Their acts of giving seem to be an attempt to divert those ageless, deathless, and constant companions into taking another path. These diversions are, as the saying goes, in the nature of 'if it hits it's an arrow, if not it's a fluke'. In order not to let the questions arise of what to give, how to give, and to whom to give, they try to focus their attention on restraining their vision.[5] They have only one goal, whether they

5 An allusion to Bhagavad Gita 17: 20–22, which describes how one should give (*daana* or giving is an important act of dharma) to a deserving person, without hoping for a return, and with dignity.

entwine their fingers in strings of sacred beads or exercise their lips and tongues with mantras they do not understand.

Ignored by this great drama, although he is its primary spectator, the old man gathers up his earnings at one o'clock and returns to his burrow-like home. His daughter-in-law boils the mixed grains or sometimes separates rice, lentils, chickpeas, and barley in order to make a rare dish like rice and dal. Usually, these grains are not enough for so many people, so Munnu's mother goes to work in others' fields, granaries, and homes. She gets her wages not in money but in grain and when she returns with it in the evening, feet heavy and hands aching, she has to fulfil the responsibilities of a housewife.

She goes to fetch water from Yamuna with an old waterpot and a shining copper pitcher that is like the last sign of some remembered happiness. Then she picks up a clay lamp from the niche in the wall above the mud stove and, dusting off the half-burnt wick made of old cloth, wets it with castor oil she has begged from somewhere, and lights it. Then she lights the stove. She solves the problem of fuel by gathering cow dung from fields and field-paths, and collecting dry branches from here and there.

When she is given millet or barley, she sets the dal to boil and sits down at the worn-down, brass-handled grinding wheel kept in a dark corner. She has to keep getting up to adjust the fuel in the stove, fill her father-in-law's hookah, or keep Munnu quiet with something to chew. Her situation is that of one who digs a well every day in order to drink every day,[6] so her housekeeping resembles the itinerant housekeeping of nomads. But her skill prevents her uncertain livelihood from becoming a hardship.

Sometimes there is no salt at home so she seats Munnu at the door and runs to the village grocer. Sometimes she nearly

6 Idiomatic for living hand to mouth.

suffocates in the smoke from cow-dung pieces and is afraid that the half-cooked roti will burn so she sets the stove aside and fetches dried castor sticks or hollow stalks from a nearby field. Sometimes her father-in-law, as he eats, asks for chillies and she goes to the corner filled with broken clay pots kept in precise order. In short, she never thinks about when, what or how, for her nature is to always be ready for any eventuality.

Her hard work renders it impossible for the people in that house to go to sleep hungry, and from time to time, they even get special dishes to eat. Sometimes, she churns buttermilk for a neighbour, brings a small pitcher of it home, grinds chickpeas, and prepares *kadhi*.[7] Sometimes, when working in a sugarcane field, she is given juice or even the dirty foam from the top of the juice, and she mixes coarse red rice in it to cook sweet rice. Sometimes she helps a gardener woman to carry her loads to market and uses the greens she is given to change the flavour of the dal. Thus, her housekeeping requires as much intelligence as is needed to make moves in chess. To slip up anywhere would be to bring the entire system tumbling down.

The father-in-law suffers from cough and rheumatism. And old age itself is an ailment. For ten to twelve days of the thirty he is unable to fulfil the duty of begging. In the remaining days too, some work comes up that may seem pointless to others but is highly important to him. If an old friend appears, coughing and hawking, to smoke with him, it would be considered the height of rudeness to get up until they have smoked not only his tobacco but even what he can beg from others. Sometimes, the old man is so troubled by the need to find out how an old associate is that he puts on a torn vest he keeps by his pillow, ties

---

7 *Kadhi* is a dish prepared from black chickpea flour and yoghurt. Munnu's mother makes a variation with substitutes.

to his waist a wallet with tobacco and a small box of lime, and sets out for the village, supported by a stick. If he comes across some neighbour kind enough to listen to him, it would be a declaration of the futility of his grey hairs not to recount to him the history of his better days. There are numberless such duties and always will be.

Ever since his daughter-in-law has been sharing his responsibility for earning a living, he lies, even more carefree, on his broken cot, explaining to her the importance of serving others. Because of his firm belief in 'as you sow, so shall you reap', he says nothing to his son but lectures his daughter-in-law to be a true and good housewife, and thus become a queen in the celestial world.

The old man's view is that life is brief but death boundless. If living for a short time in a house like a mud burrow, feeding her father-in-law and her useless husband with chickpeas and barley, grinding and cooking smoky roti on castor sticks, gets her the right to be a queen in the celestial world after death, this is a profitable deal for her. A few days' hardship and then eternal happiness! Who would be so stupid as to reject this bargain? The sharp vision of countless people in the world clearly sees the subtle benefit hidden in this invisible deal, which proves that there are very few fools in the world.

The old man takes no little pride in his intellect. Finding a capable wife for his good-for-nothing son proves that the old man is a player who equals providence, not an ounce less clever! Had it not been so, providence would have forced him to renounce the world in his old age. It is thanks to his own wisdom that he escaped the snares of providence and is now Munnu's grandfather, eating food earned by his daughter-in-law's labour and cooked by her, and smoking tobacco as he proudly reclines on his string-bed.

It would be grave injustice to call a boy good-for-nothing whose manhood purchased such a hardworking and cultured bride. Obtaining a wife and creating offspring are the goals of a man's abilities. Why should a man who has reached this goal unnecessarily bear the burden of further proving his worth? From a strictly utilitarian perspective, Hathai's actionless life is not useless.[8] By making good arrangements for his own and his son's lives, his father has erased Brahma's numbers. Unless Brahma launches his weapon of death, he can also organize his grandson's life and set out for the celestial world with his whole clan, having eaten food prepared by his granddaughter-in-law.

The life-story of this highly capable old man's daughter-in-law is a strange one. She was born in the home of a poor reciter of religious narratives in a village near Rewa.[9] Her mother died when she was a child and her father took care of her along with his *Satyanarayan Katha* volume. With the book wrapped in red cloth under one arm and the child in a bright pink skirt and veil under the other, he would travel to distant villages to recite the stories.

He would establish the child in a corner and demonstrate his scholarship by loudly reading a mix of correct and incorrect Sanskrit words, but as he read, he would not fail to keep an eye on the money offered to the nine celestial bodies and on the little girl sitting still and dozing. Tying up the spices and sweet things offered in a torn and dirty shawl, and taking *panchamrit* in an earthenware cup, he would set out for home at night.[10]

---

8 Mahadevi ironically uses the term *nishkarma* (actionless) here, with a play on the philosophical term *nishkama karma* (desireless action).

9 One who recounts the sacred stories for the Satyanarayan Puja of Vishnu, performed on special occasions or once a year or once a month.

10 *Panchamrit* is a mixture of five sacred liquids: milk, curd, sugar syrup, honey, and ghee.

If the offerings were enough, they would both eat them to avoid the difficulty of preparing a meal, or else the child would eat the spiced sweets and drink the five liquids while the father would go to sleep on an empty stomach.

Poor and motherless little girls do not take long to grow up because necessity and nature combine to substitute for time, making them sensible beyond their years. Buta had started to do small chores when she was six, and in her seventh year, she began to manage her father's house.[11] She would fetch water in a large pitcher and fill smaller vessels, collect dry twigs and cow dung, and knead wet flour to make burnt roti.

It would be untrue to say that she had no difficulty in doing these jobs but the pleasure of helping her father outweighed her pain. She would scrape her knees plucking high-up branches, fall and break her nails while fetching water, and burn her fingers when making roti. Suppressing the strong desire to cry, she would quietly put mustard oil on the injuries and wrap her burnt finger in wet flour.

Her father was in the seventh heaven. What greater cause for pride could he have than his Butiya running the house! When he went for his recitals, Butiya would run to keep up with his long strides. At the hearers' house, she would lay out the necessary items before her father and sit like a statue in a corner until the recital was over. She no longer dozed. Delighted and amazed by her father's profound scholarship, she paid full attention to the narrative, considering which character she would prefer to be.

On the way back, the father would carry the book and the five liquids, while the daughter followed with the coconuts, areca

---

11 Buta means a small plant. Butiya is the affectionate diminutive.

nuts, five sweet things, and other items in a bundle on her head.[12] She would ask so many questions about Leelavati, Kalavati, and others that the reciter could not help being astonished at his daughter's intelligence.[13] But there was a shade of sorrow in his astonishment. Had Butiya been a son, he would have made him the best reciter in the world, but since she was a girl, she was another's wealth. The best that could be hoped was for her to marry into a good family.

Before he could return another's wealth by getting her married, the story-reciter received the summons that no one can refuse. While he was tormented by fever, his *guru-bhai* arrived,[14] who can be described in Tulsidas's words as 'a wretch with neither wife, home nor property / Shaved his head and became an ascetic'.[15] In the absence of any other relatives, the story-reciter entrusted the burden of his daughter to this itinerant guru-bhai and departed to recount his life-story in another world.

Despite her good sense, the nine-year-old Buta knew little about life and death. Since there was no one else in the house to weep and mourn, she thought her father's great sleep was ordinary sleep, so it was easy to send her away to play in someone else's house. When she returned and found the house empty, her new uncle's reassurances could not quiet her weeping. She believed but also doubted what she was told—that her father had gone in a palanquin to see a doctor. The story seemed not impossible because her father knew a doctor who lived several villages away,

---

12 The five sweet offerings are *rava sheera* (semolina pudding), *kheer* (rice pudding), *sirini bhoga* (banana pudding), panchamrit, and fruit.

13 Leelavati and Kalavati are mother and daughter in the Satyanarayan story.

14 '*Guru-bhai*' literally means 'older brother' but is generally used to mean one who studied with the same guru.

15 The quotation is from Tulsidas's description of fake ascetics.

but the knowledge that her father had never before left her to go anywhere cast doubt on it.

Finally, she discovered the truth and, having wept bitterly for her father, the only companion of her lonely life, she took on the burden of serving her new uncle. His nature was so hard and his behaviour so devoid of sympathy that he could not take her father's place, but the sensible Buta did not let this appear in her conduct.

When the new uncle, who was fond of wandering, sold the old, unplastered house and proposed to go to a distant region, the child swallowed her tears with difficulty and agreed. In that house, the memory of her father had saved her from knowing that she was alone. She would, as usual, bathe her father's *shaligram* and put it in the small box, dust the Satyanarayan volume with her sari, wrap it in its red cloth, and hang it on its peg, and after plastering the place where her father sat with cow dung, would spread a grass seat on it and imagine him sitting there.[16]

But to go against the wishes of the man in whom her father had demonstrated his trust on his deathbed by leaving Butiya to him, would be an insult to her father. So, one day, carrying her father's books and papers in an old veil, as well as her toys and a couple of pots, she set out with her new uncle, leaving behind the familiar village. A moneylender had bought her house but how much he paid and how it was used, only her new uncle knew.

It is only possible to ask what she did not see in her nomadic life for it would be useless to ask what she saw as the bounds of her vision were very widespread. In their wanderings, they reached Prayag at the time of the Magha Mela and took a boat to the Arail ghat.[17] People say that he intended to sell the girl, but

---

16 *Shaligram* is a small, flat stone that is a symbol of Vishnu.

17 The Magha Mela is an annual festival held on riverbanks near temples during the month of Magha (January–February). Larger numbers of

it is hard to say whether this is true or is mixed with speculation. During the festival, each person has to pay two paise as tax at the ghat. Uncle did not have the coins so he tried to avoid paying. Perhaps it was his confusion and the girl's fearful expression as she unwillingly followed him that led one of the keepers of the ghat to ask, 'From where have you abducted her?' Whether or not this is to be considered a sign of his guilt, it is certain that Uncle left Buta and went to fetch change from a shopkeeper but has not returned to this day.

The unfortunate child, exhausted with waiting, put her head on her bundle and began weeping aloud. The ghat-keepers got worried, and after appealing to the custodians of the law, when they finally found a Brahmin family willing to take on the burden of the girl, they never returned to ask after her.

In this new house, she put her father's books in a niche, made his shaligram a member of the Brahmin's assemblage of icons around Krishna, and again absorbed herself in service. The old Brahmin's daughters were married, and his son and daughter-in-law were busy proving that they deserved the status of elders. In the orphaned child they all obtained a servant who sought nothing for herself.[18] She meekly kept taking on herself all the work of the house. She did everything—from washing the old man's ritual utensils to his wooden clogs, from massaging the old woman's back to tightening her string-bed, from picking the lice out of the daughter-in-law's head to sewing her undergarments, from filling the son's hookah to oiling his leather shoes. Her temperament was gold so the fire of sorrow made it shine brighter rather than reducing it to ashes or coal.

---

pilgrims take a sacred dip on the occasions of Amavasya (moonless night) and Makar Sankranti, the festival in honour of the Sun God, during this period.

18 *Nishkam sevak*, playing again on the Gita's idea of work or service without desire.

At this time, Hathai's father proposed to make this modest, hardworking girl who hardly spoke his daughter-in-law despite her background being unknown. There was no one in her in-laws' family apart from the two men, so she was married with one veil and a few glass bangles. One of the old woman's ancient chintz skirts was paired with the veil. Thus, dressed in old and new things, decked with glass bangles, adorned with a finger's breadth of vermilion, and wearing a small peacock crown of tin foil and green paper, the bride stood at the door of her father-in-law's dark mud house. There was no one to welcome her into the disrepair of that house which contained nothing but broken pots and spiders, mice, and lizards.

The neighbouring women examined her, established her on a torn straw mat, lectured her on a wife's duties, and returned to their own empires. Her foster mother had not forgotten to give her a basketful of delicacies. She was not hungry but the two men enjoyed the wedding feast. The exhausted Hathai lay down in a corner where the darkness was tremulous with the twinkling lamp. Buta lay curled up at his feet until morning.

Hathai went in search of his friends as soon as he awoke and the old man, on his way to Yamuna, said, coughing, to the bride, 'Bride, take care of the house, I'm off.' The bride inspected the house, then took up a broom and declared war on the spiders and crickets. By the time the old man returned with some rice and lentils, she had cleaned and plastered the house, and bathed in Yamuna. She set some khichri to cook in a pot and covered it with a broken plate while her father-in-law sat on the threshold, telling her the story of his better days. Then Hathai too returned, with *sev* and gur in a leaf-cup.[19]

---

19 *sev*: Thin, crisp deep-fried noodles made from black chickpea flour and eaten as a snack or a topping.

The bride put her hand into each of the broken clay pots and found mango powder, which she ground with salt and chillies into a chatni. Concealing a housewife's earnestness behind the bridal veil, she spread out the broken straw mat, and having filled crooked pitchers with Yamuna water, rattled the door-bolt to call her father-in-law who was smoking tobacco outside. When she sat down to serve the two of them with the delicacies and gur-sev in a leaf-cup and khichri in a broken plate, an unknown maternal affection welled up in her heart. It would be hard to find anywhere a house and inhabitants who so well exemplified the saying, 'a house without a housewife is the dwelling of ghosts'.

Taking care of those two strange souls in this house, she has grown from a thirteen-year-old child to a twenty-three-year-old young woman, from a new bride to a mother. The range of her care has expanded but no one has ever thought about taking care of her.

I made her acquaintance by chance in that ruin and our intimacy grew deeper each day. First, I invited Munnu and his mother to accompany me to an exhibition. When the mother, decked in a cotton sari washed with cleansing mud, and the son in his grandfather's torn towel covering his nakedness, arrived in front of my big room, they thought that was the exhibition and began to prostrate themselves before the statues there. In the evening, when Bhaktin brought them to the exhibition, they almost swooned in that marketplace of splendour. Since then, Munnu's mother often says, 'I'm going to my parents' home,' and comes to see me.[20] My house is her only parental home. My heart is troubled when I think of this.

As soon as the problem of food arose, the question of livelihood became urgent. Hathai was lectured into going to work at the fort

---

20 *Naibra* or *naihar* is the word for a married woman's parental home.

but he was not able to find a footing there.[21] For one thing, his temperament was opposed to work, and for another, he knew only one way to use his earnings.

Finally, Munnu's mother, with great embarrassment, asked me if there was any work she could do at the school. I repeatedly said that I would be happy to keep her with me for life but she refused to come unless she was given a job. I then found her some light work, but rest was like a crime for her. She would go in the bullock-cart to fetch girls from the interiors of their homes and bring them to school. In the remaining time, she would sew a short-sleeved jacket for one of the drivers, make a quilt for one of the women who worked in the school, and if there was no other work, set to cleaning every corner of my house. Munnu, in a new kurta-pajama, would eat his meal and then write *a*, *i*, or play with the cats and dogs or sometimes sit at the door of my office. At night, mother and son would sleep on a rug near my bed. Despite all my efforts, Munnu's mother refused to give up her practice of sleeping on the ground.

I had thought that her days of hard labour were over, but this was not to be. One day Munnu's mother, her sari pulled down to her brows, said with embarrassment that she wanted to go to Arail. The old man would not eat for two days at a time and his son would disappear for several days. Going and seeing them once in eight or ten days was not enough because the system there fell apart without her. I saw the truth in what she said and made arrangements to send her back.

This time, I was unable to go to Arail for quite a while. When I went, preparations for the Magha Mela were afoot. Munnu's

---

21 This fort is on Yamuna's shore, near the confluence of rivers where pilgrims bathe. It was constructed by a Mughal emperor, probably Akbar, when he renamed Prayag Allahabad. Later, it was held by the British.

mother was not at home so I made enquiries. I found out that she crossed the river every day to work as a manual labourer. Many people were employed there to flatten the ground for the Magha Mela. She too carried baskets of mud on her head. She got an hour's break every day but how could she come home? The boatman charged two paise per ride. She already spent an *anna* going up and down. If she returned during the break, she would have to spend another anna.[22] So, she stayed hungry and thirsty all day, carrying mud from morning to evening, and came home at dusk after buying flour and lentils. She was a Brahmin woman so she could not carry packed food. It was hard enough maintaining her purity among the other labourers.

Neither her community nor her family was pleased that she, a Brahmin woman, should carry mud, but she paid no attention to anyone's arguments on this score. Her hunger and thirst were her business, so she neither insisted on carrying food with her nor did she agree to waste money coming home at lunch time. But several people's lives depended on her labour, so she could not give anyone else the right to decide about this. If this woman, raised in the heat of labour, thinks it better to carry mud than to take to the Brahmin trade of asking for alms, this is her personal compulsion.[23] But if society, following the beaten path, allows such arrogance to flow unchecked, none of its paths will remain. So the labouring Brahmin wife is a thorn in the side of the community of Brahmin alms-seekers who are irradiated with Brahm-energy. When she returned in the evening, covered

---

22 An *anna* was a currency unit, equal to one-sixteenth of a rupee. The word derives from the Sanskrit *anna*, meaning food or grain.

23 There is a play on the word *tapa* here. It means heat but also refers to the heat of devotion, *tapasya*.

in dust from head to toe, Munnu's mother lit the lamp, fetched water, set dal to boil, and came to see me.

This system caused great hardship to poor Munnu because his mother had to leave home in order to save him from dust and mud, and to obtain food for him. She would cook food either at night or at five in the morning. After eating with his father or grandfather, he did not know what to do all day.

Sometimes he would go with his grandfather to the bank of Yamuna, sometimes he would play with other idle children, and sometimes, sitting under the pipal, he would screw up his eyes in a fruitless attempt to distinguish his mother in the crowd on the opposite shore. Large men who cross over look like small insects. His little heart churned, wondering what would become of his weak and thin mother who was shorter than all of them. His only consolation was that when she reached this shore, his mother became again the same smiling mother. Why do people become so small when they cross the river? He asked everyone this question, from his long-bodied Thakur Dada [paternal grandfather] to the smallest child, but no one understood the significance of his curiosity.

Whenever I went to Arail, he spent all his time with me, so all the details of this lonely child's temperament became known to me. He is an intelligent child. His way of observing each thing and giving his opinion about it is different from that of other children. Once at night, when he saw a train cross the Yamuna bridge and called out, 'Guru-ji, Guru-ji, Divali is running along,' I was surprised. When I asked what he meant, he nodded wisely and said, 'That is a railway train, Guru-ji. In the dark it runs like lamps.' It is true that at night the body of the train is invisible and, in the darkness, it looks like a running string of lamps, but who would not be surprised at this poetic truth from Munnu's lips!

He also has a special love of music. He would not only learn by heart any devotional song he heard but would also try to sing it in the same *raga*. Shyness prevents him from displaying all his knowledge to me. When he tries several times to start, keeps stopping, and then says in tones of defeat, 'Who knows why in front of Guru-ji I forget everything,' it becomes hard to hold back one's laughter.

Observing these children roaming about in the heat with nothing to do and the women fighting for no reason, I developed a desire to open a school, where women could learn to spin and weave in their spare time, children could study, and old people hear the newspaper read aloud. There could be differences of opinion about such a school in Arail, but when an idea comes into my head, I have to express it in action.

After spinning wheels, looms, and books had been collected, a search began for a regular teacher because I could only be there once or twice a week, but this problem too was solved. When Bhaktin began to grow frail due to old age, I had appointed Anurup to be her assistant. This Ahir [cowherd] lad was literate and wanted to study so it was necessary to teach him. When he passed the primary exam, it seemed proper to give him a more important job than assisting Bhaktin, so I taught him how to teach and arranged to have him run my strange school. An old lady who knew spinning and weaving also agreed to stay there.

But the looms and spinning wheels could not be kept on my doorless platform. All the homes in the settlement were too small for the families inhabiting them. I did not have the resources to arrange land for a building.

Then I remembered a concrete house, which was lying empty, whose back portion, because it was of mud, kept collapsing in the monsoon. I found out that its owner had not bothered to visit it for twenty-two years. In the month of Magha, when people from his family came there for a few days, the smoke from their cow-dung fire emerging from windows covered in cobwebs looked like a long sigh from that abandoned ruin. The rest of the time, it stood like a ghost, devoid of activity and cloaked in mystery. The priest who had the key to this emptiness was delighted by the proposal, and the prospective students, playing in the dust, began to cling to its walls and call it theirs. I found out from the priest that the owner of the mysterious house was Thakur Gopalsharan Singh of Nayi Garhi, so I set labourers to work cleaning it, and I wrote to him.

I had no doubt that he would agree. When my utilitarianism turned out to have no value in his eyes, I felt more annoyed than surprised. Now I have achieved much greater knowledge of the world. Let alone great artists, I do not talk about usefulness even to someone who can rhyme one line or imagine a small incident. If artists go around whitewashing trash as I do, what will become of their labours aimed at immortality?

Finally, I sent the spinning wheels to one village, gave the looms to another, found the old woman another job, and fulfilled my promise to Anurup by setting him to work as a teacher spreading literacy. I still go to Arail and sit on the platform, listening to Munnu's songs and his mother's stories. Those plastered buildings raise their heads with pride, announcing the emptiness of rights, and the broken-down ruins listen with detachment.

Emerging from one of its corners, a child says, 'Seeing you after many days, Ma,' and another asks, 'When will our school open, Ma?' All my anger wants to retort, 'You unfortunates! Your village is a criminal one, your fathers and grandfathers have destroyed their lives to earn it this reputation. Go—gamble, learn to steal, but do not dare interfere with the rights of decent men.' But the surprised, fearful expression in those liquid eyes shadowed by dusty brows and dirty lashes chokes me up, so without looking around I go towards the boat.

Thakuri Baba

When I informed Bhaktin about my decision to perform *kalpavas*, she could not believe it.[1] She tried to demonstrate my lack of foresight by asking a string of questions concerning how I would come to teach every day, how I would return, how much the tanga driver would charge, and how much the ferryman would charge.

Bhaktin knows that contesting my decisions strengthens them but she cannot control her tongue. Seeing that I was unmoved by the unbroken deluge of her questions, she pulled a face and said, 'When the age to perform kalpavas comes, one does it.[2] Have you vowed to obtain all the merit of religious rituals in one day?'

It is hard to explain to Bhaktin that I do not do this for ritual purposes, so instead of making a fruitless attempt at explanation, I kept quiet and accepted her mistaken conclusions.

---

1 *Kalpavas* is the ancient Hindu practice of camping on the bank near the *sangam* or confluence of rivers in Prayag, starting on the day of the sun-worship festival Makar Sankranti, and continuing through the Hindu month of Magha, which covers parts of the months of January and February. Practitioners follow ascetic rules, such as celibacy, giving alms, collective singing and worship, eating only once a day, and bathing in the river.

2 She means that asceticism is only for old people.

Bhaktin knows that my silence is not a sign of defeat but of victory, so she is not as disturbed when I argue as when I am silent, because opinions can be changed through argument but silence leaves no room for that possibility.

Finally, against the advice and consent of a minister like Bhaktin, reed-grass mats and bamboo sticks for making a dwelling were collected in bundles near the steps down to the river, and the ferrymen began doing the work of Vishwakarma, the divine architect. At the centre was a neat and clean ten-foot long and equally wide room, and on all four sides of it an eight-foot wide verandah. The northern verandah was for me to read and write, and in the south Bhaktin set up the empire of her kitchen. In the western verandah she put up a rod to hang pots of coarse flour, and a rope to hang dhotis and quilts. The verandah into which the door of the room opened was made a sitting-room for guests. After everything was ready, that leaf hut was furnished with Bhaktin's sacking mat and my straw mat, her dim lantern and my lamp twinkling in a brass lampstand, her pewter bucket and my copper pitcher shining like a flame, her pots filled with turmeric, coriander, flour, and lentils, and my Sanskrit tomes replete with ancient, subtle wisdom.

Thus began my and Bhaktin's kalpavas. There were many leaf huts around us but they were no more than makeshift.

How important kalpavas was in the past is evident even today. Perhaps at that time, it was an important way for people who lived in different parts of the country to get to know each other, exchange ideas, and blend their cultures. These rivers have been the life-giving blood vessels of the country, which is why it is natural and inevitable for these assemblies to take place on their shores. We have forgotten the how and why of this relationship, but we continue the ritual without understanding it. I like kalpavas because the expansive knowledge it gives me in a short time is not obtainable by any other means. And continuous curiosity about life has become part of my nature.

When mango seeds thrown around in the summer take root in the rainy season, they find me the most alert of gardeners. No one sets a more watchful guard over bird nests built in any corner of the house than I do. Any number of wild trees, plants, and birds survive and flourish because of my love of life. Even the spurge plant, whose milky sap can blind one, stands proudly beside the mango tree I have carefully planted. The thorny nightshade, adorned with thorns that pierce and that refuse to be plucked out, claims its rightful spot next to the maize plant covered in gold-coloured silken bunches and bright, tender pearls.

I don't know how many times the twinkling eyes of puppies shivering in the cold have compelled me to bring them home. Agonized fish drawn from the water in a net, the fluttering of wings in bird-sellers' tiny cages, the pathetic helplessness of panting dogs in vehicles like black iron prisons have inspired me to all kinds of strange actions. It would be surprising if such an eccentric person were indifferent to human life; her desire to know much of its sorrows and joys, life and death is naturally limitless.

Bhaktin has to bear the unnatural burden of my natural tendencies. She throws out the trash that falls from a nest, cleanses herself, and stands ready to worship the sun, when a puppy suddenly dirties the courtyard. After cleaning up the mess, she bathes again and is about to offer water to Shiva-ji when she is told to give grain and jaggery to a beggar. Having fulfilled this duty, she closes her nose and sits down to say her prayers when I call her to accompany me to visit a sick person. Despite enduring this disordered life, she never rebukes me. Yes, she sometimes screws up her lips and asks with pretended solemnity, 'Is there any exam in these skills? If there is, I will get a degree certificate in my old age!'

Though she has not received a certificate for her fulfilment of duty, Bhaktin knows its importance. Even a normal illness worries her. 'If I die what will become of her? Who will feed her? Who will look after this museum of hers?' Who would not laugh, hearing Bhaktin worry about my museum while contemplating her own death!

Kalpavas is very important to Bhaktin because of her unbreakable piety but she knows that my habit of putting together a family from odds and ends will not allow her the time required to break the bonds of attachment.[3] From a village fair to the kalpavas, every place is a school for me, but in them I learn to increase attachment rather than the way to non-attachment.

A day before Sankranti, I had just sat down in the evening and opened the Yoga Darshan when unusual clouds, interwoven with strands of lightning, began to grow dense.[4] Bhaktin had just lit the mud stove when a group of rural pilgrims entered her verandah. Bhaktin is my devoted follower but an aggressive combatant with the world. Why should she pardon such an unannounced invasion? She emerged from her kitchen like a whirlwind, displaying the dexterity of her verbal arrows secured for just such an occasion, and this disturbed even the throne of my straw mat.

I got up and saw a crowd of children and middle-aged women and men, under the leadership of an old man. It was hard to understand why these disorganized newcomers, laden with bundles, vessels, hookahs, mats, baskets, pitchers, and other household items, had entered my verandah. When signs of guilt

---

3 She uses part of the idiom: '*Kahin ka eent kahin ka rora, Bhanumati ne kunba jora*' (With a brick from one place and a stone from another, Bhanumati put together a family).

4 The *Yoga Sutra*, composed by the ancient sage Patanjali, is the foundational text of classical Yoga philosophy.

appeared in Bhaktin's angry expression and her sharp tones were lost in a light tremor, the newcomers quickly understood that I was the sole owner of that straw-and-grass palace.

Their aged leader took two steps forward and said in a calm but affectionate voice, 'Daughter, won't you allow us long-distance travellers to stay here? We have walked a long way. This life is just a night's stay—"at dawn we all have to leave"—isn't it so? The Maharaj invited us to stay up there but we will have to climb up and down.[5] And down below it is so crowded there isn't space for even a sesame seed. Where are we to go now, at twilight? What to do?'

The old man's tone and his way of talking strongly attracted me. Despite reading refusal in Bhaktin's eyes, I said, 'Stay here, Baba! This room is enough for me. If necessary, Bhaktin will cook outside. The verandah is big enough for all of you. It's a night's stay indeed.'

I brought my straw mat and books inside, lit a lamp, and sat down to read, while they began to set up their living arrangements. Bhaktin fights with others only because she worries about my comfort, but once she is sure that I will not be incommoded by a particular person or activity, all her opposition vanishes. The possibility of my peace being disturbed by the crowd had given her a harshness that melted along with that possibility. She constructed a stove of bricks and stones under the niche where the grain was kept, and tried to occupy as little space as possible, to allow those invaders to settle themselves comfortably.

That night, I did not have a chance to observe that new world. The next day was the Sankranti holiday. I am not modern enough not to bathe and not traditional enough to obtain merit by bathing with a large crowd. So, I got up before dawn, awoke Bhaktin, and

5 Maharaj is used here as a polite term for an ascetic.

went, under the cover of fog, towards Ganga who made known her identity through her constant tossing and turning.

When I returned, golden rays lying across the fog looked like a light net of gold thread on a white muslin sheet. My big but quiet leaf-cottage to the south of the river steps was unrecognizable today. The unstable world under it looked like a restless host of desires entering the helpless heart of a calm ascetic with one unwary breath. As I approached, I carefully examined those who had disrupted the peace of my cottage.

The old gentleman had asserted his right to my study verandah with the grandeur appropriate to a general. A torn rug of uncertain hue and a mud-coloured, cross-stitched bedsheet lay wrapped together. A dirty and torn cotton bundle kept it company. A black hookah made of a coconut, crowned with a red pipe, leant against a pillar. A red-bordered black tobacco pouch hung from the wall. A dhoti and a black, cotton-stuffed quilt on the clothesline that was stretched from pillar to wall announced the master's majesty. His knotty lathi was slick with frequent oil-baths. The clogs of wood and rope kept carefully at the foot of his bed said that the master had chosen them as a middle way between the untouchability of leather shoes and the rusticity of wooden-soled slippers.

In short, the old man seemed to have set up this show to embarrass my collection of books. He had perhaps gone to look for a *neem* twig to clean his teeth, which gave me the chance to assess the instruments of his power with the sharp vision of a spy.

The crowd at the other end of the verandah was a strange one. A Surdas sat as if in meditation.[6] The smallpox marks on his face indicated how he might have lost his sight. The tense and

6 A polite way of referring to a blind man, since the famous poet Surdas was blind.

swollen veins on his neck, contrasting with his weak and dark body, suggested that he wanted to compensate for his handicap with his throat. One end of the bamboo rod, to which the reed-grass blinds were attached, stuck out like a peg, and on it now hung a *chikara* and a pair of cymbals.[7] The other goods consisted of a shawl, a piece of sacking, and a small pitcher whose edges were crooked and worn down.

Beyond the border of the sacking an elderly man, seated in virasana, whose tilak proclaimed his status as pandit, had opened up a colourful basket. In form and hue, the basket seemed to be a prison-house for Shiva or for a shaligram, and perhaps to lighten the weight of the deity, he was extracting from the basket a stone to grind sandalwood and a fistful of half-ground sandalwood. The *Hanuman Chalisa* was on top of the books and papers kept on the cloth imprinted with Rama's name, suggesting that his deity had to constantly combat ghosts.[8]

Two young boys sat wrapped in a tattered black blanket, trying to forget the unpleasantness of sitting on cold sand. The eyes of one were fixed, *hypnotized*, on a bundle hanging from the thatch that perhaps contained sweetmeats like jaggery, while the other gazed at the pandit's activities as if trying to understand them.

Another elderly man basked in the sun. An old, thin sheet concealed his weak body but his bony shoulders and withered hands with veins standing out on them told the true story. His feet, their cracks filled with muck, seemed stronger than his skeletal body. Destiny, like an ill-trained child, had written so much in the lines on his face that it was hard to read their import.

---

7 A *chikara* is a two-stringed folk instrument somewhat like a *sarangi*.

8 *Hanuman Chalisa*, a forty-verse devotional song in praise of Hanuman, is one of the two most popular prayers among Hindus worldwide and is supposed to drive away negative forces.

The economic condition of the women's *department* did not seem much better. Two old women sat on the cold ground, propped up by a large bundle, one dozing, the other extra alert to her surroundings. Round, smooth anklets on the feet and a couple of flat silver bangles on the hands of the dozing one indicated some love of adornment remaining in her shaven head. A couple of large *rudraksha* beads on a black string around the other's neck were no more than a nod in the direction of women's tradition of ornamentation.

One of them, dim-eyed, her nose drooping towards her chin, had a sad indifference on her face. But the other, her ears sticking out of her dhoti, closed and opened her lips as she looked around with small black eyes, her round nostrils swelling, as if she was examining the forms, colours, smells, and words that were scattered around. A large pumpkin and a big curved knife propped up on it expressed the attachment to food in those two unattached hearts, and the black pot of ghee dangling from the thatch by a rope countered their outward dryness with its shiny stickiness.

I couldn't see the elderly woman wearing an old black dhoti who was busy tacking up a clothesline with a rope unfastened from a pitcher, but the one who stood with a collection of ragged old clothes to hang on the line attracted my attention. Her brown, red-bordered dhoti, pulled down over her face to her nose, the thick, unbaked, light-yellow bangles on her wrists, and the thin, loose anklets and doubled toe-rings on her feet spoke of her different social status. The part of her face I could see, with its asymmetrical width and pleasant expression, had an attraction that made it hard for the eye to call her beautiful or the heart to call her ugly.

On one side, two dusky girls were searching for something in a basket. The dry, tangled, and dirty locks hanging over their round faces told the story of poverty. On the other side, a very dark girl in a tight, tattered kurta lay asleep on a piece of torn rug. Every now and then, she shivered, speaking of the intense struggle between cold and sleep. Another child sat leaning on a pillar, rubbing his eyes and preparing to cry. In the absence of a kurta, he had an old striped towel as a garment, but his crying as he looked at the pot tied above and the bundle below indicated that the cold inside him exceeded the cold outside. The heap of straw in the eastern corner and the dirty sheet crumpled on it showed that the sleepers had spent the cold night huddled up like bundles.

Outside, a dusky young woman was digging a hole in the sand to construct an oven. A small nose-ring on a rounded face with long, dry, and protruding bones, kept shaking and touching her lips and cheeks. The black border of her red skirt embroidered in white was splitting here and there. The feebleness of her body glimpsed through an old yellow veil was concealed by her hands' speed in removing the sand.

Two fingers on her lips, Bhaktin muttered in astonishment, 'Oh my lord! The entire fair has come here. Why leave this collection of oddities to go see the other fair?'

Glaring at her, I was wondering how to start conversing with the newcomers when the unaffected tones of the one with her veil pulled over her face surprised me: 'I touch your feet, older sister! We are giving you a lot of trouble.' My urban sophistication did not know how to respond to the touching of feet so I met the requirements of civility by saying, 'No, no trouble—it's you all who are inconvenienced by the lack of space here.'

Then I got busy arranging my room and Bhaktin, carrying sesame laddus and a khichri made of coarse rice and moong dal, went off to fulfil the duty of giving. When she returned, she cooked more khichri.

When eating, I like to bother Bhaktin, because on no other occasion will she indulge me. She is always ready to give me a good talking-to. I don't eat black sesame laddus made with jaggery because they are very sweet, so Bhaktin makes white sesame laddus with a little sugar in order to fulfil the ritual of '*modakam samarprayami*'.[9] Because of the confusion created in kalpavas this time around, Bhaktin gave more importance to the Gods outside than to the Gods of the home. It was natural for three Gods to become 330 million, so no sweets were left for Bhaktin.[10] Understanding the situation, I thought up a prank and solemnly said, 'Bring laddu for me.'

But before I could enjoy Bhaktin's agitation, a familiar voice from the day before said, 'Daughter, can I come in?' I don't follow rules of purity, and Bhaktin and her brass cooking-pot were safe inside a thick line drawn with coal. Hearing me say, 'Come this way, Baba,' the old man came forward with leaf-cups in both hands. The front part of his head was bald and shining, but at the back a few white hairs seemed to be hiding from fate's hard lines. His small eyes betrayed a combination of emotions, sorrow, thought, and parental affection, for which I can find no name. Deep lines on both sides of his long nose disappeared into his beard. The emotions expressed on his lips were hidden by an unusual moustache and the exceptional breadth of his face was made ordinary by his beard. A few black hairs among the long white hairs in his thick beard were like black threads interwoven with silver wire and broken off. His energy hid his frailty and he walked with a stoop, which drew attention away from his height. His figure, barefoot, with a dhoti up to his knees, was that of an ordinary old villager.

He had brought sesame laddu, ghee, and a flake of mango pickle. Despite my repeatedly telling him that I eat khichri without

---

9 Statement made when offering modakas in Maharashtra and laddus in north India to Ganesh.

10 Refers to the Vedic phrase *taitis koti* Gods, which can mean 33 crores or 330 million, referring to the divinity latent in all things, but is also interpreted to mean thirty-three categories of Gods.

ghee because I don't like ghee and without pickles because of my digestion, he insisted on placing the grainy ghee and the pickle on my khichri. Leaning the leaf-cup of curd against my thali, he said pleadingly, 'Just taste it, daughter. Is this all that educated people eat?'

My acquaintance with my guests began that day and gradually transformed into affection born of living together. At nine each morning, I had to cross the river, and because I did not like to make the trip in a tanga to and from the university on my own, I used to compel Bhaktin to enjoy it along with me. By the time I was free to return, Bhaktin, like Sage Narada, would have heard the tanga-driver's life-story and passed judgement on his mistakes or else visited various acquaintances and solved the world's problems.

In the morning's hustle and bustle, it was hard to eat properly, and by the time I got back, it would take time for a meal to be arranged. Somehow or other, those rustic guests understood this inconvenience, and as soon as I set foot in the leaf-cottage, a variety of dishes, always new ones, would appear. All of these foods—millet porridge in a big bell-metal bowl, coarse parched grain, jaggery or cakes of flour and molasses in small thalis, puffed chickpeas or roasted sweet potatoes in bright-coloured baskets—were community offerings because each person would keep a share for me from whatever they cooked in their kitchens. I repeatedly explained that I would have to give up attachment to life if I ate so much but none of them was convinced.

It was hard to resist their requests: 'Won't you taste it, sister?', 'If daughter just touches it, we'll be happy', 'If older sister just puts it on her tongue, all this won't be wasted'. There was nothing for it but to accustom my urban tastes to their rural foods, from chickpeas and jaggery to sweet millet cakes. After the panoply of meals, they all went for the evening bath and lamp-lighting ceremony at Ganga's shores and I imitated them, like an eager and curious spectator. Those who observe kalpavas eat only once a day and even in the severe cold of January-February, they follow the rule of not warming themselves at a fire. At the root of these rules is the high cost of wood, the scarcity of grain, and the tradition of religious austerity.

But in winter, I like the sight of wood-fires burning in the open. And there was no shortage of wood and dried cow dung. I would set up a large heap of fuel, light a bonfire outside the leaf hut, and sit down on an old cane stool belonging to the guests to warm myself. Their children, who were free of the strict rules of kalpavas, and my Bhaktin, whose kalpavas had more to do with this world than the next, sat by the fire warming their hands and feet. The true adherents to kalpavas kept as much space between themselves and the fire as would deceive Chitragupta who keeps the records of merit and demerit.[11]

The programme followed by this strange assembly was equally odd. Someone would sing a devotional song, someone else would tell a story from the Puranas. Sometimes folk idioms would be expounded upon or oral commentaries invented on matters of popular discussion. These rustics were well-versed in everything, from Kabir's mysterious paradoxes to the practical rules for buying a bullock, so their company never seemed tedious or pointless. Through these conversations I became acquainted with their life-stories.

The aged Thakuri Baba could be called a poet because he belonged to the community of minstrels, and as a poet he could be said to belong to my community. In the modern era, there is a

---

11 Chitragupta is the divine record-keeper who advises Yama, God of Death, whether to send a person to a temporary celestial world or temporary infernal world before they are reborn. Those observing kalpavas are not supposed to seek comfort.

great gap between the duties of minstrels and the public need for them, so no one knows about them or the value of their profession as poets. Their inherited trade is now just a form of individual entertainment. Reading the signs of the times, Thakuri Baba's father channelled his inherited talent for rhyming into ordinary farming and taught this policy to the two sons of his deceased first wife, shutting the door on sentiment.

When the young second wife also left for the next world, her son was a small child, but in a display of special affection for this beloved wife, his father resolved to make him Kautilya incarnate.[12] That the Herculean efforts he made to fulfil this resolve proved unsuccessful can only be attributed to fate. Perhaps the mother, who had escaped her husband's policy-making by taking refuge in the next world, showered all her emotions on her son in order to save him. Or perhaps Kautilya, angry at the possibility of a second Kautilya, perverted his intellect, but the fact is that the obstinate boy would not learn the difference between mine and thine, let alone other aspects of policy. The despairing father left the burden of this hard education to his older sons and took leave of his life.

The half-brothers were older and were householders, so the home and property remained in their control while the young brother received food and clothing in return for working as a servant. His poetic inclinations were profitable for his brothers, because art does not allow worldly, especially commercial, wisdom to develop, and without this wisdom a person may himself incur losses but will not inflict them on others. When the community began commenting on the younger brother's being kept unmarried, his brothers got him married to a well-

---

12 Kautilya or Chanakya was a famous third-century BC economist and diplomat who authored the *Arthashastra*, a treatise on economics and politics.

behaved girl and the older sisters-in-law educated her in the duties of service.

Obviously, the marriage was not a happy one. Two servants instead of one may be good for masters but not for the servants themselves. It solidifies mastership but expands servitude. The master turns the servants against one another by wielding the weapons of persuasion, gifts, punishment, and the use of secrets to divide and conquer.[13] He thus reinforces their servitude while the servants, because of their helpless irritation and feelings of inferiority, multiply difficulties for each other and block the path of escape.

Had the younger brother and his wife established a household, it would have been hard to keep them in servitude, so the older sisters-in-law complained against the new bride to her husband, constantly depicting her as a wrongdoer. The husband's heart oscillated between trust and mistrust with regard to his wife's innocence, but neither did he console her by expressing his trust nor did he resolve his doubts by expressing his mistrust.

The wife's self-respect prevented her from speaking out, so she expressed her anger by working continuously. Poor Thakuri was a poet. Bare facts found no opening to enter the canopy of his emotion-weighted imagination. If he was given a chance to sing songs of lamentation, he would sit up all night in return, guarding anyone's fields. If he found a listener who loved songs about the changing seasons, he would consider it no degradation to feed and water his bullocks. If someone wanted to hear the legend of the famous warriors Alha and Udal, he would travel many miles to tell the story. He would forget to eat and drink when reciting Kabir's poems at Holi.

---

13 Kautilya's *Arthashastra* suggests that a ruler use these four weapons of diplomacy to overcome his enemies.

Because of this love for poetry, he was not able to succeed in any other field. His was no cultured society where singers are paid fifty rupees as *fees*, so from a financial point of view, poet Thakurdin remained a Sudama.[14] He might receive some sesame and jaggery knotted up in his dirty shawl, or coarse grain, salt, and green chillies in a small stone bowl, or someone would demonstrate their love for poetry by requesting him to bake two small flour-cakes on their cow-dung fire. It would be untrue to say that Thakuri was not happy with these rewards. Nor did he know that his failure to earn, born of his poetic inclinations, was the cause of his brothers' neglect, his sisters-in-law's contempt, and his wife's suffering.

In a few years, his wife presented him with a daughter but as a result of lack of rest and nutrition, she developed postpartum fever, and due to not receiving proper medical care, she achieved liberation from her hard life, leaving behind a one-and-a-half-year-old child. That night, Thakuri had just returned from singing the Alha ballad. He had no memory of his mother's death, bidding farewell to his old father had not touched him to the quick, but his wife's breaking all bonds of affection and leaving in the first flush of her youth shook up his heart. Salt tears washed the pinkness from his eyes and cleansed them to bear witness to life. Only after he lost his wife did Thakuri become a real husband and father.

Observing that his child was neglected and imagining the consequences of this, he was compelled to separate from the joint family. He fetched his aged maternal aunt to run the house, but he himself looked after the little girl. Bela, the daughter of an Alha-Udal loving father, sat on his shoulders when they roamed about for amusement, and was tied to his back during working

---

14 Sudama was a childhood friend of Krishna. He was a very poor Brahmin, who was a scholarly devotee but was near starvation.

hours to supervise his work. Thakuri told those who laughed at him, that if a labouring mother could take her children to work, a father need not be ashamed of doing the same. He was both father and mother to Bela.

When the child was about six or seven, Thakuri brought an orphaned nephew who was of his own community but well-behaved and poetry-loving, engaged Bela to him, and began to teach him his trade. Fate was perhaps angry with this rustic poet so the prospective son-in-law, as soon as he finished his education, contracted smallpox. His life was saved but he lost the sight of one eye and the other eye had just enough light to see the world as a cloud of steam.

The father asked the daughter what she wanted to do, but she was just as stubborn as that Bela who, after the Battle of Mahoba, vowed to become a Sati on a sandalwood pyre in her father's orchard.[15] Bela did not want to give up her childhood companion so Thakuri Baba was saved from breaking his vow.

Now the poet father-in-law, his old aunt, blind son-in-law, and beautiful daughter constitute a strange family. The father-in-law has trained the son-in-law in recitation. When Thakuri plays the chikara and sings devotional songs, the son-in-law beats time on a small tambourine with two fingers, the old aunt, lost in emotion, plays the cymbals, and a lilt appears in Bela's step as she works in the house.

They have a milch buffalo, two cows of good breed, and a single-plough field, so livelihood is not a problem. This strange family performs the auspicious kalpavas every year on Ganga's

15 In the Alha-Udal story, twelfth-century Emperor Prithviraj Chauhan's daughter Bela, against her father's wishes, burnt herself to death on her husband's pyre, after he was killed in a battle against her father. The spot where she became a Sati is behind the Panchkuian cremation ground in Delhi and is marked by a small temple.

shores at the time of the Magha fair. Other devotees from their village accompany them.

Thakuri Baba is ever ready to make everyone his guest but a requirement of kalpavas is that when one eats another's grain one must give something in return, so all his guests bring bundles of food along with them. It is not necessary to trade items of equal value. It's hard not to laugh at the way these simple villagers strike a compromise between necessity and rules. One takes half a ser of flour from Thakuri Baba and gives him a lump of jaggery in return, another takes potatoes and sweet potatoes in exchange for four chillies. One brings a little curd on a leaf and takes a bowl full of rice. Another gives a tiny amount of ghee to light incense and wants a pitcher of milk.

Thakuri Baba experiences a special joy in giving so he keeps up this barter by constantly asking others what they want. He is an emotional and trusting being. As soon as he picks up the chikara, the meaning of the world changes for him. His generosity, natural sympathy, and simple emotions are typical of village life but are no longer as easy to find. Rural life is becoming so hard and painful that it is difficult to find space for humane feeling to grow there.

As always, this year too, there is a wide range of people in Thakuri Baba's group. Thakuri Baba's own family consists of his daughter, who is occupied with worldly matters as she digs the sand to make an oven, his son-in-law lost in dreams with the chikara, tambourine, and cymbals, and his aunt sitting between her pot of ghee and pumpkin, resolving the problems of this world and the next. The rest of the assembly is a mix of various communities and categories.

There is an old Thakur woman. In her husband's lifetime she was queen of the family but as soon as she was widowed, her husband's nephews snatched from their childless aunt the right to state her opinions. In village kinship, she is Thakuri's paternal aunt so he does not forget to bring her along on occasions when merit is to be earned.[16]

Another is a Sahuayin, a grocer's wife, whose husband is doing his duty in Kolkata with an oil-presser's daughter from the village. Wearing two toe-rings like a *double certificate* of marriage, and her sari pulled down to her nose to preserve the honour of brides, she ekes out a livelihood by running a small grocery store. Every winter she bears the hardship of kalpavas with her two adolescent sons and stands in the water up to her waist to ask for the same husband in future lifetimes. Her husband has ruined this life for her but she does not want to ruin the next life by desiring anyone other than him.

The third is a widowed peasant who earns a living by growing vegetables in a corner of one person's field and guarding another's mango orchard. His wife gave him three daughters. After giving him the gift of the fourth child, a son, she took leave of all the giving and taking of this world. Despite working hard day and night, she often had to go to bed hungry. After her son's birth, all there was in the house was a little rice. The oldest girl set it to cook. Had the mother eaten the rice, the children would have gone to bed hungry, so she drank the rice-water and kept the rice for the children. That night, she fell into delirium, and on the third day after, she and the newborn son were freed from the hard asceticism of life.

A year ago, the peasant fell from a mango tree, since when he has not been able to stand straight or to perform manual labour. The two adolescent girls work at making cow-dung cakes for the grocery-shop owner or plastering the priest's house, but the

---

16 She is not his biological aunt but in villages, everyone is addressed in kinship terms.

littlest girl is a noose around her father's neck. Thanks to Thakuri Baba, he and his family of three manage to come on the kalpavas but what he asks Mother Ganga for is hard to fathom.

The fourth is a Brahmin couple. Working as a priest in a Bihar village is no wish-fulfilling cow but the husband manages to eke out a living. The creator somehow hatched a conspiracy to prevent their having a son. But Pandit-ji wants to please Ganga into negating poor Chitragupta's records. His wife, the Panditayin, is a nice woman but the long wait for a child has produced sourness in the sweetness of hope, just as it is natural for milk kept a long time to curdle. She has no love for the sound of her husband's worship rituals so she buries his sandalwood spoon in a heap of grain, hides his prayer beads in a hole in the wall, or shuts his books up in her trunk.

When his maternal cousin, a widow, died, the Pandit was compelled to give shelter to her child, his nephew. He has now become the Draupadi of this Mahabharata. Instead of filling the space of a son he has made it more visible. The meaning of his aunt's sayings—had he been her own, he would have been obedient; had he been her blood, he would have loved her—is unclear since the child is too small to understand them. He listens with amazement to these principled sayings because he has not yet learnt the difference between mine and thine. He is the same as he was when his mother was alive. When the question of how he has managed to enrage his aunt churns his heart, he bursts into tears.

I spent the month in this strange kingdom so I have many memories, but one evening is especially important to me. I used to read until late at night, so my guests used to join other pilgrims' groups to sing devotional songs. One day, Thakuri Baba suggested with affectionate civility that it would be good to sing at our cottage. I am averse to noise so it is not easy for me to join singing assemblies, but that day, perhaps from curiosity, I accepted his invitation and a date was fixed.

It was perhaps the thirteenth day, just before the full moon. Clouds had gathered that morning, but on the stream of golden light at sunset they flowed away to an unknown destination like blue lotuses. After the evening bath and offering lamps to Ganga, everyone collected on the cottage verandah and on the sand outside.

Pandit-ji had planted a tulsi in a small pot of mud in preparation for the puja. Around it a small platform of sand was erected. Then the copper plate blazoned with the lord of Dwarka [Krishna] from the old aunt's basket, the shaligram from Pandit-ji's coloured wooden box, Thakurayin's Mahadev-ji [Shiva] in his silver base, Thakuri Baba's picture of Rama and his ensemble in an old frame with broken glass, Surdas's brass baby Krishna, and the Sahuayin's clay Ganesh, a memento of her husband, were all established on the platform. The devotees had compelled their Gods to join the assembly.

Seating arrangements were also well-organized. A seat was spread for me in the open verandah. To my right were the two old ladies, and a bit farther off, the Sahuayin and Panditayin. To the left was a row of children, whom the Sahuayin had wrapped in her double-layered cotton sheet to protect them from the cold. Pandit-ji sat before the Gods, with his old book opened. At a little distance from him, Thakuri Baba was tightening the pegs of his chikara and his son-in-law, seated right next to him in order to be able to hear every note of the song, was lovingly running his fingers over the tambourine.

Uncle and Aunt sat wrapped up in a torn sheet. Because of their bent backs, it looked as if they were trying to read something in the sand. A few other pilgrims had also arrived. Bela was responsible for bringing the incense, making wicks for the arati, taking out the ghee, and so on, so she was dancing around like a top.

The devotees sang '*Tulsi Maharani namo namo*' [Queen Tulsi, we bow to you] and Pandit-ji completed the puja. Then Ganga water and tulsi leaves were distributed to everyone from copper vessels. Sprinkling Ganga water on the devotees, Pandit-ji recited the greatness of Ganga in a mix of pure and impure Sanskrit, and in a loud voice sang that part of the Ramayana in which Shri Rama, Sita, and Lakshman cross Ganga. Since most of the listeners knew that portion by heart, the main singer's voice was drowned in other voices and its tunelessness hidden.

The singing began with the worship of Gauri and Ganesh. It was hard to say who among them sang well but one had to acknowledge that all the songs impressed one with the transmission of rapture. They knew by heart many songs, from those of great poets like Kabir, Surdas, and Tulsi to those by nameless and unknown rural versifiers. One would sing a line and everyone would collectively repeat it. Like waves coming silently to shore and returning with playful joy, they maintained a continuous rhythm.

The singers sang in sequence and the songs varied in accordance with the singers' lives. Two old women sang first. Thakuri Baba's aunt sang, '*so thaarhe do'u bhaiya sursari teer / ehi paar se Lakhan pukaarai kevat laa'o naiya sursari teer*' [The two brothers stood on Ganga's shore / Lakhan called to the ferryman, 'Bring the boat here']. In response to this heartfelt picture of Rama in the forest, Thakurayin sang, '*dakhin disa heren Bharat sakaare / aaju avaiya more Rama piyaare / divas ginat mori porein khiyaani / maga jovat thaake nain ke taare*' [Gazing southwards, Bharat said, 'Today my sweet Rama will come! My body is worn out with waiting, the stars of my eyes tire with watching the road']. The songs, sung with pauses to draw breath, seemed heavy with the heart's feelings. The Panditayin's '*kahan laage Mohan Maiya Maiya*' [Mohan said, 'Mother, mother'] expanded with emotion while the Sahuayin's '*chale ga'e Gokul se Balveera chale ga'e / ... bilakhat gvaal bisoorati gau'en talphat jamana neera chale ga'e*' [He's gone,

Balveera has left Gokul and gone ... The cowherds sob, the cows weep, Yamuna's waters throb in pain] held the depth of absence. Kachhi Kaka had to be persuaded to sing '*mana magan bhayaa tab kya bole*' [When the heart is full what can one say?], which was rich with fulfilment, while the blind young man's '*sudhi naa bisarai mohi Shyaam tumhare darasan ki*' [I can't forget, dark one, the sight of you] held the yearning of memory.

Thakuri Baba coughed several times to clear his throat, then closed his eyes and sang:

khele laage angana mein kunwar Kanhaiya ho!
bole laage 'Maiya neeki khoto balbhaiya ho!'
khatarasa bhog unahin naa bhaavai Rama!
Maiya maakhan roti khavaave lai balaiya ho!
saala dusaala mana nahi bhavai Rama
hasike kaari kamari udhavai unakar maiya ho!
laike bhaura chaka'i khelan nahin jaave Rama!
maange 'dede lakuti main gheri laavon gaiyaa ho?'

Young Krishna plays in the courtyard, ho!
He said, 'Mother, my brother Bal is naughty, ho!'
He doesn't enjoy the six types of taste, Rama
His mother feeds him butter and roti, and caresses him, ho!
He doesn't like shawls and scarves, Rama
His mother laughs and wraps him in a black blanket, ho!
He doesn't like to play with tops or yo-yos, Rama
He says, 'Give me a staff, I'll go fetch the cows, ho!'

That day, I understood why ordinary people feel such intimacy with Krishna's life, an understanding that would have been hard to find elsewhere. The pictorial quality of their waves of song showed that sound can produce colours and forms. One vibration, one delight, one feeling bound all of them, from children to old people.

I cannot say how long and what they sang because when the gathering ended with the last arati, I seemed to awaken from sleep. In a short while, they arranged their bedding on the verandah and lay down but I sat in my room before the flame in my brass lamp for a long time, thinking. The Sahuayin first looked in, then set one foot inside and humbly said that one should now say farewell to the lamp because its mother must be waiting for it.

Laughter rose to my lips but stopped there. Since everything is alive for them, why not imagine the lamp having a mother who waited for it? When I said I would quench it, she stepped forward and put it out by waving her sari. The poor thing was afraid that my urban lack of good manners might lead me to blow it out.

I don't remember how long I sat in the dark, thinking, but when I went and stood outside the cottage, dawn was about to break. Moonlight drenched in immobility lay spread on the waves and the sand like a lightweight white silk sheet.

The two verandahs of my leaf-cottage were washed in moonlight—I kept wondering why there was such a difference between the outer form and the heart of the creation that lay asleep on sheets, mats, and the cold floor. Have the inheritance of their hearts, their natural courtesy, their immersion in ecstasy, their hard work so little value that it is hard for them to obtain the simple appurtenances of life?

The memory of the sea of emotion in those human hearts, whose waves had gently touched me, began to draw many pictures in my brain. Many great poets' gatherings, many all-India poetry seminars are treasured in my memory. My heart said, 'Find one that resembles this one,' and my intellect grew fatigued with the effort.

Decorated auditoriums, high stages, chairpersons adorned with garlands arose in my memory. The poets gathered around them like divine ambassadors were incomplete both in form and in value. One had claimed first-class fare but had travelled by third class. Another was already in the city for work but for a brief attendance demanded a fee that would cover travel, expenses as well as a profit. A third, in order to increase the estimation of his poetry, had asked for four times the regular price.

The importance that could not be expressed in price was manifested in dress. An Anglicized silk suit dyed in the copper hues of nationalism. A flowing Indian garment of Chinese fabric enveloped in cigarette smoke appeared mysterious. One's hair, brushed upwards, appeared like a turban or a shining black marble floor. Another's straight hair, washed in Silky shampoo and artificially curled, proclaimed human victory over the creator.

The unblinking open eyes or else drooping eyelids of some traditionalists expressed their lack of interest in poetry, which led them to implore Durga's aid. The listeners seated before these wonder-workers seemed to have gathered only to test their miraculous powers. Names were called the way witnesses are called in court. The poets would come up, some smiling, some shy, some puffed up with confidence. They would recite in the third, the fifth or the sixth note, or in the absence of any notes, would speak in nasal tones, twisting the poem with all kinds of acrobatics for the listeners' benefit, and look around for applause.

Despite all their efforts, the spectators were far from impressed. Someone would say, 'Not a good voice,' one would call out, 'Enact the emotions, please,' and another, 'Sit down.' A brazen listener would ask the poet to recite one of his unrestrained erotic compositions in order to watch the women lower their eyes in embarrassment. Poets are usually determined not to admit defeat. 'You don't like that one? All right, listen to this new one—listen carefully.' Neither poet nor listener is willing to accept defeat or to modify their determination to vanquish the other.

Sometimes this exercise continues for eight hours at a stretch but even in so long a time it is hard to find any moments when the poet's emotions are able to arouse a response in the listeners, or when the two, abandoning the farce of juggler and spectator, are able to unite in the joy of poetry. What can poets say if their identity cannot become the identity and the multiplicity of all, and what can listeners hear if their manyness cannot become one with the poet?

When the assembly ends, the speaker ends up despondent and the listeners fatigued. To understand how little influence the truth of poetry has, one merely has to recall how several persons on the way back from such sessions do not hesitate to entertain themselves by visiting professional singing women. If emotion is unable to sweep away one's niggardliness, vicious propensities, and perversities, it becomes one's weakness. That is why emotions like affection and pity are the heart's strengths while negative emotions like envy and anger leave us in an enfeebled state.

Rural communities easily drown their personal divisions and weaknesses in the ocean of poetic pleasure and after such an emotional immersion they obtain a healthier state. The poetic pleasure of our polite society, with its veneer of culture, is shallow and its aim is merely cheap entertainment, so such gatherings only sharpen our feelings of difference and our personal hostilities that are expressed in efforts to outdo one another. One is a rocking cradle in which the contact of superiors and inferiors comes to rest in forgetfulness of self. The other is a wrestling match in which even a level ground produces the delusion of alertness because of the manoeuvres of losing and winning.

I knew the futility of these assemblies but it was only that day that I fully realized it. A few years after this, these polite gatherings became so intolerable to me that I had to bid them farewell. At the height of fame, it is hard for a poet to place an impenetrable veil between oneself and one's admirers. It becomes even more difficult when money accompanies the display, because money is the God of this era. Had the truth of that simple life not thrown into relief the artificiality of the other sort of life, my rebellion would not have grown so acute.

No one now asks what virtues a poet expects from audiences but everyone knows the answer to the question of what amount of money will make a poet fling away the burden of principles and start dancing. The freer the poet's desire is in the field of finance the more it is enslaved to the audience's desires. I have not yet been able to thank the impecunious community which has made me a disbeliever in this professional belief system.

When Thakuri Baba and his companions went off to bathe on the occasion of Basant Panchami, for the first time in my life I missed noise. After that, I have met them at many Magha Melas. How many times they have arranged their devotions in a boat or on the shore, how many times they have entertained me with their khichri and millet cakes, and how many times they have told me their life-stories.

Rarely have I come across a person more sensitive than he is. I have often wondered what that old man would have been like if he had lived amongst us, but the study of life has shown me that it is not easy to erase the difference between these two types of society. Their outer life is poor and our inner life is empty. Amongst them, distortions are individual but good feeling is collective. Our weaknesses are collective and our strengths individual.

Thakuri Baba is a representative of his society so his sensitivity is not an individual oddity. It expresses the sensitivity prevalent in rural life. In our society, he could have ended up in only two situations. Had his weaknesses been dominant, he would have represented society and had strength been dominant, he would have been categorized as an exception.

For the last two years, Thakuri Baba has not come to the Magha Mela. Sometimes, I feel like going to Sayyadpur to find him, because his village is thirty-three miles away from there. I have written down some of his verses, which I want to publish along with other rural songs. The collection will be enhanced if I can meet Thakuri Baba once more. The thought that I may never meet him again does linger in a corner of my heart, but I do not allow it to advance. Can a person like Thakuri Baba give up attachment to his earth?

The last time he came, he seemed somewhat feeble. He held the chikara firmly but his fingers trembled with its strings. His feet trod confidently on the earth but the tremor in his calves made his steps tottery. His voice had the former flexibility but the rumble of his cough turned it off-key. There was the same light of affection in his eyes but time's shadow had dimmed it. The same emotion of free laughter appeared on his face, but as if to remember the teeth that were gradually bidding farewell, the lips had drawn lines of memory above them.

How helpless one is in the face of time. What is the price the body must pay to accept time?

Thakuri Baba's aunt had taken her leave. Thakuri Baba was so habituated to her presence that the unnaturalness of her absence must have taken him aback. Since anyone who came within the bounds of his acquaintance became his own, what can be said of the importance of one who had been his intimate for so many years? His aunt's absence awakened in his heart another anxiety. One day, Bela would have to endure his absence and how would she live then? This was a natural thought but he rarely expressed it.

When I asked about his health, he replied, 'The time to depart is near, daughter! How long can a baked pot last? The day it falls, it's gone.'

I laughingly said, 'How will you stay in heaven, Baba! No one there will understand your riddling verses and your paradoxes nor will anyone listen to the story of Alha and Udal. You won't fit in with the Gandharva musicians and the nymphs.'

Thakuri Baba was delighted. He said, 'I know that, daughter! I'll make such a racket there that the lord will fling me back to earth. I'll again sow grain, make vegetable beds, play the chikara, and sing the story of Alha-Udal to those like you. I don't want heaven, so I'll certainly ask for another new body. This old one is falling apart,' and he began to sing, '*chalata praana kaayaa kaahe ro'i Rama*' [Breath leaves the body, why cry, O Rama?].

That kalpavas could not be repeated. Perhaps he has gone to ask for a new body, but his love of the earth is so true and his relationship to life so unbreakable that it does not seem possible for him to live anywhere else. Thakuri Baba may be said to belong to that band of Atharva Veda singers who call themselves sons of the earth. For him, life is a gift of the earth, poetry the experience of its beauty, love the pace of its attraction, and strength the name of its inspiration. It is not surprising that such a person should prefer the smallest flower in the grass to the highest conception of liberation. I wrote about Thakuri Baba all night—the faint light of dawn behind the fading moonlight seemed like his shadow.

The birds' twitterings extend over sleep's immobility like the first awakening verse of an invisible epic poet. The breeze blows like a long sigh emitted by the trees waking from deep, moveless sleep. And at this time, my memory awakens me to the dawn of a time past. I feel as if Thakuri Baba is sitting on Ganga's shore, lost in singing a song of dawn, '*jaagiye kripaa nidhaana pancchi bana bole*' [Awake, O treasury of kindness, the birds are singing].

It is hard to say whom he awakens with his dawn song.

Bibiya

My washerwoman in town calls me Jij-ji and her son Damdi calls me Mausi-ji.[1] Polite society might consider this insolence from people who do menial work, but I have never thought so. Perhaps this is because of my samskara.[2] In my parents' maternal villages, I had to call the old barber woman Badamo Nani and the old washerman Nanku Dada. No menial worker there is so unfortunate as not to be addressed in kinship terms by even the most important people. Because of this, the urban economy is unimportant there.

Ignoring my protests, the washerman would insist on taking my frock, kurta, and other clothes every morning and returning them, washed, the next day. The barber woman regularly appeared with oil and emollients, and undertook my ablutions despite my crying and wailing. The dairywoman would not only bring butter for me but would spend hours coaxing me to eat a little of it. How effective the teaching of Rammo the gardener woman was when she made flower garlands and fans for me is seen today when my flower arrangements are praised.

---

1 Jij-ji, local pronunciation of jiji or didi, meaning older sister. Mausi is mother's sister.

2 The patterns inherited from one's past lives and one's family.

Just being the son's daughter or daughter's daughter of one family made me the granddaughter of the entire village. They would refuse to accept payment for any service they did me. But when she took a liking to my mother's new striped garment, the dairywoman Muniya Mausi would hold it and make such a scene that it became necessary to take it off and give it to her there and then. The gardener woman Rammo Bua would not sit down to grind henna unless a pair of lac bangles worth one-and-a-half rupees was put on her wrists.[3]

Badamo Nani would not stand up to dance on occasions like my ear-piercing or my birthday unless my Nani extracted from her trunk a skirt embroidered with flowers or a *chikan* dupatta.[4] On Holi, it was only after Nanku Dada had played with colours in the whole village that we would realize that my father's jacket had been taken down from its peg and reached Nanku Dada's body. These familial relations were not restricted to any particular individual or generation. Many generations, past and future, on both sides, had maintained these affectionate relations and are continuing to do so.

Urban life has not managed to erase these samskara from my nature so they must be called natural, but it is hard to say how these people realized that. For a whole era, I have had just one attendant, one milkman, one washerman, and one tanga driver. Neither they nor I think that change is possible unless death intervenes.

Damdi's mother has been washing my clothes since my student days. Several of her children had died, so in order to deceive the

3 Bua: Father's sister.

4 *Chikan* is a kind of hand embroidery that in the modern period has come to be identified with the city of Lucknow in north India. Indian embroidery is first mentioned by Megasthenes in the third century BC.

evil eye, she put her son into a basket the moment he was born and sold him to her neighbour for a *damdi*.[5] On the sixth day, he was bought back for five coins, and to memorialize this trade, his mother named him Damdilal. Whether Brahma was deceived or Damdi was strong, it is true that he escaped death. Damdi is now a big boy. He is married and his wife has come to live with him but he is still childish. He sits in my courtyard and calls out to Bhaktin who is working in the kitchen, 'Bhagatin Amma, I want to drink tea. If you are making some for Mausi-ji, maybe I can have a little?'

Bhaktin's round nostrils flare, her eyebrows scrunch up, the lines on her forehead deepen, and the wrinkles around her lips tighten, but she always gives him tea. Yes, it is true that she always takes out that old glass on which the brass is visible through the Muradabadi polishing. Damdi does not let her be even after he gets the tea. He pleadingly asks, 'Is Mausi-ji not going to have a snack? Give me a bit, Bhagatin Amma! Where else can I get this? I can drink the tea you make without gur or sugar because there is such sweetness in your hands. I'll make your dhoti shine white like the wings of a stork.' It is hard not to smile at the sight of the gentleman, perched on a bundle in the yard, drinking tea made by Bhaktin in an unpolished glass.

If they take fewer clothes to wash, they will not be paid much, so they gather clean clothes into their bundle. When I say, 'That towel was taken out just this morning,' the son answers, 'Its edge has fallen in the mud, Mausi-ji! I'll tie my chickpeas in the other

---

5 A *damdi* was a small coin. The practice of pretending to sell a baby to avoid the evil eye was widespread. Pande Bechan Sharma 'Ugra' recounts in his autobiography how he acquired the name Bechan (sold) because he was sold in this way. See Ruth Vanita, trans., *About Me* (New Delhi: Penguin, 2007).

corner,' and when I say, 'I wore this dhoti just yesterday,' the mother asks, 'Is there any harm if I wear it for one day, Jij-ji?'

What can Mausi-ji do? Damdi wants to tie chickpeas in a clean towel and his mother wants to wear an already washed dhoti, and it is Mausi-ji who must pay for this. I should speak up against this injustice but a memory arises in my heart which stops the words from coming to my lips. The lines of that picture have faded with time but the colours of sorrow have not been washed away or even clouded over.

Bibiya's mother never told me about her life but her helpless expression, the bruises on her hands, and her unnatural limp indicated that her life's journey had not been easy. Perhaps the cruelty of her quarrelsome and alcoholic husband had become so necessary to her that she could not remain in this world without him. When both her parents were gone, the little girl's position became uncertain. She lived with her paternal grandmother, and her older brother Kanhai and his wife. The grandmother was old so she sometimes considered her granddaughter's mistakes unforgivable and sometimes dismissed them as unimportant. Traditional hostility ruled the relationship between the sisters-in-law, and so many siblings had died that the age difference between the oldest brother and youngest sister obstructed companionship between them.

Perhaps it was merely for a few words of sympathy that Bibiya used to come to see me off and on. Her mother used to call me Didiya [older sister]. The daughter maintained that relationship by calling me Mausi-ji.

Usually, people in the washerman community are dark and have round faces. Bibiya had a round face but a wheatish complexion. Her cheerful nature gave her a special attraction. Her small white teeth were always visible in a smile. The balls of her big eyes seemed eager to see every corner of the world. It was hard to consider the graceful and well-shaped Bibiya a washerwoman but she was the most unfortunate of washerwomen.

The indolence or delicacy one imagines with such a form was completely missing in Bibiya. It would be hard to find anyone as industrious as she. She enjoyed doing not only her own work but that of others. She would snatch the broom from her grandmother and sweep the house and yard, grab the flour ball from her sister-in-law's hand and sit down to make roti, and take the heavy iron from her brother's fingers to herself iron the clothes. She outdid everyone in starching clothes, boiling them, carrying them, washing and drying them.

But her self-respect was so excessive as almost to become a fault. She liked wearing nice clothes and she fulfilled this desire by wearing her clients' clothes. Her mother had left her quite a lot of jewellery. Her marriage had been arranged before her birth. She was married in her fifth year but her groom died before she could move to his house. In such a situation, it is considered a shame for an upper-class woman to marry but a social offence for a lower-class woman to stay single.

Kanhai lived in a village across Yamuna but he found his sister a washerman-husband in the city. One auspicious day, the substitute groom arrived at his prospective in-laws' home with his associates. Meat was cooked in a big pot and *poori*s fried in a big wok.[6] Many bottles of local liquor were opened, and the dancing went on until the men from both sides fell into a drunken stupor.

I didn't see Bibiya for many months after she went to her in-laws. I thought she was busy establishing her new household. After some months, Bibiya suddenly appeared in dirty, shabby clothes. Her face was overcast and her body weakened, but she had neither tears in her eyes nor a smile on her lips. There was

6 *Poori*: Fried bread.

no expression of guilt on her face nor was there the plea of an innocent for justice. There was just an unmoved indifference.

She said she would wash my clothes and would live in her brother's house but cook for herself. Gradually, I came to know that her husband had thrown her out. He had said he had no place for such a woman—she could live with her brother or marry again. It was natural to wonder whether Bibiya had been exiled on suspicion of infidelity but my question broke through her armour and hurt her so that she burst into tears: 'You too think like this, Mausi-ji! My mother has gone to heaven, now who is going to ferry me across!'

I was sorry when I saw her grief but was angry with myself when I learnt the details from her grandmother. Bibiya had tried her best to organize Ramai's house but he was a hardened gambler and drunkard. These faults are common amongst washermen but are considered natural if they stay within limits.

On the first night, Ramai came home very late, completely drunk. Since there was no other woman in the house, the newly wed Bibiya had to cook for him. She had prepared dal and vegetables with special care, had kneaded the flour, and was waiting to make roti. Ramai staggered in and began to make such disgusting remarks that she lost her temper. She was sharp-tongued, and to be insulted by her own husband was more than she could bear. She said, 'Go drown yourself in a puddle. You talk to your married wife as if you are visiting a prostitute—yuck!'

Despite being drunk out of his mind, the husband felt insulted. Gritting his teeth and rolling his eyes, he said contemptuously, 'Married! You have eaten up one man and now you come to another's house and pretend to be a Sati Sita! Wonderful—I fall at your feet.'

Unable to restrain her anger, Bibiya picked up the tongs and threw them at him. Trying to save himself, he stumbled and fell flat, and his wife went into a windowless inside room and locked herself in. When she emerged in the morning, he had left.

This routine continued for several days. Apart from drinking, he was also given to gambling, which is worse than drinking. A drunkard becomes a man when he sobers up but a gambler never does sober up, so there is no question of his becoming a man.

Ramai's gambling companions were from various communities. One was a market gardener, another a cobbler, a third a weaver, and a fourth an oil-presser. The things they lost and won were odd. They would stake clothes, shoes, money, pots and pans, whatever came to hand. One would win another's wife's necklace or a daughter-in-law's earrings. Another would lose his sister's armlet or his granddaughter's bracelet. In short, theft and robbery were often necessary before they could gamble.

One day, Ramai's gambling companion Miyan Karim said, his pink eyes swimming, 'Well, friend, you have got a nice girl. Why don't you stake her? If you're lucky, you'll win a heap of money!' All the others wholeheartedly seconded this proposition. Ramai agreed to stake Bibiya but then perhaps he remembered the tongs or a stick, and he made an excuse, 'I have money today. On a day when I don't, what else is a wife for?'

This news did not take long to reach Bibiya. For a proud woman like her, this was like fire to a fuse. Unfortunately, she saw Karim Miyan at her door one day. Taking out the big knife used to cut vegetables, she told him with bent brows that if Ramai did any such thing, she would stab them both in the stomach with that knife, regardless of the punishment she might have to suffer. She was not a calf that could be sold to a butcher or handed over to a Brahmin as a gift to enable crossing the river into the next world.

Karim Miyan was stunned, but the next day, he said to Ramai in the presence of the other gamblers, 'Such a woman in a decent man's house! The wretch is like a Baluchistani, pulling out a knife at the drop of a hat. Wait and see, she'll attack you too one day. How can you sleep with death in your house?'

Lakhan Ahir wagged his head in agreement and said solemnly, 'Ram, Ram, these days wives roam around killing their husbands. Now one can clearly see Kaljug embodied!' Mahangu the market-gardener showed his knowledge of the scriptures: 'Just see how Sita Rani lived. Even when she was thrown out she didn't protest. Poor thing stayed in Jharkhand with her sons.' Khilavan the oil-presser endorsed this: 'That's why she is called a Sati Satvanti! Mother earth opened up for her. This woman eats her husbands and becomes a Sati.'

Poor Ramai did not know what to say. It was embarrassing enough that his wife could not be counted among the Satis. He would have borne the burden of this shame and guilt, but it was hard to exist day and night in the shadow of fear. A woman who is not afraid to pull out a knife won't be afraid to use it. Poor Ramai was so scared that he began to stay far from his wife. Some days passed thus, but in the end Ramai declared that he would not keep Bibiya in his house. The village council agreed with him because the members were all followers of Ramai's dharma. If they had such difficult wives as his, before whom they could neither drink nor gamble, they would have had to do the same.

Bibiya had no option but to return home and live as before. It would be untrue to say that her sister-in-law's taunts did not hurt her but she wiped her tears on her grandmother's sari. She worked four times as hard as before. She woke up earlier than everyone and went to sleep later than everyone. She wore neither nice clothes nor jewellery. She neither sang nor joined in dances and festivals. Her husband's insults had wounded her but the community's slander made her life difficult. Anyone would find it hard to give up such a beautiful, hardworking woman so everyone speculated that she must have faults weightier than her virtues.

Kanhai again attempted to get her married. This time he chose for a brother-in-law an old widower with five children in a neighbouring village. But Bibiya threw a fit. She fasted for several days and wept for hours at a time. She tried to dissuade Kanhai, saying, 'Brother, I won't go. I'll break my head and die but I won't leave my parents' threshold,' but her efforts were in vain. The brother thought it too dangerous to keep a young sister at home. If she stumbled, he would be ostracized. Were that to happen, he didn't have enough money to buy his way back into the community by feasting the village council.

Finally, Bibiya's acceptance took the form of indifference. Someone put a pink dhoti on her, someone else put collyrium in her eyes, and a third adorned her hands and feet with bracelets and anklets belonging to a deceased co-wife. Bibiya then departed once more for her in-laws' home.

When I heard nothing of her for a year, I was reassured, thinking that the wild girl had been tamed. Not only I but her brother, sister-in-law, grandmother, and other relatives had all ceased to worry about her when suddenly I heard that she was back home again. This time the black mark against her was even darker but she didn't come to tell me about it. I heard that she did not do any housework nor did she step out of the house. She just lay with her face covered in that dark room where grass for the donkey and coal were stored. After much coaxing, she would eat two bites but was otherwise uninterested in eating.

Naturally, this was worrying. In some unknown quarter of the mind, a small cloud of suspicion kept arising. Gradually it overshadowed the lines of trust. Was Bibiya really characterless? If not, why couldn't she find respect in any home? Girls far less beautiful and skilful than she had established their own worlds. What was wrong with this unfortunate girl that prevented her from getting a hand's breadth of space anywhere?

While I was wrestling with these questions, Bibiya's grandmother came over, and repeatedly wiping her dimmed eyes, told me the story of her granddaughter's misfortunes. Bibiya's new husband had already lost two wives. The first had left a son behind who was the same age or a few months older than the second wife. The second wife had three daughters, the oldest of whom was nine and the youngest three.

Jhanku decided to marry a third time for the sake of the young children. He never seemed to care much about his bride. Every morning he left for the river, with his bundles and his lunch, and returned at twilight. Then he would unload the bundles, let the donkey out to graze, and leave home to return only after eleven at night.

It was said that he spent most of his time with a Pasi family.[7] There were many theories about the nature of his intimacy with them. Because of the *jati* difference, he could not establish a permanent relationship with that family but because his wives had never accused him of wrongdoing and he was good-natured, the village council never tried to penalize him. The Pasi man worked as a groom for a prosperous household in the city but his wife had suddenly developed such love for her in-laws' home that she considered it the height of adharma to leave it.

Jhanku needed a wife from his own community, if not for himself then to look after his offspring, but no washerwoman was willing to be his companion. Bibiya was in an unusual position. The poor thing was drowning in a sea of infamy so Jhanku's proposal was like a ship for her.

Thus, keeping his own heart free, Jhanku bound Bibiya in the bonds of marriage. It's true that he did not harass his new wife in any way. He didn't even want to take her to the river to

---

7 The Pasi community often engages in fowling or toddy pressing.

work, so she was engaged in the housewife's work of grinding, pounding, cooking, and childcare. No one knew whether Bibiya was happy or unhappy about her husband's indifference because she immersed herself in the house and children in a way that precluded any other emotion.

She worked from dawn to midnight and then was freed from worldly anxiety when she lay on a broken bed with a little girl on either side of her. In the morning, a new page in the old book of duty was always open. There were two rooms in the mud house, the doors of which opened into a yard. The aperture between these two rooms had no door. Jhanku would lock one of the rooms so that he could come in at night without awaking anyone. His wife kept food out for him and went to sleep. If he was hungry he ate it, if not he wrapped it up and took it with him in the morning.

Bibiya's heart, hungry for affection, filled itself with the love of the innocent children. She bathed them, plaited their hair, fed them, and put them to sleep with such love and care that strangers thought her not only a mother but an especially affectionate mother. Seeing how well the children were cared for, Jhanku became even more detached from home. He was concerned about keeping the pots of grain full but not about filling the emptiness of his wife's existence.

This would not have been too bad had not his oldest son returned from his maternal grandparents' house. Due to his mother's absence and father's indifference, he had become something of a vagrant. His temperamental peculiarities, such as using oil and perfume, wrestling, and fighting quails, are not found among washermen.

Despite gambling and drinking, a washerman does not lose the label of decency nor does he adopt inefficiency or indolence. There is no room in his profession for laziness or dishonesty.

A labourer can waste time or do his job badly but a washerman cannot. He has to return the right number of clothes to his clients, work hard to wash whites well, and remember how each thing must be starched or ironed. If he wastes the time needed for these tasks, he will not be able to complete his monthly consignments and the problem of a livelihood will become acute. Perhaps this is the reason why all washermen, good or bad, are efficient. There may be differences of degree but complete inefficiency is an exception.

Jhanku's son Bhikhan was just such an exception. His father had somehow got him married to the daughter of a poor washerwoman but seeing that her son-in-law was not likely to reform, she found the girl a hardworking husband and sent her off with him. Thus, Bhikhan could not become a householder, let alone a good one. The father was not in a position to lecture the son but finally, fed up with his behaviour, he banished him.

When his stepmother arrived, he was at his grandparents' place, achieving excellence in fighting quails and flying kites. His father didn't call him back but his stepmother's presence made him eager to return. One day, he put on a striped muslin kurta and a silk-cotton dhoti with a border, and arranged his curly hair with care. He arrived at the door with a cage of quails in one hand and a bundle of sweets for his sisters in the other. His father was not at home but his stepmother welcomed him appropriately. She gave him a drink of sugar dissolved in water, fed him dal-roti with eggplant, and laid his bed in the other room.

The father and son did not have a loving reunion because one nurtured an undefinable suspicion and the other a definite aversion. Jhanku told him in no uncertain terms that if he did not behave himself, he would be thrown out. Bhikhan tightened his lips, narrowed his eyes, and turned his head away when he heard this but did not agree to behave himself.

Characterless people are more suspicious of others than good people are. Jhanku was no exception. He now began to happily bear the burden of guarding the wife whom he had not cared for at all. He started coming home on time, keeping a stern watch on his son, and looking out for any change in his wife's behaviour. Ignoring his father's alertness, the son kept hovering around his stepmother. He would feed his quails right where she washed the dishes. Just when she went out to hang clothes to dry, he would sit outside bare-chested, to rub oil into his fleshy hands and feet. When she was on the way back from fetching water, he would hide behind the umbrella-tree and sing, '*dheere chalau, gagari chhalaka naa jaa'e*' [Walk slowly, the pitcher may overflow].

One day, while he was eating, his insinuations went so far that the stepmother pulled a burning faggot from the stove and said, 'I'm your father's wife. If I hear another bad word from you, the skin on your back won't survive.' His stepmother's unprecedented behaviour angered the son instead of embarrassing him. Men like him are very proud of their skills in seducing women. When a woman is unaffected by those skills, their pride receives such a blow that they do not hesitate to take harsh revenge.

His stepmother's speech nourished the causeless malice to which he was prone. Bibiya, though not especially pleased by her husband's conduct, did not resent it. A self-respecting person prefers respectful indifference to affectionate insults. Jhanku was not attached to his wife but he did not disrespect her the way other washermen disrespected their wives. This is more valuable to women like Bibiya than affection is, so she was deeply grateful to him. Had her cruel fate not sent this stepson along in jest, she would have contentedly spent the rest of her life in that house, but even this happiness was denied to her.

Bhikhan now began to display such artificial intimacy towards his stepmother that she grew terrified. In order not to disrupt the peace, she did not complain to the master of the house, but she did not foresee the terrible consequences of her silence. The son began to enact a strange mixture of shyness and pleasure whenever his stepmother was mentioned, and his companions started rumours about their relationship. Other washerwomen began to remark on Bibiya's base deceptions and their own purity in order to obtain necklaces and bracelets from their husbands as evidence of their good conduct. At the river, within Jhanku's hearing, other washermen demonstrated their knowledge of women's falseness.

Unsurprisingly, Jhanku lost patience when he heard everyone talking about his wife's misconduct and his own cowardice. One day, when he was returning home with a full load, he ran into his son. Jhanku pounced on him and beat him up with the donkey whip. The son put all the blame on his stepmother, expressed his own helplessness, and enacted a farce of shame about his misconduct. Thus, Bhikhan took his revenge.

Jhanku could have asked his wife for an explanation, but her wrongdoing seemed so self-evident that he dispensed with such civilities. Bibiya had never insisted on clothes or jewels, never tried to challenge her rival in her husband's love, and never sulked in protest at her husband's indifference. These mistakes proved that she was not attached to her husband, and one who is not attached must be unattached. Also, people think it inevitable for one who is unattached to be attached to someone else. To give a chance of self-defence to a person proven guilty by such logic is to reward them. Punishment is the best warning for such a person.

That night, Bibiya was beaten for the first time. Blows, kicks, slaps, and sticks were used but the criminal neither accepted her fault and asked forgiveness nor did she cry or scream. When she wished, Bibiya had the ability to respond to kicks and blows with tongs and rolling pins but she had begun to respect Jhanku so much that she was unable to lift her hand against him. Jhanku added his wife's silence to the list of her offences, and when he was exhausted with beating her, he pushed her out on the verandah, bolted the door, and fell, panting, on to the bed.

Bibiya's body was swollen from fist-blows, blue lines showed the number of blows with a stick, and pain from kicks spread through her joints. The closing of the door banished her from the bounds of forgiveness. Weeping, gasping, and stumbling, she somehow followed the field-path like the line of fate in the darkness to her parental home.

Not a single member of the village council had tried to teach Bibiya's husband his duty, but the council met to punish Bibiya for forsaking her duty. Bhikhan repeated the imaginary story of his stepmother's powerful temptations and his own innocent weakness, and asked forgiveness. His maternal uncle's and grandfather's money made up for the shortcomings in his apology.

Humans are naturally attracted towards others' weaknesses so they accept a bad person's evidence to prove the faults of a good person. A thief does not know the use of honesty and a liar is unaware of the uses of truth. It is natural for a person who is unfamiliar with or does not believe in a particular virtue not to trust a person who possesses that virtue. But society accepts such a person's false views as evidence because humans do not want to acknowledge that anyone can be faultless, and tireless researchers of faults are found primarily in the ranks of the faulty.

No one was under any illusions about the conduct of Bhikhan who was slandering Bibiya, yet in order to find faults in Bibiya's conduct they were compelled to accept his assertions as true. She could not be present to defend herself. One can easily imagine what kind of deference those counsellors would have received from that wounded lioness.

Bibiya's grandmother had died but her brother could not summon up the courage to throw his miserable sister out of the house, so the community ostracized him. At this time, I fell ill and had to go to the mountains. When I recovered and returned, I searched for Bibiya. I found out that she had disappeared, and her brother, shamed by his sister's infamy, had sought refuge with his father-in-law in Partabgarh district. No one could tell me whether Kanhai was distressed at escaping from his sister but everyone knew that thanks to his father-in-law who was a village chieftain, he had obtained the good fortune of being received back into the community.

The washermen's community in the village was divided with regard to Bibiya. Some believed in her misconduct and were hardened against her, while others, considering her mistakes the result of ineradicable destiny, were generous enough to grant her sympathy. An old woman told me that Bibiya was very upset when her brother was ostracized. To be received back into the community, Kanhai would have had to spend two hundred rupees, which he could not have saved even from a lifetime's earnings.

In these hard times, Bibiya's nephew was born. Her sister-in-law was anyway displeased with Bibiya. Now she constantly berated her, bewailing her own bad luck and her husband's folly. 'Why would my wretched fate allow me to enjoy the birth of a first child? It's not for me to celebrate with the community. Another's sin is uprooting my home. Is it right for one who has no home of her own to destroy another's household? For one who has an ounce of shame, a handful of water would be enough to drown in.'[8]

Constantly listening to the sarcasms hidden in this kind of language, Bibiya one day disappeared. Everyone believed so

---

8 Idiomatic. One who is socially disgraced should feel ashamed and commit suicide.

strongly in her misconduct that they considered her disappearance another sign of her infamy. She was not a good wife so what could she do but go off with another man? If she wanted to die, she would have drowned herself when her first husband abandoned her or hanged herself in her second husband's house. But it was not logical to kill herself after she had come to her innocent brother's house and ruined his household.

It is hard to understand any woman's crooked ways so how could a man understand the mystery of a woman who was especially crooked? How could a number of speculations be declared false on the basis of the one known fact that she had no relationship with any man in the village? Doubtless Bibiya had, unbeknownst to anyone, found a companion for her journey.

After a long time, when I went to give medication to an old invalid Pasi, some light was shed on the secret of Bibiya's journey. He told me that two days before she ran away, Bibiya had bought country liquor from him. Since she had no money, she had removed her mother's silver earrings from her ears and handed them to him. She was the only washerwoman free from addiction to liquor so the Pasi was surprised, but when he questioned her, she said that she would feast the family on the day of her nephew's naming ceremony. If her brother got to know, he would drink it up ahead of time, which was why she had to buy it secretly.

The next day, when the Pasi gave her the liquor in a bell-metal pot and also returned the change, she put the money back in his hand and requested him to keep it for now. She would ask for it when she needed it. Many of the village girls remembered her hesitatingly going towards Yamuna with a small bundle of soiled clothing. A shepherd boy had seen her drinking something from her hand at twilight and repeatedly washing her mouth with Yamuna's brown waters while laughing like a madwoman.

Then an unknown suspicion surfaced in my mind. No one prepares for a journey by buying a drink that will make one unconscious. If liquor was needed, couldn't it have been bought by her companion, of whose existence the whole village was convinced? Why had Bibiya needed to sell the last memorial of her dead mother to obtain liquor? And did she have so much money for her journey that she could afford to leave behind the money she got from selling the earrings?

No washerman goes to wash clothes in the autumnal Yamuna which rises above its bounds with huge waves. They wash clothes in the pits that become pools and ponds thanks to the monsoon's bounty. Why then had Bibiya gone to the river? The conclusion I reached from logically joining the links set me atremble.

Suicide is a person's acceptance of defeat by life. One of Bibiya's temperament does not accept defeat even when defeated. Who can say whether she made this arrangement when she found no support anywhere, in order to forget her ultimate defeat? The world had banished her; could not that dignified soul have sought shelter in the roaring waves?

I know a childless and neglected wife of a similar temperament who belongs to a respectable family, who stood all night up to her knees in water at the Draupadi Ghat but could not drown herself and was taken back home at the Brahma Mahurat, just before sunrise, by an old man who had gone to bathe there.[9] She had said that attachment to life had not caused her hesitation. Rather, it was the knowledge that people would say, 'She couldn't do anything so she killed herself,' which weighed down her feet and prevented her from advancing into the deep.

---

9 Brahma Mahurat is the segment of one and a half hours before dawn, considered a suitable time for meditation.

Bibiya was a flame of revolt that never burnt out. The thought that the world had insulted her for no reason and that she had run away rather than challenge it to battle would have carried her a long way, like a storm cloud that has not shed its burden. But all her weapons for the struggle had been broken. Even a person brave and immovable as a mountain can step away from the struggle when in a swoon without being called a coward.

The reason for Bibiya's disappearance that the world found was appropriate for the world, but I am not compelled to accept its conclusion as true. Even today, when my boat dares to cross tumultuous Yamuna, which acts like an ocean in the pelting rain, I cannot help remembering that washer-girl. One day, in the shadow of the rain's dark, cloudy garments, she threw her oar into the maddened waves and set afloat the boat of her life.

Who can say on which unknown shore the fragile boat of that *ekakini* came to rest![10]

---

10 *Ekakini* is a word with many meanings. Mahadevi uses it in her poetry to suggest oneness with the universal Self, but she also uses it, as here, to refer to a solitary woman. In 1947, Asha Sahay used the word as the title of her novel about love between two women. I translated extracts from this novel in *On the Edge: 100 Years of Hindi Fiction on Same-Sex Desire* (2023).

Gungiya

I may not have written many letters in my own name but writing letters for others has become a sort of duty of mine. Whether in my own rustic surroundings or in a mountain village, my condition has become like that of a petition-writer.

A sad mother is anxious to send an affectionate plea to her son who has run off to a faraway place. A wife captive in her in-laws' home is eager to remind her brother to bring her home in the rainy season. A lonely housewife wants the husband who has set up a new family far away to tell her how he is doing. An invalid wants to compel his brother who is a labourer in the city to send him money. An uncle asks his nephew, in honour of their blood-bond, to help him buy a bullock. A man requests his wife's brother to free his fields from a mortgage.

A boundless variety prevails amongst letter-writers. The wide variety of topics would bewilder even a seasoned letter-writer. And I have not even as much expertise in the art as a rhymester has in poetry. The ignorance of letter-senders combined with my lack of skills makes the task harder.

They speak so fast that sentences lose their connection to each other and emotions become unclear. When I ask them to slow down they think that the writer lacks ability so the letter will be fruitless. It is not easy to organize the narrative that gets lost in their incoherent terminology and disjointed sentences, or to link it to their confused and mixed-up feelings, and then clothe it in the lineaments of a letter.

It is also hard to give the narrative the form of a letter in the modern style because these rustics are not only specialists in the tradition of letter-writing but rigid followers of that tradition. Either *Shri Ganeshaya namaha* [Salutations to Shri Ganesh] or Shri Rama must be written at the start. Without it, the letter cannot obtain their approval. Whether the addressees are unparalleled in poverty or unique in ugliness, they must all be addressed as 'the successful one, deserving of all epithets'.

The topic of the letter also creates no small dilemma for the writer because as soon as one takes up one thread of a story, many other threads come to hand. The letter-sender wants to include many sub-stories in the story. The sequence of incidents bears no relation to the flow of the story but the sub-stories are inseparably bound to the main story. Someone wants money from a relative but can say this only with an account of many incidents from his life, and is not satisfied unless everyone, from the landlord and the moneylender to Ghurahu and Mangaru Pasi, has been cited as a witness to his poverty.

Letter-senders give such lively descriptions of past events that the poor letter-writer is astonished. What to write and what not to write is not left to me. I cannot make my own decisions because I will be requested to read the letter aloud at the end. They repeat their ideas so many times that they immediately notice when a negligible element of the narrative has been omitted.

One cannot get out of it by saying that there is not enough space on the paper to write all of this. Fixing their pleading gaze on the writer's face and a crooked finger on some blank corner, they will ask with such pathos for the left-out details to be written there that one cannot refuse. It seems wrong to them to leave a margin or corners empty. They desist from asking for more to be written only when the entire paper is covered with words.

It's no easy task to understand the letter-sender's feelings. As soon as one feeling is expressed, a flood of others follows. These rural people are usually more emotional than intellectual city-dwellers, therefore every element of the message arouses new feelings in them. In the course of the narrative, one encounters them laughing, weeping, angry, remorseful, carried away by parental feeling or by despondency arising from neglect, expressing sometimes philosophical detachment and at other times worldly practicality. In short, their emotions keep changing in accordance with incidents, times, and places.

The writer is not sure which emotion should be given precedence. A father wants to rebuke his clever and far-sighted son for his undutiful and neglectful behaviour. The writer, recording his harsh words, suddenly experiences the moisture of tears in those sentences. Raising one's eyes, one sees not a stern judge but a weeping, emotional, helpless father. It is difficult to say which of these two is real and even more difficult to know which one's words should be transmitted.

I often have to tear up and throw away a letter after writing it, because towards the end, the sender is different from what she or he was at the outset. It would not only be unjust to send that letter but also harmful from a practical point of view because the recipient will not understand the sender's true feelings and will form a misconception. And after solving all the problems associated with the sender, there is still one more problem. The whole village wants to add something or other to the person's letter.

One person wants to say 'I fall at your feet' and another wants to send blessings.[1] Someone's *Jai Ram-ji* has to be conveyed

---

1 'I fall at your feet' translates *palaagan*, which is not translatable in one word.

and someone else's embrace. One wants to express his poetic temperament by writing 'A letter is half a meeting' and another his philosophical bent in '*Ho'i hai soi jo Rama rachi rakha*'.[2] One considers it necessary to convey the news that he has sold a calf and another that he has bought a buffalo, a third that he has been evicted from his fields, and a fourth that her roof has collapsed. One person must recount the story of a well falling in and another that of a pond drying up.

It would be hard to find someone who does not want to send a message to someone they know, and the urban unfamiliarity arising from distance is not possible in small villages. Everyone is familiar with everyone else. Even if they do not know the addressee of the letter very well, they know the letter-sender and by virtue of this relationship, young and old all remember to write something appropriate.

One knows the paternal uncle so he is eager to send the nephew advice regarding duty, another is intimate with the nephew so must send greetings to the maternal uncle. One knows the aunt and wants to send blessings to the niece's husband, another is the girlfriend of the niece so considers it necessary to say that she falls at the feet of the paternal uncle's wife's grandfather-in-law. In this situation, whether there is a relationship or not, familiarity or not, matters not at all.

They also think it would be insulting not to have a person like me write something. Instead of the grocer's oil-stained envelopes, those that emerge from my bag shine white as a crane's wings. The pages of my notebook are big and clean compared to the paper wrapped in a bundle along with turmeric. My shining fountain pen is far more attractive than the inkpot without a

2 What Rama has designed will happen. This is an oft-quoted line from Tulsidas's sixteenth-century *Ramcharitmanas*, which has long been the most popular version of the Rama story in north India.

lid and the black dipping-pen established in a corner of the village accountant's verandah. My stamps seem more reliable than the dirty, crumpled stamps tied in a corner of a shawl. One who doesn't get anything written by a writer who has such high-quality writing materials manifests his own ignorance of the way of the world. For this reason, everyone begs me to write 'two words' for them.

Why do I need to become an itinerant post office? Will the letters I write ever reach their destinations? Isn't my envelope and stamp supply depot somewhat dubious? Isn't this petition-writing status of mine evidence of my having nothing better to do? All these questions never once arise in their hearts.

Even the most truly benevolent person who enters urban life becomes the target of the sharp arrows of mistrust and suspicion. The unreasonable suspicions that pervade urban life cripple dedication to action and pointless hypocrisy muddies the urban world-view. In contrast, the book of rural life is open to the view. There could be exceptions in some knotty circumstances, but where life is somewhat healthy, a villager's acceptance of help is simple because it is free from pretended humility, the giving of help is natural because it is without pride, and the exchange of ideas is without artifice and completes the study of life.

Seeing me writing something, an old woman asked me to write to her son who lived far away. Then others began to come too, and finally this task became a duty of mine. I rarely write letters for no reason or even when there is a reason. Therefore, even though I had to buy stamps, envelopes, and post-cards, this letter-writing was not too expensive for me.

I sit in various places. Sometimes I sit on the raised roots of a pipal tree and lean against its trunk, and sometimes on the dry leaves under a mango tree. Sometimes I sit on a wooden bed on someone's verandah, sometimes on a mat in front of the tulsi pot in someone's yard. Everyone has to follow the lead of the one who first proposed writing a letter. The letter-sender sits nearby and the others a little distance away. Those who simply send greetings keep coming and going.

One hands the irrigation water-bag to someone else and runs up to write 'I fall at your feet', another reminds me to send blessings and then goes off to thresh corn. One stands with a full pitcher on her head and a rope in her hand as she dictates her message. Another, while telling me to write '*Jai Ram-ji*', remembers that she must grind chickpea flour, and a mother returns to hear the postscript of a letter after she has given her crying son a piece of coarse bread. One, while dictating advice, stands up to relight a quenched hookah.

Everyone keeps coming and going in this way. Only the director of this performance stays from beginning to end, controlling the pace of the story, sometimes laughing, sometimes crying, and sometimes indifferent. When the letter is written, it must be read aloud. Additions must be made here and there. Letter-senders are eager to prove the letter their own by appending their thumb impression at the end. In the pragmatic world, a thumb impression is an armour to protect oneself from prevailing falsehood but all cannot be convinced that the impression is not particularly important in characterizing the letter as one's own self-expression. That is why under the name, various strange shapes and marks of the thumb appear like decorations.

Writing the address is the hardest part of the endeavour. Someone's name is Mahavir [Great Hero] but he is called Nanhku [Little One]. Another's name at home is Dulrua [Pet] but his name outside the house is Bhairondeen [Shiva's companion]. One is called Ghasita [Draggard] in his own village and Rajarama [King Rama] in the next. Another is called Sirtajiya [Crown] in his maternal grandparents' home and Dukhiya [Sorrowful] in his paternal grandparents' home. One is called Roopmatiya [Beauty] by her family and Kaluiya [Dark] by outsiders.[3]

It would be surprising if this combination of self-contradictory names and pen-names did not remind us of our poets' community. In our community too, a person who is poor and looks like a coal can be called Heeralal [Diamond] and have the pen-name Sharadendu [Winter Moon] without being mocked. Poverty is connected with the social system, looks are given by nature, and a name is a parental gift. All that is left for the poet to take full responsibility for is the pen-name. Perhaps for this reason he wants to claim a right over the most beautiful thing in the world without worrying about his own virtues or lack thereof.

It is natural for inventors of pen-names to be drawn to the words that the poetic tradition has favoured, but when there is no connection between the meaning of these words and the persons who assume them as names, a strange situation arises. Name and pen-name are bound together inseparably so that the listener cannot forget the difference between them.

But village names and nicknames are different. The name is connected with Pandit-ji's books, but the nickname presents a realistic picture of a person's looks, nature, and qualities or of other people's attitudes.[4] One who is called Labaar [Braggart] cannot be devoid of the feature the name indicates. One called Gujariya [Doll] will not be less than a doll in the brightness of her clothing. She who is given the name Koyali [Cuckoo] will be dark-complexioned but will also have a melodious voice. A

3 Traditionally, many Indians have a formal name used by outsiders and a pet-name used at home. One may also have more than one sobriquet bestowed by different branches of the family or groups of friends.

4 When a baby is born, the priest (Pandit-ji) opens a scriptural work and tells the parents what the first letter of the child's name should be.

Nathu must have worn a nose-ring in infancy. Ghure [Rubbish] would have faced severe neglect in childhood. There may be some exceptions but on the whole, nicknames fit the person rather than contradicting their condition.

But when writing a letter, it is hard to know whether a person in a faraway place gives more importance to a name or a nickname. As long as the person is in a familiar environment, observers decide on a name, but when people are free to shape themselves, their tastes and emotions towards others will decide which form of address they choose. Both the dictator of the letter and the inditer of the letter are in the dark with regard to this.

After the name, the next obstacle is that of place. The letter-senders usually know only the name of the city. Their absolute faith in the fame of the addressee always astonishes me although perhaps it should not. A woman is sure that everyone will be familiar with the beauty of her beloved son. A man is certain that the whole city will know his nephew who is a wrestler. A third believes that a singer like his brother will be known to the post office. A fourth thinks that the postman cannot possibly be unaware of his paternal uncle's skill in combating the poison of snakes and scorpions. One woman thinks that her husband's ability to heal animals is enough of an address. Another says that the scholarly attainments of his maternal uncle who has memorized the *Hanuman Chalisa* cannot remain hidden.

They neither know nor wish to believe that their dear relatives, dwelling amongst the populace of a distant city, are like drops in the ocean. After many efforts, when an address is found and written down, it becomes necessary to get the letter to the post office as speedily as possible. One immediately wraps the letter in his turban and sets off, water pitcher in hand, to walk three miles to the post office. Another prepares his bundle to undertake the walk next morning. A third puts the letter carefully in his box and goes off to do other chores, while a fourth affectionately strokes the letter with his fingers, smearing the ink on it.

Often, I have to undertake the duty of taking the letters to the post office, but the senders do not trust me as much as they trust themselves. They are confident that they will not fail to recognize the red letterbox but they suspect that whoever I entrust with the task may mistakenly put the letter in some other box. The many letterboxes and water tanks in the city make them uneasy.

The days of waiting for a reply heighten their worry. The postman visits some villages only once a week, so the letter-senders constantly make a dash to the post office. They are not satisfied with being told that there is no letter for them. One insists upon repeating his name and nickname and getting all the addresses checked until the postman rebukes him. Another arouses the postman's anger by repeating again and again every detail from his clan to his village's topographical features.

My patience is sorely tested by the number of enquiries I have to answer with regard to letters supposed to be sent to my address. One asks how many more days the answer will take. Another wonders whether I wrote the address incorrectly. A third guesses that the letter didn't reach the addressee because we didn't put all his characteristics down with his name. A fourth suspects that the stamps were old and the postman may have thrown the letter into the trash. One thinks the rain may have washed out the address and another that because the letter was heavy, it is lost and is wandering around aimlessly.

I am sometimes amused and sometimes angered by their ignorance. Their helplessness sometimes annoys and sometimes saddens me. Who has incapacitated these individuals who are longing to communicate their feelings and thoughts? How shameless are those who are proud of their own eloquence but have silenced such a large population? Such questions are natural.

Things were going on in this way, but when one day Gungiya caught hold of my sari and indicated by gestures that she wished to write a letter, I was speechless. Are there no limits to my difficulties? Must I now write letters for dumb people? How can I possibly understand whom Gungiya wants to write to and what she wants to say?

But she had no interest in the solution to these problems. Seeing me write so many letters, her heart had forgotten her sad helplessness. Gungiya found it hard to believe that one who writes the stories of so many joys and sorrows would not find a language for her visible joys and sorrows.

I had seen her so many times that I was used to her presence. When I arrived, she was always waiting for me. When I left, she would walk behind me a long way to see me off. When I wrote, she would sit nearby and watch my actions with great curiosity. I had considered her just an inquisitive onlooker so I was thrown into a quandary by her assuming the role of a letter-sender.

Gungiya acquired her nickname because she is dumb. Her given name is Dhanpatiya [Wealthy]. Her father Raghu the oilman was prosperous, and honest too. He had a pair of well-built bullocks to turn the wheel and he produced all kinds of oil from mustard to castor. Raghu was renowned beyond the village for the purity of his oil and the utility of his oil cake. Gungiya was his first child so her birth was celebrated with pomp. Drummers performed, Domni women danced and were given veils, and many canisters of ghee were expended on feasting the elders of the oil-presser community.

Her mother was fed a strengthening pudding with *chironji*, and nutritious *panjiri* sweets made with *babool* gum.[5] When she

---

5 *Chironji*: Almondette. *Panjiri*: A dense Punjabi sweet made of flour, ghee, nuts, and sugar, which is usually eaten in winter, and fed to pregnant women and nursing mothers. *Babool*: The Gum Arabic tree.

emerged into the open air with her daughter after a month and a half, the family took many precautions to avert the evil eye. The little girl was massaged so much that her hairless body looked like a ball of flour. She was rubbed with so much oil that the viewer's gaze slipped on her skin.

The roly-poly Dhanpatiya started walking when she was ten months old but she did not speak even after she was five. She could not say Ma or Dada nor did she ask for *duddu* or *happa*.[6] Her anxious parents tied talismans on her, and many rituals and ceremonies were performed, but speech did not bless Dhanpatiya. Finally, Raghu took her to town and showed her to the doctor. The misshapen palate and uvula with which she was born could have been corrected only by a special operation, which Raghu had neither the money nor the courage to undertake.

Dhanpatiya therefore grew up as Gungiya. By not giving her the deafness that usually accompanies dumbness, the creator doubled the curse on her because dumbness is more bearable if one cannot hear than if one can. She had just one younger sister, who had the gift of speech. Gungiya made up for the lack of speech with good sense. She was so sharp that she never forgot what she had once seen and never made a mistake in what she had once learnt. By the age of eight or nine, she became her mother's helper in all the household work.

Now the problem of marriage arose. To remove the blemish of perpetual virginity from the girl's life, Raghu employed the fraudulence that is the chief weapon used by parents of girls who are unsuitable for the marriage market. He got the younger girl engaged to someone in a far-off village and then seated Gungiya as the bride at the ceremony. After three or four years, Gungiya was sent to her in-laws' home and discovered a new dimension of her sad state.

---

6 *Duddu*: Baby-talk for milk. *Happa*: Baby-talk for mush fed to children.

When she could not speak and could only say *'Ay, Ay'* when she was pressed, her in-laws were infuriated at having been deceived. In the cries of 'The bride is dumb, her father has cheated everyone, take her jewels and throw her out', Gungiya saw the reflection of the cruel curse that her parents' love had hidden from her. She caught hold of her mother-in-law's feet and, despite being kicked, hid her face at those feet and kept weeping, but no one's heart melted. Fraud is fraud. What would become of justice if neither the parent nor the child was punished for this trickery? Her in-laws heaved a sigh of relief after they had divested her of all her clothes and jewels and sent her back to her father's house.

Raghu was already tormented by what he had done. To make up for the injustice, he offered to marry his younger daughter into the same family. This time, the wedding took place only after the girl had been properly seen and heard. The old women say that when Gungiya saw her sister decked in her clothes and jewels and married to her husband, she could stop her weeping only by stuffing her sari end into her mouth. After her sister left, she tried to mitigate her parents' distress by her silent service.

Many years had passed since then. Gungiya's parents had left for the next world and so had her parents-in-law. Her sister Rukiya had given birth to two children but neither lived beyond the third year. Perhaps to avoid mourning the third child, she left it motherless. Unable to make arrangements to raise the child, the father brought the newborn to his in-laws' home, put it in Gungiya's lap, and began to weep.

Only Gungiya knows what message she read in the twinkling eyes of the child that was voiceless like her, but she was unable to return the child. Her brother-in-law quietly proposed to take her home with him but he stopped, seeing the stern refusal on her face. The villagers were astounded by this mute mother's care for the child. She sold one bullock and bought two goats for milk for the child, cut up her best clothing to make his clothes, got a cap stitched for him, and melted down her necklace and bracelets to make him anklets, a waistband, and armlets. She used her savings to feast the village at his naming ceremony.

Gungiya's business had suffered when her parents died, and now she was busy looking after the baby. Thus, her property dwindled even as Hulasi [Delight] grew. The child's father asked after him for a while but then forgot him in affection for his new wife and child. Gungiya never asked the father for anything nor did she reduce her princely expenditure on Hulasi.

To begin with, Gungiya and her son were both voiceless and communicated with each other in signs. After the child learnt to speak, he was surprised by his mother's silence, and then embarrassed by it. He was wounded by the village boys calling him '*Gungi ka beta Gunga*'. He would run to hit them or would start crying. Hearing the noise, Gungiya would run out to scold the boys, saying '*Ay, Ay,*' and they would run off, yelling, 'Gunga Mausi, Gunga Mausi.'[7]

The poor thing would bring Hulasi home, sit him in her lap, feed him sweets, dust his hair with her fingers, wipe his face with her sari, and try to console him with many gestures, but this would only enrage the boy more. Sometimes he would push her away with both hands and then lie on his stomach in the yard, weeping, and sometimes he would pull her clothes, demanding to know why she was the only mute one when everyone else's mother could speak. What answer could Gungiya give? Her affection and care were no less than those of any mother in the village, but how could she explain her dumbness?

7 The two Hindi phrases mean 'Dumb woman's dumb son' and 'Dumb Aunt, Dumb Aunt'.

As Hulasi grew, he learnt from others some truths and some untruths about his life-story. Since Gungiya could not speak, many baseless rumours went unanswered. He was told that Gungiya was very angry with her sister who had stolen her husband and home. She had snatched the son from the father to take revenge on him. There was definitely some bad motive behind the love she showed Hulasi. Although he didn't fully grasp these innuendos, the child's heart began to reject Gungiya Amma.

Because most people are those whom Goswami Tulsidas describes as 'flies who destroy themselves trying to ruin others' ghee', Gungiya's small share of happiness was transformed into inexpressible grief.[8] Who would tell Hulasi that his father had abandoned him and was indifferent to his upbringing, and that his stepmother had always tried to keep him at a distance in order to secure her own children's rights? The depths of Gungiya's silent affection were beyond his understanding. And because she had over-indulged him, he considered her affection his right rather than her gift.

When, one day, he asked Gungiya why she had snatched him away from his father, a poisoned arrow seemed to pierce her heart, but how could she express her pain? Her open mouth, eyes filled with dismay, and despairing expression were an unresolved riddle for the child. Enquiries revealed that his father had obtained a job in a factory and moved to Kanpur with his family. Gungiya pawned her bracelets and made arrangements to send the child to his father. New clothes were made for Hulasi. Brightly coloured clay and wooden toys were carefully packed in a basket. Roasted mahua, jaggery and wheat balls, laddu, and

---

8 Quotation from the *Ramcharitmanas*: '*parahita ghrita jina ke mana maakhi*'.

other sweets were tied up in a bundle. A black milk-pot was filled with ghee.

A local learned man, who was called Kaka because he was a fellow-villager, was coaxed into accompanying the child. Then, one day, at a time pronounced auspicious by Pandit-ji, Gungiya, holding back her tears lest they prove unlucky, walked three miles to send Hulasi and Kaka off by train. She found it hard to return to the village. Weeping and laughing as she stood at a field's edge or sat under trees, Gungiya reached home and lay, face down, until morning, on the square platform where the tulsi grew in the yard.

She was agitated for several days. On the day she opened her door to go back to work, she saw Hulasi walking behind the dust-covered Kaka. The child's new clothes were dirty and his face downcast. She ran to embrace him, expressing her extreme grief in wordless, indistinct cries.

Finally, the result of the journey became known. After wandering for two days, they had managed to find Hulasi's father. He lived in two dark rooms in a dirty, narrow alley, with his wife and four children. The parental joy that shone in his eyes on seeing this forgotten son was lost in the shadow of his wife's harsh gaze. Husband and wife argued all night.

In the morning, he put forward various arguments to persuade Kaka to take the child back. Whatever was in Hulasi's maternal grandparents' home would come to him, but their father was the only support for these other children. Hulasi would be with a stepmother in his father's house as well as in his grandparents' home, therefore it would be better for him to stay with Gungiya and take care of the business, house, land, and money. When his half-brother grew up, he would be sent to Hulasi. Hulasi's stepmother was in favour of moving to the village, but Gungiya would not like that. Gungiya was not immortal. After her death, they would all live together and look after her trade.

Neither Hulasi's tears nor Kaka's pleas could withstand this harsh practicality. Like two defeated soldiers, they returned, exhausted. Hulasi's stepmother kept the ghee and sweets as gifts sent to her, and she distributed the clothes and toys amongst her children. So Hulasi came back to Gungiya, divested of everything. The poor thing tried her utmost to heal the child's wounded heart with the ointment of her maternal love.

She laboured hard to collect for him the things he liked, but it was not easy to repair the broken thread of trust in the child's tender heart. Humans always desire what they cannot have. Following that principle, Hulasi's heart hankered for his father, brothers, and sisters. His father had sent him back because of Gungiya's house and goods. Only when she died would they all be able to live together. These thoughts kept poisoning his heart.

Two years passed. Hulasi's behaviour had somewhat improved and he had started helping Gungiya in the trade, when fate, which amused itself by causing her misfortune, sent a Baba-ji with two or three disciples to the village. They had come there in the course of their rounds but decided to set up camp in the Thakur's mango orchard and wait four months for the monsoon to pass.

The arrival of such Babas and ascetics is a major event for villagers. One brought him a pot of milk, another a pitcher of ghee. One brought him a ripe pumpkin and another a lump of molasses. One brought old rice and another flour ground from white wheat. One expressed a wish to feast the group with *malpua*, and another with *kheer* and poori.[9]

These offerings were not selfless. All the devotees who served them wanted one blessing or another. One wanted a son in his old age. Another needed more money. One wanted to vanquish the co-owner of his fields. Another wanted a special mantra to

9 *Malpua*: Deep-fried sweet pancake. *Kheer*: Milk pudding.

get rid of his own brother. One was eager for a stratagem to bring someone else under his control. Another asked how to get his mortgaged fields back without repaying his debt. One wanted to make his creditor lose his wits so that he could grab back the jewels he had pawned. Another pleaded to be cured of illness without taking medicines. In short, all the devotees sat with hands folded before Baba-ji, cherishing a hidden desire, proper or improper.

Baba-ji seemed to have descended amongst them in order to exemplify the proverb, 'one came to sing God's praise but began to thresh cotton instead'.[10] Spreading ash on his body that was black as a lump of tobacco, placing a crown on his fake matted locks, and holding a pair of tongs as a sceptre, he sat on a mat of sacred grass to hold court for these petitioners. His manner of conferring boons was mysterious. He would give one nothing but a pleasant glance, deign to wave his hand in reassurance at another, clap the tongs to show his dissatisfaction with a third, and content a fourth with a pinch of sacred ash. Thus, no one was ever completely gratified nor was anyone reduced to despair.

Those who perceived him showing even a mild indifference to their petitions served him with redoubled fervour, and those whom he favoured brought more gifts to remain in his good books. Naturally, he was especially kind to women petitioners. When a village bride told the sad story of her husband's neglect or her childlessness, his eyes, reddened by *ganja*, grew even redder.

Three or four adolescent disciples toiled in his service day and night. One wore the loincloth of an ascetic, another had a towel draped on his shoulders. One had a shaven head and another's freshly matted locks kept slipping off his head. One would bring

10 To set out with one purpose and get distracted by another.

him sacred food but taste it on the way, and another could not help taking a drag while filling his hookah. Baba-ji was always surrounded by inquisitive village boys. Hulasi too began to pay him visits.

Baba-ji had the ability to figure out many things by observing facial expression, behaviour, and dialogue. It would be hard to say how much he knew about Hulasi but one day, pretending to notice him for the first time, he exclaimed, 'Aha! You are going to be a man of high attainments, child![11] Your forehead glows but in your heart—come here, let me look at the line of your fate!'

Baba-ji's attention drew Hulasi to him as a python's breath draws its prey. Hulasi was never able to free himself from this attraction. Gungiya too had sent gifts of sesame, jaggery, and oil to Baba-ji but she had neither the voice nor the desire to ask him questions. She grew worried when Hulasi began to spend his nights and days there. One day, she dragged him away by the hand, in Baba-ji's presence, but the next day, ignoring her orders, he returned there. She had no option but to spread her torn aanchal before Baba-ji and beg for her only child.

Whether inspired by pity or by mockery, Baba-ji ordered Hulasi to go home and never come back, and then drew a deep sigh. Hulasi was never seen there again. A few days before the four-month period elapsed, the villagers found the orchard empty. Perhaps Baba-ji had left in the night. Hearing the news of his departure and finding Hulasi's bed empty, Gungiya beat her head in sorrow. Unable to find him anywhere in the village, she ran weeping and sobbing for several miles but could not find any sign of Baba-ji. After some days, it was heard that a group of sadhus had taken the train from a railway station four or five miles away, but nothing more could be discovered.

---

11 Translates *siddha purush*. The attainments referred to are spiritual.

Gungiya's sorrow became a source of mirth for the villagers. One would tease her: 'Baba-ji has come, Gungiya!' Another would joke, 'Hulasi has sent a telegram, Gungiya!' A third would sarcastically remark, 'Take someone else's son again and become a mother of sons!'

But Gungiya knew and understood nothing except waiting for Hulasi. She seemed to be searching for something among the village boys. When a new toy appeared, she would buy it immediately and keep it in a red basket. When she saw new fabric, she would get a kurta stitched to Hulasi's measurements and fold it away in her wooden trunk. She would buy the sweets he liked and keep them in the kitchen. Sometimes she would open the door at dead of night and hear the sound of someone approaching. She fully believed that Hulasi would come back to her one day, but he never came.

These events had occurred twelve or thirteen years before I met Gungiya. Except for his dumb aunt, everyone had forgotten Hulasi. Suddenly, after many years, a person returning to the village from Kolkata said that Hulasi was working as a doorman for a Seth there. He was married and had several children. How much of this was true only the one who reported it knew, but the villagers found in this too a means to tease Gungiya. Now Hulasi was a big man, now he would show Gungiya the city, he would take her around in a car, they joked, but for Gungiya the jokes were true.

Instead of being angry with the son who had run away and never bothered to contact his mother, she felt even more love for him. What hardships must her son be facing? In that distant land, who would cook for him and look after his clothes? That group of ascetics must have definitely fed him owl's flesh and dulled his mind. When he wanted to return home, he perhaps would not have had the money to do so. But when he got the opportunity, he had become a decent man.

How would he know that Gungiya Amma was alive? He must be feeling embarrassed to write to anyone in the village. Also, he must think that no one in the village would recognize him now. But his Gungiya Amma should write to him. As soon as he got news of her, he would come running. The daughter-in-law would come too. Wouldn't the children insist on meeting their grandmother? Drowning in these thoughts, Gungiya one day expressed a wish to write a letter.

But it was not easy to write her letter. After writing, 'Blessings from his Gungiya Amma to the respected and deserving Sri Hulasi Teli', the proceedings halted.[12] When I asked if I should write 'It was very wrong of you to run away', she shook her forefinger to indicate refusal. Should I write 'Whatever you did was right'? Gungiya shook her head in disagreement. Should I write 'Your Gungiya Amma has been waiting for you for twelve years'? Gungiya nodded in agreement. In this way, like an amateur poet, I kept adding and breaking off sentences, and somehow completed the letter.

No one knew the address so I freed myself from Gungiya by writing 'Shri Hulasideen Teli, Kolkata'. She posted the letter herself. But I was not really freed because Gungiya constantly waylaid me to ask in gestures about replies to letters lost in the dead letter office.

A classmate of mine was staying in Calcutta in those days, getting herself treated by a Yunani [Greek medicine] practitioner. I wrote to her to tell her Gungiya's story and ask her to look for Hulasi. In a week's time, I received a sarcastic reply. My imagining that she could find an unknown person like Hulasi, without an address, in an ocean of people, was

12 His name is Hulasideen but he is politely referred to as Hulasi Teli (Oilman). Most Indians did not use surnames but in the modern period they were developed, often from names of professions and villages.

evidence of my lack of sense. Such an impractical person should content herself by not getting involved with others' problems. No surprise that I was annoyed when I received this sermon instead of Hulasi's address.

Some more days passed. Gungiya fell ill. She had had a mild fever for several months and it turned into TB. She stopped working only when she had to take to bed. As her cough worsened, her visitors decreased in number. A distant relative took charge of her bullocks and oil-press, and his daughter took a little care of the invalid.

Whenever I went to see Gungiya, she would ignore her fatigue and ask with various gestures about a letter from Hulasi. Then came another letter from my classmate. She had given the task of finding Hulasi to her new servant Harbhajan. Hulasi had not been found but Harbhajan was very sad when he heard Gungiya's story. His village was somewhere near hers and he too had run away ten or twelve years earlier, without telling his mother. His mother had died but he believed that he could satisfy his mother's spirit by giving Gungiya some comfort.

He had passed Class Three so he was determined to write a letter himself and wanted to send Gungiya some money. He was not happy with the idea of his employer sending money on his behalf because he thought it proper to send his own earnings. He decided that efforts to adhere to the truth might destroy the happiness of that mother who was nearing death.

After a week, Harbhajan's letter and ten rupees arrived. When Gungiya heard that news from Calcutta had come, she assumed that Hulasi was the sender so one did not need to tell her either the truth or a lie. Harbhajan's letter gave no clue about the sender or the recipient. He had written what any rustic son would write to his mother.

> Maiya [mother], I cannot repay my debt to you even if I serve you in many births. You are the arbiter of my destiny. My brain was addled, otherwise why would I have left a mother like you to roam around in strange lands? I will definitely come to your feet as soon as I can obtain leave. Don't worry about anything. Your blessings are on my head like a shade protecting me so I will never fall into hardships. Your daughter-in-law and grandson fall at your feet.

Gungiya held that dirty piece of paper in her skeletal fingers, put it on her cage-like chest, and closed her eyes, but the tears that flowed from the corners of her wrinkled eyelids washed the pillow that was sticky with dirt and oil. A month later, she was found lying dead between the open basket of Hulasi's toys and the box full of his clothes. The money was found under her pillow exactly as she had received it. I tried to find out more about Harbhajan but he did not return with his employer to her home and it was as impossible to find him in the city as it was to find Hulasi.

The creations of imagination fall short before the strange people and mysterious details of the lives I have encountered, but the sad astonishment that Gungiya awakened in my heart was never awakened again. My letter-writing did not stop. I used to write the life-stories of others for my own amusement, and now I read about others' joys and sorrows to find another individual like Gungiya. But ignorance replicates itself much more than knowledge does, so it is hard to repeat the moments that give one a glimpse of life's mystery.

Sometimes I wonder, will that image of silent but eternally vibrant parental love remain unmatched in my memory?

About the Author

MAHADEVI VARMA, generally considered the greatest Hindi woman poet of the twentieth century, was born on Holi in 1907. She took an MA in Sanskrit from Allahabad University, and became residential principal (later, vice-chancellor) of the pioneering women's institution, Prayag Mahila Vidyapeeth. She worked in the Gandhi-led movement for independence, and edited several journals, most notably the women's magazine *Chand*. She was one of the four pillars of the *chhayavad* movement in Hindi poetry, and authored several collections of poems, such as *Nihar* (1930), *Rashmi* (1932), *Nirja* (1933), *Yama* (1939), and *Deepshikha* (1942). Her prose works include reminiscences, pen portraits, essays on women's predicament (*Shrinkhla ki Kariyan*, 1942), and works of literary criticism, such as *Sahityakar ki Astha* (1962). She translated numerous works from Sanskrit to Hindi. She founded a trust to support writers in need. In 1979, she was the first woman to be made a fellow of the Sahitya Akademi. Among other awards, she received the Jnanpith Award in 1982, the Padma Bhushan in 1956, and the Padma Vibhushan in 1988. She died in 1987.

About the Translator

RUTH VANITA was educated entirely in India. She taught at Delhi University and later at the University of Montana. She is the author of two novels, *A Slight Angle* (2024) and *Memory of Light* (2020), two poetry collections, and many works of non-fiction, including *Shakespeare's Re-Visions of History: Social Collusion, Violence, and Resistance in Nine Plays* (2025), *The Dharma of Justice in the Sanskrit Epics: Debates on Gender, Varna, and Species* (2023), *Love's Rite: Same-Sex Marriages in Modern India* (2005; 2021), *Gender, Sex and the City: Urdu Rekhti Poetry 1780–1870* (2012), and *Dancing with the Nation: Courtesans in Bombay Cinema* (2017). She edited *On the Edge: 100 Years of Hindi Fiction on Same-Sex Desire* (2023) and co-edited the pioneering *Same-Sex Love in India: A Literary History* (2000). She has translated several works from Hindi to English, including fiction by Premchand, Rajendra Yadav, and Mannu Bhandari, and Mahadevi Varma's *Mera Parivar*, which is about the poet's animal companions, as *My Family* (2021).

HarperCollins *Publishers* India

At HarperCollins India, we believe in telling the best stories and finding the widest readership for our books in every format possible. We started publishing in 1992; a great deal has changed since then, but what has remained constant is the passion with which our authors write their books, the love with which readers receive them, and the sheer joy and excitement that we as publishers feel in being a part of the publishing process.

Over the years, we've had the pleasure of publishing some of the finest writing from the subcontinent and around the world, including several award-winning titles and some of the biggest bestsellers in India's publishing history. But nothing has meant more to us than the fact that millions of people have read the books we published, and that somewhere, a book of ours might have made a difference.

As we look to the future, we go back to that one word—a word which has been a driving force for us all these years.

Read.